Laurens van der Post
and Jane Taylor

TESTAMENT TO THE BUSHMEN

VIKING

VIKING
Penguin Books Ltd, Harmondsworth, Middlesex, England
Viking Penguin Inc., 40 West 23rd Street, New York, New York 10010, U.S.A.
Penguin Books Australia Ltd, Ringwood, Victoria, Australia
Penguin Books Canada Ltd, 2801 John Street, Markham, Ontario, Canada L3R 1B4
Penguin Books (N.Z.) Ltd, 182–190 Wairau Road, Auckland 10, New Zealand

First published 1984

This book was designed and produced by
The Rainbird Publishing Group
40 Park Street
London W1Y 4DE

British Library Cataloguing in Publication Data:
Taylor, Jane
    Testament to the Bushmen.
    1. Sam (African people) – Pictorial works
    I. Title
    968'.004961   DT764.B4

ISBN 0-670-80065-1

Text set by Oliver Burridge & Co Ltd, Crawley
Colour originated by Newsele s.r.l., Milan
Printed and bound by Hazell Watson & Viney Limited,
Member of the BPCC Group, Aylesbury, Bucks

Contents

Foreword

This book, and the television series it complements, started as an appealing idea, but quickly turned into a considerable personal involvement. Much of the responsibility for this lies with Laurens van der Post whose Bushman films had touched me as a child, and his books a few years later, and whose gift it is to transform an individual glimpse into a universal perception.

By a happy coincidence I met Paul Bellinger at a moment when both of us were looking towards the Kalahari for a film; we discovered a common friendship with Laurens van der Post, and at once realized not only what our joint subject must be, but also whom we must ask to present the programmes. With characteristic generosity Laurens agreed at once.

A similar coincidence led to the discovery that another friend had a connection with the Bushmen — Jeremy Ractliffe, financial director of Murray & Roberts, a construction engineering company which had already sponsored a major project to preserve some Bushman paintings. Without Jeremy Ractliffe, and also Les Mankowitz, *Testament to the Bushmen* would have remained an idea without form or substance.

The growth of form and substance was nurtured by two most generous and patient advisers — Dr David Lewis-Williams and Dr Tony Traill, both of the University of the Witwatersrand. Without David's detailed understanding of the paintings and folklore of the Bushmen, and Tony's exceptional knowledge of their language and his personal involvement with the Bushmen of Lone Tree in Botswana, whose way of life he was attempting to improve, I would have been lost. I also owe a debt of gratitude to Bert Woodhouse, another considerable expert in Bushman art, who must have photographed more of their paintings than any other person. All three were exceptionally generous with their time and expertise.

Every member of our film crew not only did a terrific job, but also managed to maintain a sense of humour and enjoyment even after several weeks of scarcely luxurious conditions in the bush, two broken cameras and a multitude of painfully infected scratches. Paul Bellinger, who was both director and cameraman, was tirelessly assisted by Cliff Bestall and Norman Mankowitz, while Peter Poole did all the sound recording, and Dodi Keller was the production assistant. Norman Mankowitz nobly added to his existing burdens by taking my stills camera with him on the men-only hunt — he took some superb pictures, without which the photographic record of our stay with the Bushmen would have been incomplete.

Izak Barnard guided us through the Kalahari, and without his unparalleled knowledge both of the Bushmen and of the bush, we could never have done what we did in the time. And throughout that time Coral Fourie and her assistants produced miraculous banquets for us every evening on a single fire.

Back at base, throughout the whole period of pre-production, filming and editing, all the organization was dealt with single-handed by Estelle Coxall. Everything from hotel bookings to monitoring expenditure came under her eagle eye and efficient hand. We could not have managed without her.

Not only in Botswana, but also in Namibia, we were given generous help and advice – by the writer Olga Levinson whose knowledge of, and concern for, the peoples of Namibia is unsurpassed; by François Stroh, then Secretary to the Council of Ministers in Windhoek; by the Department of Nature Conservation and the staff of Etosha National Park; and especially by John Marshall and Claire Ritchie who were then doing a demographic survey of the Tsumkwe area, and establishing the Bushman Development Fund to encourage some Bushmen to own and care for cattle, in order to improve both their diet and their prospects for a self-sufficient future.

But – in common with most people who have had any contact with the people of the Kalahari – my main acknowledgment is to the Bushmen themselves whose gaiety, charm and utter helplessness ate into my heart.

Jane Taylor
London, 1984

Part of the royalties of this book are going to:

1. The Bushman Development Fund,
   c/o TUCSIN, P.O. Box 11174,
   Windhoek 9000, Namibia.

2. Kagcae Development Trust,
   c/o Barclays National Bank,
   Mall Branch, P.O. Box 41,
   Gabarone, Botswana.

3. Help a Child to See,
   c/o The Hospital for Sick Children,
   Great Ormond Street,
   London WC1.

Note on Orthography

The Bushman languages contain click sounds for which no conventional symbols suffice, so new ones have had to be invented. The four main ones used in this book are as follows:

/   *Dental click.* The tip of the tongue is placed immediately behind the top front teeth and pulled away, making a sound similar to that used in mild reproof, or in sympathy.

≠   *Alveolar click.* A similar sound to the one above, but made by the end part of the tongue being pulled away from the alveolar ridge just behind the top front teeth.

!   *Alveolar-palatal click.* The end of the tongue is drawn away sharply from the curve where the alveolar ridge meets the hard palate, making a popping sound.

//   *Lateral click.* One side of the tongue is sucked sharply away from the alveolar ridge on the same side of the mouth, making a sound similar to that used to urge on a horse.

In this book all the Bushman words have been spelt in such a way that the click sounds may be disregarded.

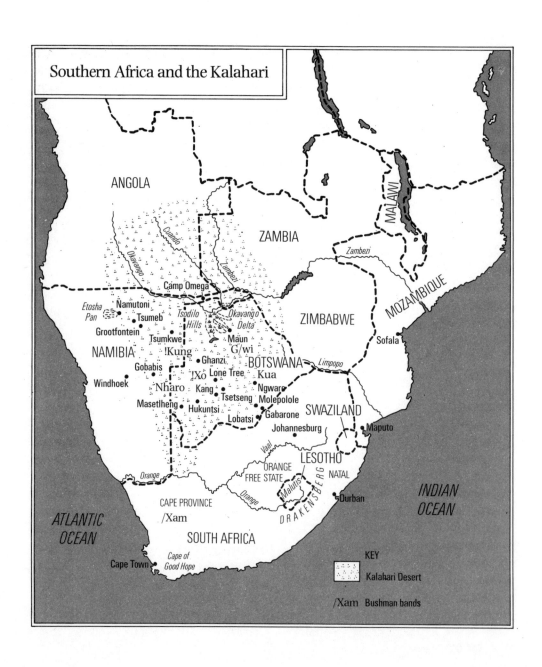

Southern Africa and the Kalahari

ANGOLA

ZAMBIA

Cuando

Okavango

Zambezi

Camp Omega

MALAWI

Zambezi

MOZAMBIQUE

Etosha
Pan   Namutoni

•Tsumeb

Tsodilo
Hills   *Okavango*
Delta

ZIMBABWE

Grootfontein

Tsumkwe

•Maun

Sofala

NAMIBIA   !Kung   G/wi

•Ghanzi   BOTSWANA   *Limpopo*

Gobabis   /Xo   Lone Tree   Kua

•Windhoek   Nharo   Kang   •   Ngware

Tsetseng   Molepolole

Masetlheng   Hukuntsi   Lobatsi   Gabarone   SWAZILAND

Johannesburg   •Maputo

Vaal

LESOTHO

Orange   ORANGE
FREE STATE   NATAL

Malutis   DRAKENSBERG

•Durban

INDIAN
OCEAN

CAPE PROVINCE   *Orange*
/Xam

SOUTH AFRICA

ATLANTIC
OCEAN

Cape Town•   *Cape of*
Good Hope

KEY

Kalahari Desert

/Xam   Bushman bands

CHAPTER ONE
In the Beginning

The Bushmen of the Kalahari Desert are the last survivors of a people who once lived all over southern Africa, and who for thousands of years were the sole inhabitants of the land. Possibly as early as 25,000 years ago — and certainly no later than 10,000 — a yellow-skinned people, with anatomical features like the Bushmen of today, began to appear in southern, central and eastern Africa, as a separate genetic development from the black-skinned peoples of Africa. Even as far north as Egypt some ancient Bushman-like skeletal remains have been found; but for the most part these people pursued a nomadic life in virtual isolation in the temperate areas to the south of the continent.

Game of all kinds abounded in the lands of these ancestral Bushmen; and in most places the earth, well watered by mountain streams and great rivers, produced an astonishing richness and variety of plants that were good to eat. Certainly some areas were dry and cruel; but for a nomadic people these were not difficult to avoid, and they could pick up their few possessions and move on to where water, vegetable food or game were more plentiful. Best of all, there was no alien culture to disturb the balance of their lives. Each band had its own clearly defined territory which was respected by all neighbouring bands. Here they hunted game and gathered plant food, and knew where to find not only water, but also the honey they prized so highly.

They understood the ways of nature in the most complete manner, for they knew themselves to be part of its intricate and divinely-ordered system. And because Nature did not have large numbers to provide for, life for the early Bushmen was not always a matter of mere survival. In times of plenty they had the leisure and tranquillity in which to make music and dance; to tell stories filled with the most beautiful and complex metaphors concerning their sense of the divine; and to cover the rock surfaces of southern Africa with similar metaphors expressed in paint.

Certain characteristics distinguished the Bushmen, then as now, from the other peoples of Africa. They are short of stature, the men marginally over five feet tall, the women somewhat under. Classically they have high, wide cheekbones and pointed chins, giving their faces a rather diamond-shaped appearance. Their eyelids have a fold similar to that of the Chinese, which led in the past to fanciful ideas of a Mongolian origin and a long migration to their southern African home. Belief in this theory was reinforced by the considerably lighter colour of the Bushmen's skin than that of other African peoples. Their colour ranges from yellow to mid-brown, tanning in the sun to a dark apricot or copper tone, and their skin tends to become deeply wrinkled at a much earlier age than that of black Africans, or of most whites. Their bodies are lean and wiry; and their hair grows thickly in tightly coiled spirals, which are commonly referred to as 'pepper-corn'.

Their most spectacular physical characteristic was one that belonged to the women especially – the protuberant, almost shelf-like buttocks that scientists refer to as steatopygia. This feature seems to be less common now than it was in the past; or perhaps it is simply less noticeable under the western-style clothes so many of them wear. Bushman women are very modest about their behinds when outsiders are around, keeping them well covered; but in their paintings it is portrayed with obvious delight in a feature they regarded as extremely attractive.

Between 4,000 and 2,000 years ago, another group of people gradually emerged in southern Africa – the Hottentots. They had the same ancestors as the Bushmen; they were indeed so closely related to them that it might not have been easy to distinguish one from the other for they shared the same physical characteristics. Even their languages – which abounded in astonishing diversity – sounded similar, for all contained click sounds. The difference between them was not a physical or linguistic one so much as the fact that the Hottentots had added the herding of cattle to the hunter-gatherer mode of existence that had been common to them both.

The Hottentots, like the Bushmen, were nomads; but their wanderings were governed not only by their need of water, game and vegetable food, but also by the need to find grazing for their cattle. The better diet that the milk provided gave them a greater stability than the Bushmen ever had, and this resulted in their usually living in larger groups – some probably several thousand strong, as compared with the Bushmen for whom one hundred would have been a large band. This in turn led to their becoming more centrally organized, and many groups had hereditary chiefs. The Bushmen, on the other hand, had no chiefs or rulers, but were led by those in each generation whom they deemed the wisest and the best.

Hottentot cattle now competed for the grazing that had once supported only the wild animals of Africa; so the game moved elsewhere. The Bushmen, if they did not move too, were deprived of their sources of meat; so some hunted instead the domestic cattle of their Hottentot neighbours, who retaliated angrily. Sporadic shooting of cattle as game, and also more wholesale raiding of larger numbers of cattle – possibly by Bushmen who wanted to become cattle herders themselves – took place with increasing frequency. These clashes between the Bushmen and the Hottentots were a model in miniature of those that were to erupt between the Bushmen and the two later intruders into their territory – the Bantu-speaking black Africans who came in from the north from about the third century AD onwards, and the Europeans who settled in the south in 1652.

A century and a half before this, Portuguese sailors had started to ply down the west coast of Africa in their carracks and caravels, searching for a trade route to the East Indies. In 1497, following Bartholomew Diaz' lead nine years earlier, Vasco da Gama rounded the Cape of Good Hope [2]* – or the Cape of Storms as it had hitherto been known. A few days earlier he and his crew had a somewhat unfortunate first encounter with a group of Hottentots who, after their initial fear had been allayed, had been so friendly that a Portuguese sailor called Fernando Veloso had gone with them to their village to find out more about them and the way they lived. Suddenly overcome with panic that they might, after all, be cannibals, Veloso beat a hasty retreat to his ship, followed by some of the uncomprehending Hottentots. By the time he was within sight and hailing distance of the ship, Veloso was in such a state of terror that his comrades thought he was in mortal danger and poured off the ship to attack the unfortunate Hottentots.

It was an inauspicious beginning to the relationship between Europeans and the indigenous people of southern Africa; but fortunately such misunderstandings were not universal. By the beginning of the seventeenth century it was mainly the Dutch and the British who landed at various points on the coast of this part of Africa, because it was a convenient stopping place on trading voyages to the east for their respective East India Companies. They made contact with the Hottentots who gave them cattle to swell their provisions in return for iron, copper, tobacco, brandy and beads.

It was not long before a regular trade developed, and the Europeans were acquiring ivory and ostrich feathers as well as cattle from the Hottentots. They established special ties with one or two individuals, and used them as intermediaries and negotiators. The British even took one, Coree, to London so that he could learn English and thus be of even greater use to them. However, this initiative backfired as Coree, besides learning English, also learned the paltry value of the baubles that were being offered to his people in trade. Nothing daunted, the British tried the experiment again some years later with Herry, whom they prudently sent to Bantam in the East Indies, instead of to London, for his linguistic education.

When the Dutch first settled at the Cape in 1652, to set up a permanent refreshment post for the traders of the Dutch East India Company, there was already an established trade operating with the Hottentots. And Herry, with his partial command of English, was immediately at hand for the useful (to the Dutch) and profitable (to Herry) role of interpreter and intermediary. It was also a time when friction between the Hottentots and the Bushmen was at a high point; so the attitude of the Dutch to the Sonqua, or Sana, as the Hottentots called the Bushmen, must inevitably have been coloured by the Hottentots' view of them. They lost no opportunity to complain of the Bushmen's cattle-thieving. They also called the Bushmen 'Obiqua', which meant robbers and murderers.

However, the Commander of the Dutch East India Company's settlement, Jan van Riebeeck, was under strict instructions from the Company to conciliate 'the

*Numbers in brackets refers to colour plates.

natives' and to establish good relations with them all. At this stage the colonists would have had no means of distinguishing Bushmen from Hottentots on purely physical grounds, and in any case they did not immediately come into contact with the former. When they did, they tended to regard them as simply another group of Hottentots who happened to live in a rather different and, as time went on, considerably more unfriendly manner.

The first contact with Bushmen seems to have been made just three years after the Dutch had landed. Jan van Riebeeck wanted to find out more about the people who lived further inland. He was beginning to find the Hottentots and Herry not quite as cooperative as he had hoped, and he thought it might be valuable to make friendly overtures to those peoples who were in conflict with them.

In the garrison at the Cape was a freebooting soldier called Jan Wintervogel, who agreed to lead a party of seven soldiers, and to try to form alliances with other tribes and to look for precious metals. They set out on 15 March 1655 and some days later Wintervogel recorded that they came into contact with 'a certain tribe, very low in stature, and very lean, entirely savage, without any huts, cattle or anything in the world, clad in little skins.' These strangers were about to attack them with bows and arrows, but Wintervogel went forward, gesturing in a friendly manner and offering them tobacco. The Bushmen put down their arms and accepted the tobacco, which they knew exactly what to do with. The only other information that Wintervogel gathered, apart from the above extract from his journal, was that they were on unfriendly terms with all their neighbours.

In 1660 another party, this time of thirteen members under the leadership of Jan Danckert, left Cape Town on 12 November. Near the Olifants river to the north of Cape Town, they met various Bushman groups, some of whom dropped their bows and arrows and fled; while others came to meet them and were friendly, showed the explorers the way, and gave them honey.

The next contact, however, was far less agreeable. In 1662 an exploratory party under Corporal Pieter Cruythof set off northwards from Cape Town. One night, as they lay sleeping around their fire, a volley of arrows was shot into the camp. It was never known who fired the arrows, for the attackers disappeared into the night. Shortly afterwards, when the expedition came across a Bushman camp where there were only women and children, Corporal Cruythof ordered his men to kill them all in retaliation for the supposed involvement of their menfolk in the attack on their camp. Cruythof's second-in-command, Pieter van Meerhof, refused, and his mutiny was supported by all the other members of the expedition. Back in Cape Town the authorities approved of their stand, and took the first opportunity to demote Cruythof. This clement attitude towards the Bushmen did not last long.

From time to time the colonists would go on hunting expeditions, penetrating much further afield than the area they had annexed for farming, and over the next few years there are a number of accounts of white hunters being killed by Bushmen. In 1676 three members of a group of four Europeans were killed at the Breede river to the east of Cape Town, where they had been hunting 'sea cows' (hippopotamuses). The survivor of their party, and a Hottentot chief known as Captain Klaas, reported the murders, and the Council of the colony decided to send out a punitive expedition. What nobody seems to have considered was whether the Bushmen might have had a rightful grievance against the hunters and farmers who came into this land which had once been theirs and theirs alone. The Europeans, with their highly developed sense of property and acquisition, had simply come in and regarded the land and all it contained as their own.

Bushmen had little sense of property – what need of property when everything you require is provided by Nature, and all you have to do is to take it and share it with your family? But they did have a sense of territory – the area within which they hunted game – and each group respected the territories of their neighbours. To do otherwise was a clear act of aggression. Small wonder then that the Bushmen should have responded with force when this new kind of white-skinned human being invaded their hunting grounds without so much as a by-your-leave, and shot large numbers of the animals on which their livelihood depended. But to the whites, the death of their three compatriots was an act of unwarranted murder, and it called for retribution. On this occasion retribution was not effected, because the commando, which consisted of fifty infantrymen, twenty-three cavalry, fifty non-military colonists, and a large force of Hottentots, did not so much as catch a glimpse of their quarry. The Bushmen's knowledge of the terrain, coupled with their pursuers' ignorance of it enabled them to vanish, as it were, into thin air.

Occasionally the Bushmen, in their nomadic wanderings, would settle for a while near the lands now farmed by the white settlers, and would shoot sheep and cattle there, as previously they had shot game. On one occasion when this happened, early in 1678, the Dutch immediately called on the Hottentot captains to capture the 'robbers', and in due course five Bushman prisoners were delivered to the Commander who rewarded the captains with goods to the value of £5. The Bushmen were tried by the colonists' Court of Justice, convicted as highwaymen and sentenced to death.

In 1684 another party of Europeans who went out hunting beyond the area of settlement was attacked by Bushmen. One of the men was killed by a poisoned arrow, sixteen head of cattle were stolen and two wagons were burnt. The new Commander of the Cape, Simon van der Stel, asked two Hottentot captains to act against the Bushmen. One of them was the same Captain Klaas who had reported the murder of the three Europeans some eight years earlier. After some delay he went out to find the Bushmen, and afterwards reported his success to the Commander and Council.

He said that, having located the Bushmen, he was about to attack when they sent three women to ask for peace. He sent them back with a present of tobacco and a request that their leader and ten other men should come to him on the following day. When the men duly arrived, Klaas received them with every appearance of friendship, and had a sheep slaughtered for them. On the next day, while the Bushmen were dancing and rejoicing, Klaas ordered that they should be surrounded and seized. He asked them if they intended to continue killing the white men, and when they said that they did, he had them killed immediately – with the exception of three who managed to escape. So delighted was the Council with his actions that 'it was resolved to reward the said Klaas for his faithful services with two bunches of copper beads, a roll of Virginia tobacco to the weight of twenty pounds, an anker of aniseed arrack, one hundred and fifty pounds of rice, and a pair of coarse stockings.'

Captain Klaas was naturally encouraged by such praise and liberality to continue his punitive expeditions. And as the Dutch appropriated larger and larger areas of land, pushing back the Bushmen as they did so, the Bushmen responded by ever-increasing depredations on the herds of the intruders. Captain Klaas was therefore kept hard at work. While the expeditions of the Europeans against the Bushmen were, to begin with, almost completely ineffective, those of Klaas and his Hottentots succeeded in wiping out large numbers of the 'robbers'.

As the situation rapidly escalated, so stronger measures were taken by the colonists themselves, instead of relying on their resident military force. In 1715 a commando system was introduced – a mounted volunteer force of Dutch settlers under a military commander. Over the next one hundred and fifty years it was used with increasingly deadly effect. Whenever Bushmen raided a farm and made off with cattle and sheep, a commando would go out to recover the stolen property and to kill as many Bushmen as possible. As one colonist with a certain conscience protested, 'I have had several conversations with individuals who have been engaged on these expeditions, and they talk of shooting Bushmen with the same feelings as if the poor creatures were wild beasts.'

By the middle of the eighteenth century a new element is apparent in the records of these commando raids – the capture of women and children to become slaves. Sir John Barrow, at the end of the century, wrote bitterly of the practice: 'The government of the Cape, which seemed to have been as little acquainted with the temper and disposition of its distant subjects as with the geography of the country, formed all its resolutions, respecting the Bosjemans, on representations made to it by the persons who were immediately interested ... it decreed that such of the Bosjemans as should be taken alive in the expeditions made against them, were to be distributed by lot among the commandant and his party, with whom they were to remain in a state of servitude during their lives.' Nothing could have been more calculated to push the Bushmen to revenge.

Throughout the last quarter of the eighteenth century, the conflict between the colonists and the Bushmen intensified, each side visiting retribution on the other as fiercely as they knew how. In the end it was a battle that the Bushmen could never win, for the colonists had guns. In 1774, one commando expedition alone accounted for 503 Bushmen dead, and 241 taken captive.

Among a long catalogue of terrible raids, a peculiarly unpleasant note is struck by one Adriaan van Jaarlsveld who, in 1775 decided to adopt a similar stratagem to that employed so successfully in the previous century by Captain Klaas. On 4 August, he recorded:

> . . . we met, unawares, one of these cattle plunderers, and also saw a great many of these thieves at a distance. In order to create no suspicion in the mind of the thief we had caught, we behaved peaceably to him in order to get the other thieves in our power. Wherefore it was thought good by everyone in the commando to inform this Bushman that we came as friends and were only journeying to the above-mentioned river to kill sea-cows. We gave him a pipe and tobacco, and sent him to his companions to offer them our peace. . . .
>
> *6th.* . . . on the road we unexpectedly met with five thieves and addressed them in the same way as we did the first one; and as a token of peace, we killed a sea-cow for them. . . .
>
> *7th.* Sixteen Bushmen came to us at Rondekop from the mountains to the south, when we killed some more sea-cows, to entice the thieves with their flesh, because I knew no other way to pay them for their continual murdering and stealing our cattle.

The next day van Jaarlsveld and his men killed another twelve sea-cows and then withdrew to wait for the Bushmen to come for the meat. They returned at dawn, killed one hundred and twenty-two Bushmen, and took twenty-one of them prisoner. The pride with which this treachery is related makes nauseating reading.

Over the years that followed, thousands of Bushmen were killed. When the British first annexed the Cape in 1795, there was no relaxation in the ruthlessness with which the Bushman depredations were answered with commando expeditions; yet the survivors continued to raid the stock of the white farmers. By the end of the eighteenth century, however, there were simply not enough Bushmen to resist further. The colonists were now able to extend their territory, and they pushed what was left of the Bushmen further to the north.

At about the same time, it had begun to occur to the new British authorities that the Bushman raids had almost always been in years of drought when they had virtually no food. Therefore, having not quite eliminated the Bushmen on the northern borders of the Colony, the colonists now adopted a new policy. They supplied the remaining Bushmen with food by shooting game for them, and they provided livestock in the territory to the north which they had set aside for the Bushmen to live in.

In the Colony itself, those Bushmen who had been captured as children and had grown up on white men's farms came to be known as 'tame' Bushmen. If the reasons for, and method of, their capture stick in our throats, it must also be said that they were often treated kindly and, with their natural sense of fun, became great favourites with their masters. The Revd A. Faure, an early-nineteenth-century missionary wrote in a letter that:

> . . . the farmers on the frontiers are entirely dependent on the Bushmen for their welfare. . . . Such farmers as possess Bushmen have been in the habit of committing

to them the charge of their flocks, and they have proved such faithful shepherds, that the farmers have not hesitated to give them some hundred ewes and other cattle, to sojurn with them beyond the limits of the colony. The Bushmen having received a reward of tobacco, dakka (or hemp leaves for smoking), and, perhaps one or two ewes leaves the habitation of the colonist, drives the cattle into distant parts, with the fertility of which he is well acquainted; and, after an absence of some months, returns to the farmer his cattle in such an improved condition, that had they not his particular mark upon them, he would with difficulty credit that they were the same animals. . . . Many farmers on the frontiers declared to me, that were it not for the Bushmen, they saw no means of breeding cattle.

Outside the Cape Colony it was still possible to meet 'wild' Bushmen who did not immediately fear for their lives at the sight of a white man. Throughout the nineteenth century increasing numbers of Europeans went on their travels in southern Africa. Some were missionaries, intent on bringing the gospel to the 'savages'; others were hunters whose great ambition was to kill as many, and as great a variety of, wild animals as possible in order to bring back the trophies to an astounded Europe. Still others seemed to regard southern Africa as a more adventurous form of the Grand Tour; and there were also a few botanists and zoologists. All wrote their books of travels and commented on the things they saw and the people they encountered. Because of the Bushmen's universally bad press, it was with a special *frisson* of excitement mixed with fear that they came upon Bushman groups.

The Bushmen's language came in for some adverse comment. Arbousset (a French missionary) described it as 'harsh, broken, full of monosyllables, which are uttered with strong aspirations from the chest and a guttural articulation as disagreeable as it is difficult . . . they cluck like turkeys'.

Several European travellers in southern Africa reported conflicts they encountered between the Bushmen and various groups of black Africans. R. G. Cumming, for example, wrote of a number of occasions when some Bechuanas went out against the Bushmen, whose territory they had appropriated, in exactly the same way that the Europeans had done further to the south. On one occasion:

In the year 1847, a Bechuana chief, named Assyabona . . . despatched a strong party of his tribe, armed with guns and assagais, to accomplish the destruction of a strong horde of wild Bushmen, whose robberies had become so daring and extensive that they were the terror of all who dwelt a hundred miles around them. On this occasion a great number of Bushmen were destroyed, having been overtaken on open ground. One determined fellow, having hastily collected the quivers of his dying comrades, which were full of poisoned arrows, ensconced himself within three large stones, from which position he for a long time defied the whole hostile array of Bechuanas, shooting two of them dead on the spot, and wounding a number of others. Though continuing gallantly to defend himself, he seemed aware that he could not possibly escape. . . . He was eventually finished off with a shot in the forehead.

Ironically, some of the Europeans, in particular the missionaries, remonstrated with the Africans about their treatment of the Bushmen, reminding them 'that this part of the country originally belonged to the Bushmen'.

Black, Bantu-speaking Africans were probably already south of the Limpopo river by the third century AD; and they gradually penetrated further into southern Africa over the centuries that followed. There are, of course, no written records to chart the course of their relationship with the indigenous Bushmen, but it seems likely, from both archaeological evidence and oral tradition, that to begin with they remained at peace with each other – at least for most of the time. The newcomers not only kept cattle, but they tilled the earth and made tools and weapons of iron. While their numbers remained small, competition for the land and its resources did not become an issue; in fact there seems to have been a fair amount of interchange, and even intermarriage, between the two. The clicks in some of the Bantu languages – Zulu, Xhosa and South Sotho – developed from their contact with the Bushmen.

At this stage, in what is now Natal, the Bushmen lived throughout the lowland areas, probably migrating to the Drakensberg mountains only in summer to escape the oppressive heat and humidity of the lowlands, and to follow the game. But as the Bantu-speaking population increased, and took over more and more ancient Bushman land for their own farming, so the Bushmen withdrew to the Drakensberg area on a more permanent basis; and so the incidents of conflict between them increased. For with less territory, and depleted game, the Bushmen inevitably took to hunting and raiding the cattle of the black farmers.

The Africans seem to have regarded the Bushmen with a curious blend of respect, fear and contempt. The respect was reserved for their supernatural skills, especially in healing and rain-making; the fear was for the deadly effect of their poisoned arrows; and the contempt was general, possibly a psychological defence mechanism aroused by their respect and fear. Canon (later Bishop) Henry Callaway, who worked among the Zulus for many years in the mid-nineteenth century, recorded a fascinating account by a Zulu of this mixed attitude towards the Bushmen:

> They are dreaded by men; they are not dreadful for the greatness of their bodies, nor for appearing to be men; no, there is no appearance of manliness; and greatness there is none; they are little things which go under the grass . . . and the man feels when he is already pierced by an arrow; he looks but he does not see the man who shot it. . . . The Abatwa [Bushmen] are fleas, which are unseen whence they came; yet they tease a man. . . . The bow with which they shoot beast or man, does not kill by itself alone; it kills because the point of their arrow is smeared with poison, in order that as soon as it enters, it may cause much blood to flow; blood runs from the whole body, and the man dies forthwith. That then is the dreadfulness of the Abatwa, on account of which they are dreaded.

The final elimination of the Bushmen from the more southerly areas of southern Africa occurred in the central fifty years of the nineteenth century in the west of Natal, in Basutoland and the Orange Free State. It was, in fact, a combined black and white operation, sometimes the two working in concert, sometimes independently.

In 1824 a group of English traders established the first settlement in Natal, and made contact with the Zulu king, Shaka. Thirteen years later several thousand Dutch colonists known as Boers, who were dissatisfied with British government in the Cape, crossed the Drakensberg mountains into Natal to set up their own republic. They called themselves the Voortrekkers. In the areas they had farmed previously on the frontiers of the Cape Colony, they knew all about Bushman stock raids, and about the commando raids which their own people had organized in swift retribution.

The Voortrekkers claimed large areas of Natal as their own, which brought them into disastrous contact with the Zulus; and they also went on great hunting expeditions into the Drakensberg which disturbed the Bushmen in their last refuge in Natal. Within six months of the Voortrekkers' arrival, the Bushmen started to descend on their new farms on the edge of the mountains, and to make off with their horses, cattle and sheep, sometimes with up to three hundred head of stock. They usually raided at night, or in such bad weather that pursuit was impossible. The farmers never knew when they would come, and were never adequately prepared. But they were just as determined as they had been in the Cape Colony to get together a commando to go and retrieve their stolen property. In the early days most of these punitive excursions were led by one Jacobus Uys. They were not often successful, largely because the complex topography of the Drakensberg was well known to the Bushmen but not to the Boers.

In 1842, only five years after the Boers had arrived, the British occupied Natal and the little Boer Republic of Natalia was soon obliged to submit to them — exactly what they had crossed the Drakensberg to escape. The British colonists were extremely hesitant to take action against the Bushmen in the face of strong opposition from Britain to such oppression. To the Boers this was mere dilatoriness; and their fury increased as they lost more and more cattle to the Bushmen against whom virtually no action was taken. However, as the British administration became more firmly established, and land titles were granted to increasing numbers of both British and Boers, so the need to protect this 'property' became more and more of an issue.

In September 1846 a small military post under Lieutenant Gibb was established on the farm of a Boer called van Vuuren. At the same time an attempt was made to negotiate with the Bushmen. A party of four men was sent out and they made contact with a notorious group of Bushmen, offering to give them a place where they could live permanently and without harassment, as well as sheep so that they would not be dependent on hunting game, or on stock-theft. Their reply was brief and to the point, and shows the tragic gap between the thinking of the Europeans and that of the Bushmen: 'That is what we cannot do, it is a life we like and it becomes a necessity, for we live by hunting and must follow the game, as it moves about the country.'

Meanwhile the raids continued; but the retributive commando raids were spasmodic for they could rarely be organized with sufficient speed and efficiency to have much effect. The Crown Prosecutor, Walter Harding, tried to organize resistance where he could, but many farmers were unwilling to leave their farms for a long hard raid that might well be totally ineffective.

In 1848 a new military post was established on the Bushman's river, some way to the north of the existing van Vuuren's Post. An armed African police force was also started 'for the protection of Her Majesty's subjects from the robberies they suffer from the Bushmen inhabiting the lower range of the Drakensberg', and was called the Natal Native Police. Several expeditions were sent out after Bushmen, but successes were so occasional and so limited that the force was disbanded after only three years. Walter Harding's military expeditions, however, were proving rather more successful.

Feelings ran high in Natal over the Bushman question, with most people agitating that something must be done to settle it once for all. The editor of the *Natal Guardian*, Charles Barter, used his paper to support the view that the Bushmen should be totally eliminated so that the colonists could live without fear of their property being stolen. If anyone spoke in defence of the Bushmen, it was private and unrecorded. The universal opinion seems to have been that they were irredeemable thieves and scoundrels.

In the mid-1850s about five thousand new British colonists arrived in Natal, and this additional weight of numbers increased the confidence of the colonists to take action into their own hands. Two semi-military volunteer units were formed, the Durban Volunteer Guard and the Natal Carbineers, both of which acted with considerably greater dispatch and effectiveness against the Bushmen than any previous force had done. The story is all too familiar; the Bushmen could not survive year after year of being hunted down with firearms.

In August 1872 the last known Bushman raid into Natal took place, this time against a Zulu leader called Sakhayedwa, whose people retaliated immediately and with deadly effect. For the first time one of the Natal newspapers, *The Mercury*, expressed some sense of communal guilt: 'Could nothing have been done to bring these unfortunate creatures – thorough outcasts of humanity; shot down as dogs whenever the opportunity offers – to live the quiet pastoral life of the Kafir? . . . By educating a few of these people, in time they might become messengers of good to the last of the race of the once formidable and numerous Bushmen.'

It was a plea that came too late to save from extinction the Bushmen of this part of southern Africa. A small number of individuals and groups, who had somehow survived the massacres, lived on for a few years more. But by the beginning of the twentieth century there was hardly a Bushman to be found in Natal, Basutoland or the Orange Free State; they had disappeared as completely as they had from the Cape Colony. From this time on, they were to be found only in an area so inhospitable that no one who did not have the knowledge of the earth that the Bushman had could survive there – the Kalahari Desert.

CHAPTER TWO

Gods and Storytellers

In northwest Botswana, just in the angle where the Namibian border turns east along the Caprivi Strip, stand the only hills in the Kalahari Desert, ramparts of rock rising clear and commanding above the flat surrounding bush. They are called the Tsodilo Hills. At one end stands the tallest of them, known as the 'male' hill, a great inhospitable cone, little more than 1,000 feet but seeming higher from the sheerness of its rise [21]; straggling away from it is the 'female' hill – in fact a cluster of little hills, imposing with craggy protuberances, yet with a sense of gentleness in its undulations [20]. At the far end, somewhat apart, stands a third hill, the smallest of the group [4].

I first saw the hills on an early filming trip when we were flying in a small plane from Tsumkwe in northern Namibia into the Caprivi, and the pilot circled them for us to see. There is an inherent arrogance about flying, an encapsulation that disallows any opening of yourself to the surrounding world; yet even as we flew around the hills, like Olympian *voyeurs*, we were all silenced for a long moment (rare for a film crew) by some strange numinous quality that seemed to emanate from these solitary outcrops of rock. Four months later we returned to the Tsodilo Hills with Laurens van der Post to complete our filming; and as they came into sight there was the same short intake of breath, and the sense of something awesome as we had experienced before; and as Laurens van der Post had experienced twenty-eight years earlier, the first white man known to have set eyes on these hills.

The Tsodilo Hills are a place of special sacredness to the !Kung Bushmen who live in this area of the Kalahari. As with all things that have great significance to them, the Bushmen have stories about the origin of the hills. One story relates that they were once a man and his two wives; but the man loved one wife more than the other and this caused a great quarrel. The wife who was less loved hit her husband on the head with a heavy stick which made a deep wound, and then she ran off into the desert. The Great God said that since there was no peace among them he must turn them to stone. Thus the man became the largest of the hills and the wound on his head became the great gash on its face; the unloved wife became the smallest hill that stands apart; and the loved wife, together with her children, became the cluster of hills that stands in the middle.

Other !Kung tell similar stories with variations in detail; one version has the smallest hill as the child of the 'male' and 'female' hills. Such a plurality of legends is very characteristic of the Bushmen for whom no one person's story or perception of the supernatural, is regarded as inferior to another's – each tells its own truth and can illumine some aspect of the divine.

There is one thing that is more or less universal in !Kung beliefs about the Tsodilo Hills – that they are a place of strong *n/um*, or supernatural power. It is believed that the Great God, Gaoxa, made the hills and lived there himself; there too he created and kept cattle, sheep and goats, as well as all manner of wild animals. They say this must be so for their hoofprints can be seen in the rocks – and there are indeed some strange marks which look like the prints of some fiery creatures impressed deep into molten rock. Even the paintings on the rock faces are said by many Bushmen to be the work of Gaoxa; and the whole place is filled with special magic. No person should complain there of hunger or thirst, or if plagued by wind, thorns, flies or the incessant bees.

Few of the early European travellers in southern Africa became unduly knowledgeable about the customs and beliefs of the Bushmen. They tended to come to Africa wearing their own cultural spectacles, through which they saw things only in relation to the ideas they had been brought up with. To set those ideas aside, and to start thinking again from scratch, would have seemed impossibly eccentric; and indeed such a notion would never have entered the head of any man for whom religion and civilization were simply two sides of the same coin. Yet such a new beginning was what they required of the Bushmen.

Views on the state of religion of the Bushmen varied quite considerably, mainly because they tended to be expressions of mere opinion rather than based on any kind of objective investigation. One of the earliest references to the inhabitants of the Cape is by Linschoten who, in 1596, published a treatise on the Indies, which also included a description of southern Africa since it had to be circumnavigated in order to reach the Indies. At this stage he had no means of distinguishing Hottentots from Bushmen, but he noted that the people he saw had huts that could be moved about like tents, and clothing made of the skins of animals. He said they were wild, barbarous and untrustworthy; they used bows and arrows; ate the fruits of the earth and the flesh of wild animals; they were without religion or any knowledge of God. All this, it seems, without a single interview.

After the Dutch had established their colony in 1652 and people ventured further into the interior, so the books proliferated. One of the earliest writers of this period, a German called Peter Kolben who travelled to the Cape in 1704, stated that the Hottentots (among whom he included the Bushmen), 'firmly believe there is a God, who made all Things . . . they believe in a Supreme Being, the Creator of Heaven and Earth, and of every Thing in them; the Arbiter of the World, through whose Omnipotence all Things live and move and have their Being'.

Andrew Sparrman, on the other hand, a Swedish zoologist who travelled extensively in southern Africa between 1772 and 1776, stated categorically that the Bushmen (whom he did distinguish from the Hottentots), 'are not sensible of the existence of any being who is the origin and ruler of all things; for on being questioned, they say they know nothing of the matter. . . .'

Despite the fact that he did not think highly of their religion, Sparrman was generally sympathetic towards the Bushmen and their plight. He saw them as weak and insignificant in the face of powerful neighbours – both black and white, but especially white – and 'doubted whether any body will ever trouble themselves with the conversion of these plain honest people, unless it should appear to have more connexion than it seems to have at present with political advantages'.

For the most part he was entirely correct. When the London Missionary Society turned its attention to South Africa in 1788, it was principally concerned with the various black people – or 'Caffers', as they called them. However, one or two individuals undertook to work among the Bushmen, and in 1814 a mission was established at Toverberg, just south of the Great (now the Orange) river, outside the then limits of the Cape Colony. The Revd Robert Moffat, David Livingstone's father-in-law, writing in 1842, tells us that 'the light and power of the Gospel at an early period of the mission, accompanied the proclamation of its glad tidings, and a number of these barbarous people, when they heard the word of life, believed. And here a Christian church arose, extensive gardens were laid out, and these cultivated with the Bushmen's own hands.' Horticulture, it seems, was pretty close to godliness.

Not long afterwards another mission to the Bushmen was established not far from Toverberg, and was called Hephzibah. The missionary there was a Mr Smith, assisted by a 'native' teacher, Jan Goedman. The numbers of Bushmen at the two missions reached about seventeen hundred at one point as the first-comers brought in their relatives and friends for food, and found there a kindness that was not at all what they had come to expect from the 'Christian' colonists.

A fellow-missionary of Mr Smith's wrote in a letter that 'some of the Bushmen who Mr Smith baptized, had acquired very rational ideas of the principles of the Christian religion. . . . They were zealous in trying to convey the same inestimable blessing to their unhappy countrymen, who live without God and without hope in the world.' He concludes that 'the conversion of this race of immortal beings is not impossible', an opinion greatly at variance with that of the majority of colonists who regarded the Bushmen as little better than wild animals and vastly more troublesome.

The missions to the Bushmen were of short duration. By 1816 the colonial government had abolished them and reverted to a policy of overcoming the Bushmen by the gun rather than by the Word. Moffat sadly bemoans the fact that 'God, in his infinite wisdom had other, and far more extensive ends to accomplish, than simply a mission to the Bushmen.'

The Revd John Philip, one of the most attractive of the missionary writers, was more practical and shrewd in his assessment of the abolition of the missions: 'The country was given out to the colonists, and it must be cleared of Bushmen, as if they had been so many wild beasts; this could not have been done under the eye of a missionary station.' Yet even Philip, with all his care for the Bushmen, did not really get to know what they believed and thought, and was 'never able to discover from my intercourse with the natives, or from any other source, that this nation had ever attained any distinct notion of a Supreme Being, or that an idea of a future state of existence had at any period prevailed among them.'

This opinion was shared by most other nineteenth-century travellers, whether or not they were missionaries. Livingstone, however, was refreshingly different. He admitted that his own ignorance had on one occasion led to his completely misunderstanding what a Bushman had been telling him: 'If I had known the name of God in the Bushman tongue the mistake could scarcely have occurred.... I have not had intercourse with either Caffres or Bushmen in their own tongues.'

To have been able to converse with the Bushmen in their own language might indeed have been very illuminating both to Livingstone and to others who constantly passed off as superstition not only behaviour that might legitimately be regarded as such, but also anything that they did not understand. In the former category, perhaps, comes the Bushmen's preoccupation with throwing the bones (or dice as some writers called them). Bushmen still use them very widely today; they consist of a few pieces of bone — when there are five, as we encountered, two are flat (small pieces of rib), two are roundish (vertebrae), and the fifth any shape that is totally different. Some groups use leather discs instead of bones. The man throwing cups the bones in his hands, shakes them about, blows into his cupped hands and finally casts them to the ground with a sweeping movement that makes both hands continue upwards and outwards. He and the other men present then ponder the message of the bones, usually with much discussion. Frequently he will throw the bones several times before coming to a conclusion on what the message is [39].

One of Livingstone's Bushman helpers 'took out his dice, and, after throwing them, said God told him to go home. He threw again in order to show me the command, but the opposite result followed; so he remained and was useful.'

We had a similar example of the unreliability of the bones, with the group of Bushmen with whom we spent some time in the southeastern Kalahari. One afternoon, after Ramonne, Be/tee, Kotuko/tee and others had laid a snare for a small antelope, they all came back to their camp, sat down in a semi-circle, and Ramonne proceeded to throw the bones to ascertain whether anything would be caught. After several throws and much debate between them all, Ramonne declared that the snare would not catch anything because there had been too many people there. We couldn't help feeling that there was a high degree of perfectly sensible personal opinion coming through in the judgment; but in the event neither bones nor personal opinion proved accurate as a steenbok was caught in the snare that very evening.

The Bushmen's lack of understanding of the nature of the white man's God was at best held up as an object of kindly amusement. John Chapman, on his travels in the mid-nineteenth century, came upon some Bushmen who, 'seeing our cattle, thought they must be game belonging to God (Torra), and were doubtful whether it would be safe to discharge their arrows at them'. My own suspicion is that on this occasion the Bushmen probably feared the presence and wrath of the white man more than that of his God; and Chapman seems to be somewhat credulous if he really believed that Bushmen did not know ordinary cattle when they saw them. They had, after all, been making off with white men's cattle for the best part of two hundred years. On another occasion Chapman was using a new-fangled camera when a Bushman 'took me by the button-hole, and asked whether God (Morimo) was in there — pointing to the camera'.

Two different words for God are quoted here, of which the former is probably the same as Thora, which is used today by some !Kung groups in the northwest. Morimo is the Tswana name, and is not generally used by the Bushmen except by way of explanation to those who might not understand one of the many names that they themselves employ, most of which in any case may not be spoken out loud. Each language group has its own names for God.

Korakoradue, the grand old man of the group of Kua Bushmen we spent some time with in the southeastern Kalahari, talked a little of God but was reluctant to go very deeply into the subject. We would have needed more time than we had available for him to feel free to explore such a subject. But he told me that their Great God was called Bise. At first he said that Bise lives in the sky, but later added that maybe he comes from the ground and lives in the earth.

He said, 'Most of us human beings cannot see him, but he is there when we sit around the fire, and at other times too — he is always there — especially in the dark. If there is a medicine man, he will be able to see Bise. Bise only speaks to his people through the medicine men, and he cares for us only through the medicine men.'

I asked Korakoradue if, when a person dies, it means that Bise has ceased to care for him, and he replied,

Sometimes it is because Bise loves him that he makes him ill, and then he dies because Bise wants him. In the olden days, Bise took those who died to where the sun sets. If a person is a cripple, that also is Bise's work. He makes him a cripple because he loves him; and if he loves him even more he will take him to himself.

We observe that when the moon is small it rises where the sun sets; but when it is full, it rises where the sun rises. When we see the morning star, it tells us that Bise is making a new day. In summer the sun is high above us, but when winter comes the sun goes to the north, it does not give so much heat and it sets earlier. All these things we just observe with our eyes, yet they are the work of Bise.

As many as eight different names have been recorded in some groups, not denoting different gods, but possibly used in connection with different aspects of God's character or function. The !Kung group with whom the American anthropologist, Lorna Marshall, worked for several years in Namibia had one earthly name for God — ≠Gao!na (old ≠Gao), a common name for a man — by which he was most frequently referred to, and seven divine names which are never given to human beings. Of these she found that Hishe was often associated with God as the Creator; Huwe seemed to relate to God's greatness; Gani ga was used when they wanted to show special respect or ask for special help; !Gara and ≠Gaishi≠gai when they were remonstrating with God. Of the other two names, Kxo was hardly used, and //Gauwa we will come to later. But there seemed to be no hard and fast rule about this usage of names – it was, rather, a 'vague tendency'. What she did find was a general reluctance to say any of the divine names out loud.

These !Kung believe that ≠Gao!na, the Great God, lives in the eastern sky where the sun rises. He created himself first, saying, 'I am Hishe. I am unknown, a stranger. No one can command me.' Then he created a Lesser God who lives in the western sky where the sun sets; and after this two women, as wives for himself and for the Lesser God. He created the earth and water, the sky and rain – both the gentle 'female' rain and the fierce 'male' rain – thunder and lightning, the sun, moon, stars and wind. He created all the plants that grow on the earth. He created the animals and painted their individual colours and markings, and gave them all names. Then came human beings, and he put life into them; and ≠Gao!na ordained that when they died they should become spirits, //gauwasi, who would live in the sky with him and serve him. He set the pattern of life for all things, each in accordance with its own rules.

The !Kung pray to ≠Gao!na not as a remote being, but as intimately involved with their lives, sometimes calling him father. They pray for rain, for success in hunting, for healing both of physical and social ills. Only a really great medicine man might see ≠Gao!na face to face, but this is said to be very rare; much more frequently ≠Gao!na may appear to anyone in a dream to encourage or advise.

The Lesser God, while not the personification of evil, is more inclined to do evil and to bring harm to man. He has all seven divine names of the Great God, but not his human name. Among the !Kung, to name a child after a person implies a degree of identification with that person. So the Lesser God, who shares all seven divine names, is not regarded as a totally separate being but, with a kind of dualism, as the dark aspect of the deity. The divine name by which he is most commonly known is //Gauwa, which is also the singular form of the !Kung word for the spirits of the dead. He is associated with sickness and death, and when medicine men hold a healing dance (see Chapter 9), it is against //Gauwa that they fulminate.

The belief in the Great God's permeation and ordering of all things is also found among the /Gwi Bushmen of the central Kalahari. Their Great God is called !Nadima; he is the supreme being in the universe, the creator and lord of all things, who can be commanded by no one. Yet George Silberbauer, who worked among them for many years, found that the /Gwi, unlike the !Kung, regarded !Nadima as somewhat remote from them. He knows their needs and actions, but chooses of his own accord whether or not to favour them; therefore the /Gwi do not pray to him, for it will make no difference. The Lesser God is called //Gamama, and he has neither the omnipotence nor omniscience of

!Nadima; he can take life but he cannot make it. He is generally hostile to man and sends illness and misfortune which !Nadima may, on occasion, choose to counteract. If he does, it will only ever be effected in accordance with the laws of the system that he himself created. Within this system man has to find his own way of life as part of a complex and integrated whole which !Nadima alone can comprehend. All things – the sun, moon and stars, all plants and animals, and man himself – have their own unique place in !Nadima's finely-ordered system for the universe.

Fables, myths and legends – like those collected in the mid-nineteenth century by Wilhelm Bleek, with his sister-in-law Lucy Lloyd, and so luminously expounded by Laurens van der Post – are the metaphorical form in which much of the Bushmen's religious beliefs are expressed. In the past, as in the present, the stories are peopled with a colourful range of characters, some human and some animal, drawn with great subtlety and wit.

Among some of the !Kung Bushmen in the Kalahari today, the central god/ hero figure is usually called Kauha, one of the lesser names of the Great God. He, like the Mantis of the extinct southern Bushmen, is endlessly trying to trick and deceive, especially members of his own family; he gets things wrong, frequently fails in his enterprises, and is generally seen as a fool as well as a trickster. But there are other aspects of the stories today which are not found in those Bleek collected. Both groups of stories pay considerable attention to food; but the !Kung stories involve that other great human theme – sex. The lack of such stories in Bleek's collection may simply reflect nineteenth-century European inhibitions, rather than any lack in the /Xam repertoire. Many of the !Kung stories are gross and extremely bawdy, and are a source of enormous enjoyment and laughter both to those who tell them and those who listen.

According to one story told to Megan Biesele, another American anthropologist, Kauha wanted to sleep with some beautiful women, but every one whom he asked refused him. So he decided to play a trick; he turned himself into a springbok, lay down in the veld and died. Soon some women passed that way gathering roots, found the dead springbok, and decided to carry it home. They packed it into a kaross and took it in turns to carry it. First it was carried by a woman whom Kauha did not desire, so he made himself very heavy on her back until she handed the burden over to a woman whom Kauha very much wanted to sleep with. As this woman carried the kaross, Kauha slipped further and further down her back until he was level with her buttocks, and then he began to enter her. The woman yelled and could not think what was happening to her. Then, after much complaint, one of the other women took her share of carrying the meat and experienced no trouble at all. Again came the turn of the woman Kauha wanted, and again he slipped down and entered her. She kept pushing him away and up onto her back, but every time he came down again and continued his interference until the woman became thoroughly alarmed.

When the women finally reached home, they told the others about this strange meat which interfered with one woman but gave no trouble to the others. When they came to skin the springbok and cut it up, they found that it had no blood or guts but was just a solid piece of meat. What was worse, it tasted bad, so they threw it away.

Kauha is not only lecherous, but also vindictive. One day he was cross because the women of his family only gave him raw //xaru bulbs to eat while they ate delicious cooked bulbs. So he persuaded his brother-in-law, !Kõ!kõtsi/dasi, to go gathering //xaru with him for their own consumption. His brother-in-law's name means 'eyes on his ankles', because that was where his eyes were, and not on his face. When they came back from gathering they played a game, still played by some Bushmen, which involves transferring a small bead along a series of holes in the ground. Kauha could not understand how his brother-in-law could win every time when he did not appear to have any eyes. When !Kõ!kõtsi-/dasi took a nap, Kauha flicked sand into his face but got no reaction; then he flicked the sand all the way down his body, and when he reached the ankles the eyes blinked. Kauha determined to blind those eyes.

The following day, when !Kõ!kõtsi/dasi and he were cooking the //xaru bulbs in a big hole filled with coals, Kauha asked his brother-in-law to stamp down the tops of the bulbs so that they should not reach above the top of the hole. As he did so, Kauha raked the coals over his eyes, whereupon the eyeballs popped out and started singing, 'Kho-Kho-Kho-Kho-Kho-tsuninini!' [Tsuninini, come and eat me and your mouth will disappear!] Kauha then ate one of the cooked //xaru bulbs, but as he put the second one to his mouth he found that he could not put it in because his mouth had already disappeared.

In most of these stories everyone recovers from the awful things that happen to them, even death, and live to harm, and be harmed, another day. But the character of Kauha is so greatly at variance with the !Kung concept of the Great God that it is difficult for those of us with western preconceptions to see any real identification. Yet this seems to pose no problem for the Bushmen whose cosmology is perhaps too complex and subtle for our more stereotyped perceptions. Or perhaps our own subtleties are in such a different mode that we fail to perceive theirs.

The same duality is found in Lorna Marshall's !Kung group in Namibia, for whom the main protagonist of the stories is, like their Great God, called ≠Gao!na. One story is about ≠Gau!na discovering fire, which was then unknown except to one man, /Kai /Kini, who alone ate cooked food. One day ≠Gao!na came upon /Kai /Kini's home and asked for some food. He thought it was delicious and came back secretly the next day to see how it was cooked. Lying hidden, he saw /Kai /Kini get out his fire sticks and rub the male stick against the female stick to produce fire. ≠Gao!na then came out of hiding and went to eat the cooked food with /Kai /Kini's family. Determined to steal the fire sticks, he persuaded /Kai /Kini to play a game, and at an opportune moment he seized the sticks and ran off with them. He broke them into little pieces and threw them all over the world so that all men could make fire and cook food. Presumably to punish /Kai /Kini for keeping the secret to himself, ≠Gao!na turned him into a bird.

The /Gwi Bushmen have a completely different story about the discovery of fire by the god/hero of their tales, Pisiboro (also one of the names by which the Great God is known). Pisiboro saw red-hot coal under the wing of the Ostrich who was then a person of the early race. He stole the coal, and from it gave fire to men. The burning coal itself he threw high into the air, but twice it fell back to earth. At the third attempt, the coal stayed in the sky and became the sun.

The stories of the Bushmen — of whatever language group, whether past or present — point to a special relationship between the Creator and a particular animal. With the southern Bushmen it was the eland. With the !Kung, as well as with many other groups in the Kalahari today, it is also the eland; though with some groups, in places where the eland is rare, it is the gemsbok that has this pre-eminence.

J. M. Orpen, who collected some Bushman stories in the Maluti Mountains in the 1870s, was told by his guide, Qing, how Cagn (Mantis) re-created the eland after it had been killed by his two sons. Indeed he made not just one new eland but many; and when one of his sons later tried to hunt them, he was not able to kill any for, as Qing said, 'they were able to run away because Cagn was in their bones'. Furthermore, when Orpen asked Qing where Cagn was, he replied, 'We do not know, but the elands do. Have you not heard his cry, when elands suddenly start and run to his call? Where he is, the elands are in droves like cattle.'

It is this special relationship with the Creator that gives the eland what one of Bleek's informants called 'its magic power'. In every aspect of the Bushmen's lives, in the various rituals still practised in the Kalahari today, and also in the paintings of the now extinct southern Bushmen, it is the eland above every other creature that is regarded as the supreme source of supernatural power, the greatest link with the divine.

CHAPTER THREE

Painters and Metaphors

How long paintings have adorned the rocks of southern Africa is almost impossible to gauge. Many have doubtless disappeared with time, and for the rest dating is notoriously difficult without destroying the painting itself. The most effective method is to apply radiocarbon dating techniques to other objects associated with the paintings at the same site and in the same cultural layer. This was done at the Apollo 11 Cave in the Huns Mountains of southwestern Namibia, excavated by Eric Wendt in 1968 to 1972, and it produced an astonishingly great age for the paintings — between 27,500 and 25,000 years old. This makes them the oldest dated works of art in all Africa — only 6,000 years (at the most) later than the earliest rock art in France and Germany.

The Apollo 11 paintings, in two colours, depict a variety of animals both real and imaginary (half human, half animal). We cannot at this early date talk about 'Bushman' art, but the inhabitants of the cave were clearly hunter-gatherers, so it must be possible to suggest some kind of ancestral relationship between those people and their art and the later Bushmen and their art.

All over southern Africa Bushmen have painted and engraved on the rocks for thousands of years. The earliest dated Bushman paintings have been ascribed to about six thousand years ago; however, the vast majority of what we can see today was almost certainly executed within the past two thousand years, and most of it probably since the turn of the last millennium. Zimbabwe, Zambia, Botswana, Angola, Namibia and South Africa, all have rich examples of Bushman art. People have been at pains to identify different styles, and even individual artists; but to me, far more astonishing than the differences, is the homogeneity of the art over such a vast geographical area and over such an extended timespan. What connection could the !Kung of the Tsodilo Hills have had with the /Xam Bushmen of the Cape, or those of the Drakensberg? Even their languages would have been mutually incomprehensible. Yet their paintings, like their stories, are in a similar mode and are filled with the same spirit. Something very powerful must have taken hold of them at an early stage; powerful enough to have survived their variations in language as well as their geographical diaspora.

Some of the later paintings can be fairly easily dated as they relate to the coming of the white men. Bushmen observed the galleons in which they arrived, and they painted them. They painted the wagons and cattle and sheep of the early Dutch farmers; and also the farmers themselves and their wives, dressed in clothes that must have amazed and amused the Bushmen [26]. Later came the British soldiers in their uniforms; all were faithfully represented on the walls of the Bushmen's caves.

To the rest of the world the paintings remained unknown until the eighteenth century. But once the Europeans had penetrated the fastnesses of the mountains of the Cape, they came upon caves filled with paintings of men and animals, and were astonished at the richness of the art. It was so unlike anything that they had previously encountered that they were not quite sure how to award praise or criticism, and usually ended up with a curious combination of the two. Criticism often consisted of a statement about the primitiveness of the Bushmen, which in turn earned them a surprised and patronizing praise for the remarkable success of their untutored attempts.

Sir James Alexander, writing about his travels in southern Africa, assured 'the intelligent reader' that he would 'readily perceive that these rude attempts of uncivilized artists are not utterly devoid of merit . . . though defective in proportions'. He later reported seeing in a cave in the Cedarberg Mountains to the north of Cape Town, a painting of 'a flock of sheep with their lambs represented in red ochre, the outlines of which were surprisingly accurate; whilst higher up there is another cave in which Boschmans [Bushmen] are seen combating with javelin, bow and arrows; these traces of a rude people, who have long since disappeared from the locality, are very interesting.'

Alexander's book was published in 1838, by which time, he says, the Bushmen had 'long since' disappeared from the Cedarberg. They had been pushed as far away as possible from the Cape Colony, and the only traces of their millennia-old habitation there were their paintings on the rocks. In the Malutis of what is now Lesotho, in the Drakensberg of Natal, and in the plains of the Orange Free State, they survived for some few years longer.

George Stow, the first person who consistently recorded and made copies of Bushman paintings, visited the eastern Cape in 1869. There he met an old Bushman called 'Gcu-wa, 'the artist of the family [who] still carried two or three of his horn paint-pots slung at his belt. He was the artist who painted the representation of a Boer commando, which adorned the wall of his brother's rock shelter, and it was said that it was intended to commemorate the first attack the Boers ever made upon their tribe'. But 'Gcu-wa was by then one of a 'miserable remnant' of Bushmen in the area, consisting of three men, three women and about five little children.

Stow also tells us that 'the last known Bushman artist of the Malutis was shot in the Witteberg Native Reserve, where he had been on a marauding expedition, and had captured some horses. He was evidently a man of considerable repute among his race. He had ten small horn pots hanging from his belt, each of which contained a different coloured paint. The informant of the writer told him that he saw the belt, that there were no two colours alike, and that each had a marked difference from the rest.'

Unfortunately Stow does not appear to have seen a Bushman artist at work, otherwise our ignorance of how they worked might have been less profound. All the reports from the nineteenth and early-twentieth centuries are either second-hand, or of not pure-bred Bushmen. Thomas Baines, one of the few accomplished artists to have encountered Bushmen in the mid-nineteenth century, might have been expected to go into some detail about their technique, but he limits his observations to one tantalizing remark: 'A true child in art, he will paint with his feather, dipped in grease and coloured clay'.

Dornan, in the first quarter of this century, paid a half-bred Bushman to paint for him, who

> first took a pebble and rubbed the surface of the granite boulder on which he was going to paint as smooth as he could, and wiped away the dust carefully. Then he took a burnt stick and drew the outline of the figure, in this case a zebra. Next he took his lump of dry paint, his crayon in fact, and rubbed it over the figure, roughly filling in the outline. Then he brushed away all the dust, and then he took a small feather brush, some liquid paint which he heated in a small hollow pebble, and laid this carefully on the figure, and the painting was complete. He painted a zebra, a tortoise, a porcupine and some guinea fowl, and it took him the best part of three hours to complete the set of pictures, for which he was paid five shillings. The figures were quite small, only about three inches high, and he did not work hard, as he stopped to smoke more than once.

One of the most fascinating and detailed accounts of a painter at work comes from Marion Walsham How, whose family had been in Basutoland since 1861. In 1930 she met an old man called Mapote, one of the many sons of Moorosi, a great Sotho chief in the mid-nineteenth century. While Mapote himself probably had no Bushman blood, his father had had some Bushman wives, so he had half-Bushman half-brothers. He told her that he and these half-brothers used to paint at one end of a cave, while the pure-bred Bushmen painted at the other end.

Although he was very out of practice, he agreed to do a 'Bushman' painting for Mrs How, and carefully selected the right kind of rock on which to do it. It had to be porous enough to absorb the pigment, but also smooth enough to work on. His brushes were made of reeds with birds' feathers stuck into the ends of them. Mapote said that the red pigment ought to be Qhang Qhang (haematite, or oxidized red ochre mixed with various other iron oxides), which, he said, had to be prepared at full moon outside in the open by a woman, who must heat it until it is red hot and then grind it to a fine red powder. However, since no Qhang Qhang was available, he used ordinary unoxidized red ochre obtained from the local shop. For black he burned some sticks and mixed the resulting charcoal with water; and for a white pigment he used a local white clay with a high silica content, powdered and mixed with the thick white juice of *Asclepia gibba*. This is unlikely to have made a very long-lasting pigment, and may account for the complete loss of parts of some paintings that had once been white. But the Bushmen used whatever was available in their area, and where gypsum was to be found, a much longer-lasting white pigment could be made.

Mapote's most difficult request was for the blood of a freshly killed eland to mix with the red ochre; but as Mrs How was unable to provide this, he agreed to make do with the blood of a freshly killed ox, supplied by the local butcher. As soon as all his pigments were prepared, Mapote then painted an eland because, he said, the Bushmen of that area had been people of the eland. He does not appear to have drawn an outline first, as Dornan's artist did; he simply started painting with his feather brush at the eland's chest, and continued working with great fluency, using a different brush for each colour.

Feathers were not the only instrument used to paint with. Mrs How's grandfather, the Revd D. F. Ellenberger, was told of an artist in the Malutis who used brushes made of wildebeest hair; while other reports say that bones were used, hollow and tapering to a point, and filled with liquid paint. The blood used by Mapote as a fixing agent must have made his paint liquid initially, but it would have tended to thicken as the blood coagulated. Some artists evidently used animal fat, as Baines reported, and the result would have been much less fluid. Dornan's artist used a 'lump of dry paint' which was presumably rather like chalk, and then he painted over this with liquid paint. He does not say how either was made.

Some of the earth pigments were found by the Bushmen inside stones which they cracked open to reveal a soft centre of reds or yellows or browns. The Basotho had a high regard for Bushman medicine men, and would go to great lengths to obtain Bushman pigments which they believed had special magical properties. This may, perhaps, give some clue to the role of the painters in Bushman societies. If their pigments were so sought after for their magical properties, it seems likely that the painters themselves were deemed to have some share in that magic. This could account for Stow's observation that the Bushman artist shot in the Malutis 'was evidently a man of considerable repute among his race'.

In the remarkably egalitarian society of the Bushmen, the men of greatest repute have usually been the medicine men, those believed to have supernatural power in healing, the control of game for hunting, or the bringing of rain. To acquire this supernatural power, or n/um, the medicine man has to enter a state of trance which is regarded as the central religious ritual of the Bushmen. Only in trance can the n/um inherent in such things as the sun, rain, honey, giraffes — and pre-eminently the eland — be transformed for the benefit of the community. Even today in the Kalahari, about half the men in most Bushman bands are, for some period of their life, medicine men; so it is quite possible that many of the southern Bushman artists of the past may also have been medicine men. Certainly in the paintings which portray the performance of rituals such as rainmaking, there are some features which seem to indicate that the particular painter understood what it was to go into trance.

One of the most common misconceptions about Bushman painting is that it consists largely of animals and hunting scenes. In fact, on a purely statistical count, the majority of figures are human (between fifty and sixty per cent); and of these only a small fraction are of men hunting. Clearly it was the animals and the hunting scenes that captured the imaginations of the people who first copied or photographed Bushman paintings, and their selection has conditioned our understanding of the art.

Most of the paintings with human subjects show groups of people involved in some activity: men on the march; men and women dancing or sitting about apparently talking; or two or three men, painted almost on top of each other, running full tilt, their legs at an angle of 180 degrees to underline the speed with which they are moving. Among the dancing groups there are a number of paintings that appear to portray rituals in which some of the people are in a state of trance.

There is a remarkable painting at Sani Pass in the Drakensberg Mountains which shows some people dancing, several running, and others standing and clapping, while a number of others are bending over, overcome with gushing nose-bleeds – a sure sign of a man in trance [31]. One of these men is in such a deep state of trance that he has fallen flat on his back. Underneath these figures are two animals surrounded by a line which looks rather like the outer edges of a net. These have been identified as rain animals, imaginary creatures (here in the form of eland) which the medicine men of rain, while in trance, would lead across the area where the rain was desired. No real animal was involved – it was all in the realm of the supernatural – so this painter has clearly introduced these rain animals as a symbol of what he believed was happening during a rain-making ritual.

Several stories involving the rain were collected by Bleek and Lloyd in the 1870s and the metaphysical, almost dreamlike, form of the stories illuminates the metaphors of the paintings. Dia!kwain, a Bushman from the Katkop Hills of the Cape, told them,

> Mother used to say that people pull the water-bull in order to lead it over their place, that the rain may fall upon their place and the wild onions sprout there,.so that they may live. If the rain did not fall, they would starve. . . .
>
> That is why they want the water's people to make rain fall for them, that they may dig and feed themselves when rain falls on the wild onion leaves, for these are what they eat, the Bushman's food. So they beg the water's medicine men to make rain fall for them. . . .
>
> Therefore they speak to the medicine men about it, and these promise that they will really make rain fall for them. Then they go and sling a thong over the water-bull's horns, they lead it out, they make it walk when they have slung the thong over its horns. They make it walk along and kill it on the way, that the rain may fall. They cut it up and the rain falls at the place where they threw it down.

Other paintings of rain animals show them as amorphous creatures, barely recognizable as animals at all, and certainly not of any known species. Sometimes they are shown with no human figures or activity associated with them, but with perhaps a single or multiple zig-zag line surrounding them – possibly a symbol of trance – and some lines streaming downwards which look like rain. These rain animals are pure metaphor, a single image which conveyed to the

Bushman who painted them, as well as to his own people who looked at them, the whole range of beliefs and rituals associated with the making of rain.

Of the paintings of animals that the Bushmen executed, by far the most numerous, and the most beautiful, are those of eland. Other animal subjects pale into insignificance by comparison with the care lavished on depictions of the Great God's favourite creature. In the Drakensberg we filmed in a rock shelter that had with justice been named Eland Cave [23], for while there were many other animals depicted on the walls, the dominant subject was the eland. One panel in particular drew all eyes. It started at the bottom right hand end with an eland cow lying down and looking over her shoulder, as though curious about something coming up behind her. Thereafter the scene sweeps up through a vast array of eland in all manner of postures, culminating in an eland of Herculean proportions. All mature eland bulls are huge by comparison with their cows, but this painted eland exceeds all comparison, clearly showing the significance that this great antelope had acquired in the Bushman's mind.

There are many instances of eland being painted out of all proportion to the other animals around it. At Bellevue in the southern Drakensberg, for example, a group of massive eland are pursued by diminutive men on diminutive horses. It seems it may have been the spiritual value, rather than the merely physical, that was portrayed.

Not only in size is the eland distinguished by the Bushman painters, but also in the care with which it is painted. No other creature is painted with such attention to subtle shading and line definition, to perspective, and to the representation of inner vitality. The eland is painted from the rear, from the side and from above, indeed from every angle the artist could think of. It was truly a favoured creature.

Next in numerical importance in the painting, after the eland, are all the other antelopes — rhebok, hartebeest, springbok, reedbuck, etc. — counted as a single group. In the Drakensberg the number of rhebok painted is far greater than in other areas, putting them in second place after the eland. It is, however, very rare to find a blue wildebeest, astonishingly so considering that it was the commonest antelope and the most abundant source of meat for the Bushmen. Why it was avoided as a subject can only be guessed at. Bleek appears to have been told only one story about the wildebeest, and this portrays it as an interferer and hinderer. Possibly in the uncollected mythology, which has died with the southern Bushmen, the wildebeest represented even more clearly something that was to be avoided. However, as this avoidance does not seem to have applied to the wildebeest as a source of food, it is clear that the painters were not merely depicting potential meals, even when this was a matter of survival. If they had been, they would surely also have painted more women with digging sticks gathering the plant food which, far more than the occasional meat that the hunters provided, kept the Bushman bands alive. The women are indeed painted, but not so frequently as their economic role might warrant. Clearly economics had little to do with the choice of subjects to be painted.

Another rarity as a subject in the art is the gemsbok, stated in the /Xam mythology to be an animal beloved of Mantis, though not so beloved as the eland or the hartebeest. Perhaps a reason for the omission of the gemsbok is that in most of the area where it is not only common but also regarded as especially important – the Kalahari Desert – there are, with one exception, no rock surfaces and no paintings. But in the hills in the west of Namibia, where Bushmen also lived in the past, we find gemsbok painted on the rocks, testifying to the significance with which it was invested by the Bushmen of that area.

The only place in the Kalahari Desert where there are rocks on which to paint is the Tsodilo Hills where, as we have seen, some Bushmen believe that the paintings were executed by the Great God himself. Eland, gemsbok, various other antelope, zebra and giraffe figure there, painted in red. But the most unusual feature is the number of rhinoceros, a very rare subject in Bushman painting; both black and white rhinos are clearly identifiable. All the paintings at Tsodilo are in monochrome, and are very simple in composition and technique, both of which facts indicate that they are probably of a fairly early date. Almost all the paintings are of animals, with only a few rather crudely painted human figures. The most beautiful and best preserved figures, mainly of eland and giraffe, are on a rock face about one hundred feet above the base of the 'female' hill [22]. In among these animals there are a few human hand-prints, where the artist had covered his diminutive hands in the red pigment he was using, and pressed them against the rock as a permanent signature to his work [27].

A !Kung Bushman from Namibia called ≠Toma (whom we shall meet again in Chapter 10) told John Marshall, the doyen of Bushman documentary film-makers, a story of how these hand-prints came to be there. He said that they were made by a man long ago who was hunting a giraffe. As he crept silently along, he occasionally put his hands on the rock at the places where we now see the prints. The last hand-print, right beside the painting of a giraffe, marks the spot where he finally shot his poisoned arrow at the giraffe that he was stalking.

All along the base of the 'female' hill, and forming a painted procession up the rocky climb to the spring at the top, are hundreds more animals. They seem to reflect very closely the stories told by the Bushmen connecting the Tsodilo Hills with the Great God's act of creation of all the animals of the earth.

We have already seen how the Bushmen of the Cape had marked the arrival of the white men in their paintings. Similarly, in the Maluti and Drakensberg Mountains to the northwest – among the first areas where the Bushmen came into contact with the encroaching Bantu-speaking black peoples – we see the shields and assegais of these other newcomers. Some of these paintings may well date to an earlier period than those of the whites in the Cape, since the blacks arrived several centuries earlier. It seems, perhaps inevitably, to be only the conflicts that were portrayed; though there are some paintings of Bushmen and Bantu (identifiable either as Zulus or Basotho by the shapes of their shields, and by the assegais that they carry) sitting down together in what appears to be a friendly manner.

Less friendly in tone are the paintings of stock raids, in which Bushmen are seen making off with the cattle and horses of their black or white neighbours. By the mid-nineteenth century both British and Boers had established themselves in Natal, the Orange Free State and Basutoland, and their distinctive clothes can be seen in a number of paintings at that time. Men in uniform shoot guns at Bushmen who drive off herds in the opposite direction. In other paintings we see shields and volleys of assegais, as Zulus or Basotho attempt to stop the Bushmen in their raids.

Many of the paintings of stock raids by the Bushmen, and of commando raids by the whites seem to have the immediacy of narrative. There are details of clothing that are so accurately observed – the jaunty set of a hat, for example – that I feel I am present at an event that really took place. Stow's reference to the artist 'Gcu-wa would seem to confirm that at least some paintings were about actual events. He was told that 'Gcu-wa's painting of a commando raid 'was intended to commemorate the first attack the Boers ever made upon their tribe'.

Patricia Vinnicombe, who worked for several years between the late 1950s and the early 1970s on Bushman paintings in an area of the Drakensberg, found some fascinating correlations between some of the paintings and information in the Natal Archives. In the Lotheni valley early in January 1847, the Crown Prosecutor, Walter Harding, led a commando of twenty-two men – five Cape Mounted Riflemen and seventeen Boers – against a group of Bushmen. In a rock shelter above the Lotheni river there is a Bushman painting of a group of twenty-two horses, most of them ridden by men dressed in a generally European manner, all heading purposefully in the same direction. The correspondence both of the number of men involved in the commando and of the location make it tempting to speculate that the artist was recording an actual event.

Yet there are many other paintings, especially those involving eland, where enigmatic figures associated with a particular scene have long baffled students of Bushman art. It seems clear that, as with the rain animals, we are in the realm of painted metaphor. Nothing in our own western cultures can help us to decode the metaphors; the only hope lies in what has been collected of Bushman folklore. David Lewis-Williams has spent several years meticulously researching the ethnography – mainly that collected by Bleek, both published and unpublished – in an attempt to decode the art according to the Bushmen's own concepts. One of the paintings that has had new light thrown on it is a superb scene in a shelter at Game Pass in the Drakensberg [30].

The painting shows a great bull eland staggering, its head lowered with the approach of death. Another indication that it is dying, also taken from real animal behaviour, is the hair which stands on end all along its neck and over its hump, under its belly and down its tail. A semi-human figure, with an antelope's head and hooves, stands behind the eland and holds its tail, his legs crossed in the same way as those of the dying eland. Behind this figure is another who is dancing, bending forward with his arms stretched out behind him, a characteristic posture of a man in trance. Two other figures further to the right also have antelope features, and one of them has hair standing on end in the same way as the dying eland.

'Death', or 'half-death', is a metaphor that was used not only by the southern /Xam, but is also used by present-day Bushmen in the Kalahari Desert to refer to the trance state. So the figures in this painting, whether human or antelope or both, are all linked by images of death and trance. Through the antelope-man who is holding the eland's tail, the dancers are acquiring the 'magic power' of the eland which, in trance, they can transform in order to heal sickness or conflict, to bring rain, or to control game.

There are lamentably few records from the nineteenth century of southern Bushmen explaining some of the paintings executed by their own people. Even those that do exist are couched in metaphorical language that must have been as enigmatic to the interviewer as the paintings themselves. The prime example is J. M. Orpen's questioning of his Bushman guide, Qing. He asked him about the meaning of a painting showing men with rhebok's heads, to which Qing replied, 'They were the men who had died and now live in rivers, and were *spoilt at the same time as the elands* and by the dances of which you have seen paintings' (Orpen's italics). Orpen seems to have treated 'died' as literal, or at any rate he does not appear to have questioned the word which, as we have seen, was also used to refer to trance. Equally, he did not apparently pursue the meaning of the phrase 'live in rivers', or he might have discovered that, in the /Xam mythology, being under water was another metaphor of the trance experience. As Lewis-Williams explains, 'the struggle, gasping for breath, sound in the ears, sense of weightlessness, inhibited movement, distorted vision and final loss of consciousness are common to both experiences.'

Orpen did, however, question Qing about when the elands were 'spoilt', and was treated to a description of the ways of the god/hero, Cagn, and his close relationship with the eland. To the Bushmen, the verb 'to spoil' has, like 'to die', a double meaning, one of which is to go into a deep state of trance. Qing later went on to tell Orpen that 'the men with rhebok's heads . . . live mostly under water; they tame elands and snakes. . . . They are people spoilt by the __ dance, because their noses bleed. Cagn gave us the song of this dance, and people would die from it, and he would give charms to raise them again.'

It seems that Qing was trying to explain to Orpen, by heaping one opaque metaphor on another, that these rhebok-headed creatures represented medicine men who had gone into trance through the medium of the dance, and by association with the elands which they had 'tamed'. Cagn himself was involved with the whole process, both by giving men the songs of the dances, and by providing the way to come out of trance.

Orpen did not have the means at his disposal to decode either the paintings or the explanations. Yet despite this inability to penetrate their meaning, he was convinced, as was George Stow whom he consulted, that some paintings had 'a mythological meaning, or [were] representing certain quasi-religious acts'.

Not only had Orpen consulted Stow, but Bleek was then invited by Orpen's publisher to comment on his paper – a remarkable coming together of the three main students of Bushman mythology and art in the nineteenth century. Bleek wrote: 'The fact of Bushman paintings illustrating Bushman mythology has first been publicly demonstrated by this paper of Mr Orpen's. . . . This fact can hardly be valued sufficiently. It gives at once to Bushman art a higher character, and teaches us to look upon its products not as the mere daubing of figures for idle pastime, but as an attempt, however imperfect, at a truly artistic conception of the ideas which most deeply moved the Bushman mind, and filled it with religious feeling.'

Furthermore, Bleek showed the paintings that Qing had commented on to the Bushmen who were staying with him at the time, including the same Dia!kwain who had told the story of the water-bull. Of one painting that contained both an animal and some human figures, they said that it represented a rain-making ritual. The human figures, they said, were putting a rope around the rain animal's nose, and then leading it over the area where the rain was required. The vertical strokes, they told him, indicated the rain that fell as a result. It could scarcely fit more exactly to the rain bull story.

In Eland Cave we filmed, besides the great eland frieze, a strange and enigmatic painting. It was a small group of figures, rather set apart from the rest, which looked as if it had once been part of a larger design, now crumbled or faded out of existence. At the bottom were a few eland, and among them a small running human figure, painted in red, evidently a hunter. From the midst of these rose two human figures, yet they were no ordinary figures for they had an elongation to every limb that put even El Greco in the shade. These wonderful figures, complete with the distinctive, protuberant Bushman behind, towered up the rock face, each ending in great broad shoulders and a small white head. There was about them, as Laurens van der Post commented as we filmed him there, something Olympian if not utterly divine [28].

Elongated human figures are not uncommon in Bushman art, and their meaning has been the subject of some speculation. It has been suggested that the elongation has a psychological explanation: either that it portrays the Bushman's sense of his own spiritual value, in the same way that elands are often painted so large; or conversely that it represents the Bushman's wish for extra inches; or that these figures do not portray Bushmen at all, but taller people of different origin. To me the most convincing explanation is that they represent men in trance. Among the sensations that medicine men have said they have felt while in trance are a sense of weightlessness and rising from the earth, and a feeling of elongation in their limbs.

In this particular painting in Eland Cave there are a number of other features that would also seem to associate the elongated figures with trance. One is their evidently intentional connection with the group of eland at their feet, the most usual source of a medicine man's n/um; then, higher up and to the left of the two great figures, is a large eland bull with its head lowered with the approach of death which is, as we have seen, a metaphor of trance. In addition, the figures themselves have small, white heads of a curious and simplified shape — also believed (from the frequency that such heads appear in scenes depicting trance rituals) to be a metaphor of trance.

Perhaps the paintings of stock raids, and of some animal and human figures and groups, are indeed narrative paintings, or depictions of everyday life — the 'innocent playthings' that Arbousset thought them to be. But where what appears to be, say, a simple domestic scene is set in close juxtaposition with an eland or some antelope-headed figures, or perhaps an elongated figure, the possibility remains that these apparently simple scenes may also be some kind of metaphor, as yet impenetrable to us. There are so many other representations of human or semi-human figures in an enigmatic association with eland — and also other creatures unknown to natural history — that the conclusion seems inescapable that similar metaphors exist in very many Bushman paintings. Whether they will ever be decoded, or whether some will remain enigmatic, the future alone will reveal.

CHAPTER FOUR

The Desert's Dusty Face

The Kalahari does not look like a desert. The barely undulating earth stretches away in every direction as far as the eye can see, covered with knee-high Bushman grass, corn-coloured from the sun [53]. In the early mornings, and in the evenings, the feathery tops of the grass catch the low beams of the sun and reflect them back like a sea of shimmering light. Scrubby green bushes are scattered about, interspersed with occasional acacia and terminalia trees. In some areas, like that around Masetlheng pan in the southwest, the grass was shorter and stouter and greener, with heads like wild wheat, and the impression was altogether gentler — rather like some great European park except for the very African shape of the acacias.

Beneath this vegetation, and in some places showing through it, the Kalahari Desert is a vast basin of sand — varying in colour from white to deep orange — which extends for over 200,000 square miles and occupies about one third of the vast plateau of southern Africa. Most of it is between 3,000 and 3,500 feet above sea level. It stretches from the Orange river in South Africa, takes in most of Botswana and the eastern part of Namibia, and reaches into central Angola as far as the watersheds of the Cuando, Zambezi and Okavango rivers.

For thousands of years the Kalahari has provided everything that the Bushmen required. Its earth supports an astonishing variety and abundance of plant food, including several plants with water-storing tubers that remain a source of fluid throughout the long dry season. The vegetation also provides food for considerable numbers of animals, in the past exclusively for wild animals, now for an increasing number of cattle which are effectively driving away the herds of antelope which were the main source of meat for the Bushmen. The desert also provides the poles and thatching grass for their huts, the fibres for their string, the wood for their bows and arrows and for their fires.

The Kalahari can truly be called a desert for it has no running water at all, and no permanent standing water. The ancient watercourses are now dry sandy beds; and the great pans which dot the surface of the Kalahari are, for most of the year, expanses of hard, caked, dried-out mud [5]. Only after the rains do they contain any water, and even then they are shallow and last sometimes for no more than a few weeks after the rains have ceased, before reverting to their normal encrusted aridity. The annual rainfall averages from around eight inches in the south to around twenty in some parts of the north, and almost all of it falls

between January and March. In late April 1982, when we arrived in the Kalahari to film, all the pans that we saw were already completely dried out — the
result of several years of drought.

Drought and the establishment of boreholes have between them done more
than anything else to change the life of the Kalahari Bushmen. In years of
drought, when all their traditional sources of water have dried up, many Bushmen have travelled to a borehole. There they have come into contact with a cash
economy, and many of them have decided to stay and work for the local farmer
rather than go back to the hard life of the hunter-gatherer. Today probably no
more than about one thousand Bushmen out of a total of between fifty and
sixty thousand live in the age-old way, and they are almost all in the Central
Kalahari Reserve in Botswana. In the rest of the Botswana Kalahari, and in
Namibia, most Bushmen have been encouraged to become sedentary, and they
live within easy reach of a borehole. Several groups have retained some elements
of their old way of life, but very few have either the skills or the inclination for a
complete reversion to the life of hunter-gatherer.

Traditionally, the Bushmen's main sources of water have been the various
waterholes that occur with more or less frequency throughout the Kalahari —
wells whose water is held near the surface in places where the underlying rock
is not so deep as it is in most of the desert. A few provide water throughout the
year, every year; others dry up only in times of extended drought; while the
majority fill only during the seasonal rains, and dry up after a few weeks, or
perhaps months.

In some areas where hollow trees exist, these provide another source of water
when the pans have dried. During the rains, water collects inside the hollow
trunks and, because it is not exposed to the sun, does not evaporate quickly.
Some of the great baobab trees (*Adansonia digitata*) in the north of the Kalahari
are hollow, and form veritable cisterns of hidden water after the rains have
ceased. In the south no baobabs grow, so when we went out with a few of the
band of Kua Bushmen with whom we spent some time in the southeastern
Kalahari, it was for hollow *Boscia albitrunca* trees that we were looking.

This Kua group had been nomadic until about twelve years ago. Now they
live within two hours' walk of Dinonyane borehole (the name means 'place of
birds'), which is an hour's heavy driving along a dirt track from the little settlement of Ngware. Cultivation of the land has reached as far as Dinonyane now,
and the earth yields thin and scattered crops of mealies (maize). Beyond Dinonyane, where the Bushmen live, no crops are grown, but the Kgalagadi people
(a sub-group of the Tswanas, the majority of the population of Botswana) have
moved in with their cattle which they can graze on the abundant Bushman
grass, and which they water at the borehole.

Because of their situation so close to what has become farming territory, this
group of Bushmen showed an interesting mixture of the old ways and the new.
All the adults remembered the nomadic life, and still did many of the same old
things in the same old way, yet with certain differences. Western-style clothes,

usually in rags and tatters, are immensely popular, but they still have their traditional skins and sometimes wear the two together. They build their huts in the traditional manner but, instead of living together, the various families have separated, though they are still all within hailing distance of each other; and from time to time each family moves as the fleas, lice and other vermin in their huts become oppressive, and builds a new hut a short distance away. Although the larger antelope have been driven from the area by the incursions of the cattle of the Kgalagadi, the Bushmen still trap the little steenboks and duikers that remain in considerable numbers. Most important, perhaps, when tubers and melons are plentiful, as they were when we were there, they do not bother to go to the borehole very often, but rely on the plants and on water found in hollow trees, all of which are closer to home.

Koto, the youngest man of the Kua band, led the search for hollow trees. With him was his wife, /Kongo, and their two children, Samgo, a boy of four or five, and Aegu/tawasa, a baby girl; and also two unmarried girls, Aa//xama and Tsherokhoisa. They took with them two empty ostrich eggshells in which to collect the water – still one of the most commonly used containers.

We walked for about half an hour, Samgo alternating between riding on his father's shoulders and trotting along beside his mother. Then Koto spotted a small tree that looked likely, and went to check. It was indeed hollow, and still had water in it. Koto immediately put his sipping stick into the hole through which the rain had entered. The sipping stick was the straight, hollow stem of a shoulder-high desert plant called *Kalanchoe rotundifolia* (though in other areas of the desert *Leonotis microphylla* or *Panicum kalahariense* perform the same function). Another similar stick was put into the hole at the top of one of the ostrich eggshells. Then Koto began to suck on the exposed end of the stick in the tree and, as soon as his mouth was full of water, he drained it down the other stick into the ostrich eggshell [7]. When the water started to run over the top, he plugged the hole with a bung of grass.

When both eggshells were full /Kongo sucked some water up from the tree and turned to Samgo. He stood with his head tilted up and his mouth open, his hands held out behind him, twitching with anticipation. /Kongo leaned down and gave him some water straight from her mouth into his. He took three mouthfuls with considerable relish, but when /Kongo bent down to offer him a fourth, he turned his head sharply away and suddenly burst into tears. Koto rushed to comfort him for no Bushman can bear to see a child cry, while /Kongo turned to Aegu/tawasa, securely fastened at her side in a kaross, and gave the water to her instead, by the same method [8]. All thirsts quenched, we turned and walked back to camp. Aa//xama carried the ostrich eggshells, now full of water, while Koto paused from time to time to gather some more stems of *Kalanchoe rotundifolia* for future use.

Some weeks later, and far to the west of the Kua Bushmen, we came to a place between Hukuntsi and Masetlheng pan where there was a sipwell. The place was called Bohela-batho, which means 'where the people end'. From the depressed manner of most of the people who lived there, almost completely lacking the usual Bushman humour and delight in life, the name seemed as though it could be all too true. Few people now still have the skill to suck water up from where, deep down, it saturates the sand above the underlying bowl of rock; the boreholes that are an increasing feature of the Kalahari have made it unnecessary. But one old lady at Bohela-batho, called //Gamsi, said she would show us how it was done.

The only problem was that the drought had been so bad for so long that even the sipwell, usually reliable, had dried up; so we would have to cheat. We went with //Gamsi and several of the people from her village to the sipwell, a deep depression caused by centuries of scraping away the sand to get a few inches closer to the water-table. At the bottom we dug a deep hole, poured a flask of water into it, filled it in again and covered it with a thick layer of dry sand. //Gamsi tied a wad of moistened grass around the end of her hollow sipping stick, dug a hole (which was very shallow compared with what she would have needed had we not been cheating), put the grass-covered end of the stick into the hole and filled it in. Then she took another wad of grass and held it in her left hand immediately below her mouth, and over the end of a thin, straight stick which was to conduct the water into the ostrich eggshell container; then she started to suck.

For several minutes she sat there sucking noisily, but with no apparent effect. Then suddenly water began to pour like a miniature waterfall from her mouth, into the filter of grass, along the guide-stick, and down into the ostrich egg-shell [9]. It seemed uncanny, and even miraculous, despite the fact that at the back of our rationalistic minds we knew about the scientific explanations of capillarity. But in our mechanized world it is an increasing wonder to find a human being who can still, with such freedom and such lack of external apparatus, harness the laws of nature. In a few minutes more it was all over; //Gamsi must have sucked up almost the total quantity of water that we had poured into the earth. With no more ado, she pulled her sipping stick out of the sand, picked up the ostrich eggshell, and walked back towards the village.

With water such a precious and uncertain commodity, it is hardly surprising that the life of the nomadic Kalahari Bushmen has always had it as its lodestar. In the long dry season, as one source of water after another dries up, the bands move to the waterholes that keep their water longest. They settle there for a few weeks, gathering whatever bulbs, tubers and melons are available at the time, gradually covering a wider and wider area in their search for vegetable food as they deplete the supplies within easy reach of their camp. If the plants become scarce, the band will move to another waterhole, which might be two or three days' walk away, where they will again settle as long as a supply of plant food is available.

But in some parts of the Kalahari there are no waterholes that remain productive throughout the dry season. For anything up to nine months of the year, the various /Gwi Bushman bands who live in the central desert have to obtain their water exclusively from plants, and from what can be squeezed from the stomachs of the animals that they kill.

Throughout the Kalahari it is the plants that have provided the staple diet of the nomadic Bushmen, not only as food, but also as a source of water. Meat is an occasional luxury, and standing water a seasonal one. In times when both water and plant food are plentiful, Bushmen can afford to migrate to follow the game. But when the waterholes have dried up, and only the water-storing plants remain, it is these that govern their movements; for the water that the plants provide is the bottom line of survival for the Bushmen.

The number of times in a year that a group will move to a new camp site is dictated by the amount of rain that has fallen during the rainy season, and the resultant availability of standing water, plants and game. In a good year they may move only twice; though they may also, while still in a fruitful location, make an intermediate move to a new site only a hundred or so yards away, if the old site has become unduly bug-ridden. In a lean year, however, they may move as often as nine or ten times, with a couple of days' walk between each site.

The Bushmen have never accumulated property because the demands of the nomadic life have precluded it, and their necessities can be found wherever they go. They can move quickly and easily because their possessions amount to so little: the skins they wear; a leather bag and a digging stick each for the women; a bow, a quiver of arrows and a pair of fire sticks for the men; and a cooking pot for each family. In the central Kalahari today, among the few Bushmen who remain truly nomadic, possessions (or the lack of them) remain much as they have always been, the only addition being a few items of tattered western clothing. Even the Kua Bushmen we were with, sedentary now for several years, have acquired little more. One thing they have lost, however, is the bow and arrow, for their hunting consists almost exclusively of snaring.

When on the move, Bushmen walk through the desert in single file, looking utterly at one with the nature around them. The men carry their hunting equipment, and have toddlers riding on their shoulders; the women carry babies at their sides, and their belongings wrapped in a kaross, either slung on their backs to the side of the baby or else in a bundle on their heads. Children run around together, but always within eyeshot of their parents, for to become detached from the group is one of the greatest dangers of the desert.

When they arrive in the area they have decided on for their next camp, they must then choose a suitable site. This, as everything, is a subject of much discussion, and everyone has their say. Invariably they choose a place where there are bushes and trees to give shade in the heat of the day. As soon as a site is decided on, they put down the children and their bundles, and immediately set to work to clear the place of grass.

The most important thing, we were told by the Kua Bushmen, is to light their fires, for it is the fire – today almost as much as in the past – that is home to each family, far more than the hut. The men got out their fire sticks and showed us how they made fire in the traditional manner. The base stick is of very soft wood.

They made a notch in it and inserted the sharpened end of the hard stick which they then rotated between their hands at astonishing speed [15]. The friction of the hard wood on the soft base produced a little smoke; then a fine dust of burned wood oozed out of the hole in the base and spilt over onto the small pile of dry grass that had been placed underneath the sticks. When enough of this had collected, Kangao picked up the grass, carefully folded it over the hot wood-dust, and blew gently into the centre [16]. White smoke began to pour from the grass [17], and then suddenly it burst into flame [18]. Kangao's hands were so hardened that he held the flaming grass for several moments before putting it on the ground and piling dry sticks, in increasing size, on top of it. Bushmen still make fire in this way, but infrequently and more as an act of remembrance than an everyday practice. Increasingly, matches, and even lighters, are being used as Bushmen come into more permanent contact with blacks and whites and a cash economy.

The life of each family still revolves around its fire [19]. On it, and in it, they cook their food; around it they sit and eat and talk, tell their stories, sing and dance under the moon. At night they sleep around the fire, huddled in skins to keep out the cold night air of the desert, gradually inching nearer and nearer to the fire as the night wears on. Frequently they get so close to the fire that their shins get burned; almost all the Bushmen that we saw had the mottled scars of old burns all down their shins. This is no new phenomenon, for more than one nineteenth-century travel writer remarked upon the 'scars that they continually have on their shin-bones'.

The huts are hardly ever used to sleep in. Only in the rainy season do the Bushmen shelter inside them at night, and then only if it is actually raining. In the dry season there is no rush to build huts. Probably the day after they arrive at a new camp site they will build one hut, enough to store the goods of the whole band for a while, until they get around to building another, possibly several days later. The building of huts is very much a communal activity, and was completed more quickly than we had thought it was going to be. The men went out into the veld and pulled down dead but strong branches for the basic framework, and carried them back to the camp in huge bundles over their shoulders [10]. Meanwhile, the women gathered large armfuls of grass from the immediate vicinity of the camp [11], while one or two of them dug a circle of small holes for the ends of the supporting poles to be put into. As soon as the men returned, the poles were put in place, the tops meeting in the centre so firmly that nothing seemed to be needed to bind them together [12]. Smaller, forked branches were laid over the main poles, leaving a gap in one side as an entrance; and on top of these branches the grass was laid, and hooked well into the forks to keep it in place [13].

The whole job, from beginning to end, was completed within two hours [14]. A few ostrich eggshells, full of water, were put inside to keep cool, and also the tubers and melons that the women had already collected. Then the hut seemed to be forgotten, while life continued around the hub of each family's fire. Three days later they made another hut, mainly, it seemed, to accommodate the increasing hoard of plant food they had accumulated.

In the rainy season, however, a nomadic Bushman band will build many more huts – one for each individual family, who will have its own fire beside its hut. The huts are built in a rough circle, the entrance of each facing towards the centre, which is the communal area for the whole band. Here the children play together, and discussions concerning the band take place, and here they dance and perform their healing rituals.

Bushman bands have rarely been very large – between twenty and forty seems to be a reasonable average. For the nomadic life, large numbers are un-wieldy; but as bands become sedentary they often get larger. Each band has its own defined territory, within which its members hunt, gather plant food and use the available water resources. It is not the land itself, or the waterhole, that they think of as theirs, so much as the right to use the resources. Three or four individuals are usually regarded as the 'owners', an hereditary entitlement which may be held by either men or women. But even with these people, the 'ownership' is not an individual right; they are the representatives of the whole band. Other Bushman bands, or individuals, entering the territory should ask permission of the 'owners' to use the resources of that territory, be it water, plants or game.

The structure of a band tends to be fluid, but the grouping is usually on the basis of kinship or friendship. At the centre of the Kua band we were with, were two brothers: Kangao, who was the elder, and Be/tee who often took the lead, especially in talking. One of their sisters, /Ganakadi, was married to Kotuko/tee, who was one of the two men who was turned to in matters requiring physical action, and especially manual dexterity. The other (and main) man of action was Ramonne, who was not related to anyone else. He and his wife, //Khoe/tee, had five children of whom the eldest (a daughter) had married and gone to live with her husband's band. Another brother of Kangao and Be/tee had been married to N//kobo/to, but he had left her and their children with this band, and had remarried and gone to live with his new wife's band.

Another extended family grouping in the band centred on /Wa/tee. He had had two wives until about five years ago when one of them had died giving birth to her fifth child. His surviving wife, Namgãe (who had six children), was the sister of another man in the band, Phorana, who was himself married to /Wa-u/tee, a younger sister of /Wa/tee. Not only were the two families thus doubly related, but Phorana's and /Wa-u/tee's eldest son was married to /Wa/tee's and Namgãe's second daughter. Cousins (even double cousins) are acceptable marriage partners.

The usual pattern with this group was for women from other bands to be brought into their band on marriage; and when one of their women married, she would usually go to her new husband's band. But there were several excep-tions to this rule. N//kobo/to, as we have seen, remained with the band when her husband left her, while he moved to the band of his new wife. Also Kotuko/tee

1. (*previous page*) The Drakensberg Mountains, clad in early morning mist. The Bushmen of old came to the cool mountains in summer, following the game, and in their rocky shelters executed their paintings.
2. (*above*) The Cape of Good Hope, or Cape of Storms – to Francis Drake 'the fairest Cape in all the globe'.
3. (*below*) View to the lowlands from Cathkin Peak in the Natal Drakensberg.

4. Aerial view of the Tsodilo Hills. The 'male' hill is on the left, the 'female' hill next to it, and the small third hill at the end of the group.

5. One of the great pans that dot the surface of the Kalahari desert. For most of the year, they are expanses of dried-out mud, and contain water only for a few weeks after the rains.

6△

7▽

8▽

6. (*opposite*) Kua women trekking. They carry little more than their leather skins and digging sticks.
7. Having sucked water from a hollow tree with a tubular sipping stick, Koto transfers it to an ostrich eggshell container.
8. When the eggshell is filled with water, /Kongo sucks more water into her mouth and gives it direct to her baby fastened at her side.
9. (*above*) The water //Gamsi has sucked up from the sipwell is dropped through a filter of grass and runs along a stick into an ostrich eggshell.

10△

11▽

The building of a Bushman hut is a communal activity.

10. Men return to the campsite carrying strong branches which they will use to make a framework for the hut.
11. Kua women gather grass for thatching.
12. The men start to build the hut by placing the ends of the poles in a circle in the ground.

13, 14. (*opposite*) Both women and men share the job of thatching, and of putting finishing touches to the completed hut.

12▽

13△

14▽

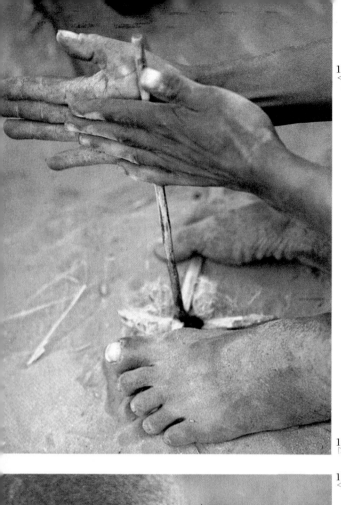

15
◁

16
▷

17
◁

18
▷

The fire is the focus of the Bushmen's social life. They congregate around it, cook food in it, sit near it by day to talk and work, and by night for warmth. Kangao showed us how to make fire in the traditional manner.

15. (*opposite*) A base stick of very soft wood has a notch cut into it in which the sharpened end of a stick of hard wood is rotated at speed, producing a dark and burning wood dust which falls into a wad of dry grass.
16, 17. The grass, with the burning dust inside, is blown until white smoke pours from it.
18. Suddenly it bursts into flame; then dry sticks are piled over it to make a fire.

19. (*below*) Kua Bushmen sit around a fire outside their hut. Their fires are always economical. The boy on the left has a disease which affects the scalp of many Bushmen today, mainly during puberty.

20, 21. The Tsodilo Hills are a place of special sacredness and supernatural power to the !Kung Bushmen. They say that the Great God, having formed the hills, created there all manner of animals.

22. (*opposite*) Some say that it was the Great God himself who painted these animals on the rocks.

23. (*opposite*) Eland Cave in the Natal Drakensberg. There are other animals depicted on the walls of this cave, and also human figures, but the dominant subject is the eland.

24, 25. (*above and below*) Laurens van der Post stands beneath a magnificent frieze of eland in Eland Cave. Above his head to the right is an eland cow lying down and looking backwards; then the frieze sweeps up, showing eland in every posture, to the great bull at the top.

26. Some paintings show the Bushmen's view of the people who came to live in their territory, such as this Dutch couple from Klipfontein in the Cape (now in the Africana Museum, Johannesburg).
27. This Bushman artist 'signed' his work with hand-prints in the red pigment he had painted with. Or were the prints made, as one !Kung story tells, by a Bushman hunter long ago?

28. Elongated figures, like these in Eland Cave, are not uncommon, but their meaning is unclear. Do they represent the Bushmen's sense of spiritual value? Or are they medicine men in trance?
29. In this dance scene, a later artist superimposed elands over human and animal figures to emphasize the link between Bushmen and elands – their most potent source of supernatural power.

30. A rain-making ritual. Above the larger rain-animal, medicine men are seen in varying degrees of trance — one prostrate, another bleeding profusely from the nose.

31. An elaborate visual metaphor of the 'half-death' of trance. A medicine man, with antelope head and hooves, holds the tail of a dying eland, legs crossed like those of the eland.

had moved into the band when he married /Ganakadi. However, another sister
of Kangao and Be/tee had moved 'far away' when she married; but her son,
Kwa, had joined the band where his uncles were, together with his wife.

A great deal of visiting is done between neighbouring bands. A family will
decide to go and stay, often for several weeks, with another band where they
have relations. So the people actually living together in a band at any given
moment may not all be permanent members. Permanency is not, in any case,
absolute, as it is not uncommon for people to change bands.

Bushman society is remarkably egalitarian. They have no chiefs or rulers,
and leadership may not even be vested in one individual. Among the Kua band,
as I have mentioned, Be/tee seemed to be recognized as the leader when it came
to matters requiring a spokesman; but when there was something practical to
be done — like setting a snare, engraving ostrich eggshells, or throwing the
bones — it was almost always Ramonne who naturally took the lead. In Bushman society leaders emerge, not by heredity, not by being more powerful or
authoritarian than the others, but because of their manifest integrity, perception
and decisiveness. Leadership confers no honours — the leader is simply one
among equals — and it is always, at least in its outward manifestations, the
prerogative of the men.

Francis Galton, who published his book of travels in 1853, gained a somewhat different impression of male leadership from some of the Bushmen whom
he met: 'I am sure the Bushmen are, generally speaking, hen-pecked. They
always consult their wives.'

In fact the balance of power between men and women seems to be a har-
monious one. Women have an equal right to express opinions when decisions
affecting the whole band have to be made, and it would be a foolish man indeed
who failed to take these opinions into account in the final decision. Women are
the major contributors to the economy of the band, but work is generally fairly
equally divided with the men. When Richard Lee, an American anthropologist,
was working among a !Kung group, he discovered that men actually worked
longer hours than women, but that women were more effective per hour spent.
Men tend to do the heavier work; we saw this while they were building the huts
when the men went some distance to collect heavy poles, while the women
gathered thatching grass for which they had to move only a few yards. Also the
men will often help the women with heavy loads, especially with carrying
toddlers on their shoulders. Their leadership is far from domineering, but protective and supportive and refreshingly unpatronizing.

One thing that particularly fascinated me were the Bushmen's names and
their meanings. Among the Kua group we were with, the children tended to be
named after some event that had occurred at the time of birth. Almost always
this had to do with occasions when they had killed an antelope — the most important events in their lives. As I asked about people's names, I very quickly
learned the Kua words for the various antelopes, which tended to come at the
end of the name. But other events were also recorded in the children's names, so

that fascinating details of a family's history could be gleaned simply by an enquiry into the meanings of the names.

Be/tee's name refers to a blue wildebeest that his father had killed at the time that he was born; and he told me that his wife's name, Khangdu, means 'eland killed in a hailstorm', for she had been born in a freak hailstorm at a time when her father had killed the greatest antelope of all. Their eldest child, a daughter, they called Aa//xama, which means 'the beating at the place of the hartebeest'. At the time she was born Be/tee came upon a hartebeest that had been shot and wounded by some white hunters; he killed it and was in the process of skinning it when the white men found him and gave him a beating for appropriating their game.

Their next child, a son, was given a Tswana name rather than a Bushman one because at the time of his birth Be/tee was having an argument with some Kgalagadi neighbours about a truck; Tshipikan, he told me, meant 'the case of the iron truck'. With the next son we were back in the hunting context: Dyuogãe refers to a steenbok that Be/tee had trapped in a time of great heat and drought when the child was born.

With their next daughter, Bia≠tebe, we returned to local politics, but this time expressed in the Bushman language. At the time she was born the family was living some distance away, and they were very short of food. Be/tee asked a neighbouring Kgalagadi farmer for some corn, but he refused and had him beaten up.

By the time their next child arrived (a son), they had moved back to the place where they had lived before Bia≠tebe was born. Be/tee had set a snare and the following morning, at daybreak, he crept towards the trap and saw a steenbok standing near it. As he crouched there watching, he saw the very moment when the steenbok put one leg into the snare and was caught. He skinned it and took it home, and at that moment Noa-adigãe was born.

Iogãe (the name of the next son) means 'hole of the steenbok'. At the time of his birth Be/tee had gone out hunting and saw a steenbok running. He followed it and came to an antbear hole, and saw the spoor of the steenbok going into it. He dug and found the steenbok inside.

The next son, /Gae≠tebe, was the merriest child in the whole group, and easily my favourite. His sunny disposition was in complete contradiction to his name which refers to yet another altercation that Be/tee had had with some local Kgalagadi farmers. As I was never able to get any explanation of the event, I suspected that Be/tee may have felt, but did not wish to admit to the feeling, that on this occasion not all the blame had been on the side of the Kgalagadi.

Last in this large family was a baby boy who was only about ten days old when we arrived. When I asked Be/tee about his new son's name, he said he had not finally decided, but he thought he would give him a name that referred to the fact that at the time of his birth he had caught a steenbok in a trap, but the dogs of the Kgalagadi got to it before he did and ate it all, leaving only the bones and the skin.

There did not seem to be any sex distinction between the names that referred to antelopes, but some girls had the feminine suffix -sa tacked onto the end of their name. It was interesting to discover that throughout the group only the adults and the older children had names that referred to the larger antelopes. From the age of twelve or thirteen downwards, the children were named almost exclusively after the small antelopes – steenbok (gãe) or duiker (kwa) – or after incidents unrelated to hunting, such as arguments with the local Kgalagadi (≠tebe). Thus we could trace, through the names, the period when the encroachment of the cattle had driven out the eland, hartebeest and gemsbok that had once been as common in that area as in most of the Kalahari Desert.

With the !Kung, however, among whom we spent only a few days around Tsumkwe in Namibia, there is a completely different system of naming children. They have a standard range of accepted names – boys' names separate from girls' – from which the parents select one for the new child. But even though the name does not relate to a specific event, as among the Kua, the choice is not as arbitrary as it is among most western societies. It is not a question of choosing one name that merely appeals more than another. The first rule is that no child shall be named after its father or mother; the second that it should be named after one of its relatives. The first son is always named after his paternal grandfather; the second son usually (but not always) after his maternal grandfather. The same pattern applies to daughters being named after their grandmothers.

The !Kung believe that the sharing of a name with another person involves some kind of sharing of identity with that person. So anyone who has the same name is regarded as a kind of close relative, even if there is no known blood relationship. As their behaviour towards each other is closely tied up with their concepts of relationship, it is very important for a !Kung, especially when meeting someone new, to discover what his or her name is, and the names of all close blood relatives, so that the correct pattern of behaviour can be established.

As there are relatively few names in use among the !Kung, there are a great number of people who have the same name; so distinctions, in the form of nicknames, are tacked on to the end of the name. The ≠Toma who told John Marshall the story of the hand-prints at the Tsodilo Hills is known as ≠Toma Word because of his wise talking; and when the Marshall family first arrived in his area in 1951, he gave John his own name to which John's special distinguishing nickname was attached which related to the length of his face – ≠Toma Cheeks. It immediately created a special relationship between them, which has endured through the years. It also enabled the other !Kung in the area to know in what sort of relationship they stood with him.

The naming of the various members of the Marshall family can only have been arrived at after much voluble discussion in ≠Toma's band. Never have I come across people with such a genius for chatter and consultation as the Bushmen. I would have given anything to have known what the Kua Bushmen were saying during the time we were with them, and would doubtless have heard some very perceptive, and probably unflattering, remarks. What they allowed

us to hear through our interpreter was always shrewd, but also always cour-
teous and kind. Whatever their discussions — whether about people, about the
plants they were gathering, the snares they were setting, the visits they had
made to neighbouring bands, or the bones they were throwing — they were
always pursued at great length, and accompanied by frequent shrieks of
laughter. Even at night, from our camp some distance away, at whatever hour
any of us happened to wake and listen, we could hear a constant hum of chatter
coming from the Bushman camp.

Talking is, in fact, one of the great Bushman remedies when quarrels and
tensions arise between members of the band. In such a small and close society
tensions between individuals can, if not quickly resolved, tear the band apart.
But such tensions are unlikely to pass unnoticed, and from an early stage will be
commented on and discussed in such a way that the problem is frequently resolved before it builds up into a quarrel of significant proportions. If it does get
out of hand, one method of dealing with the situation is for one of the parties to
the quarrel to go off and visit friends or relations in another band for a few
weeks, or even months. By the time he or she returns the contentious issue may
no longer seem so important.

Dancing is also regarded as a great healing and unifying force in such tensions.
The Bushmen dance for everything; they dance to celebrate a birth, they dance
at marriages, they dance for the rituals of a girl's first menstruation or a boy's
first kill in the hunt. And often, when no particular reason presents itself, they
dance just for the fun of it, clapping and chanting and stamping around the fire
with increasing verve as the night wears on.

CHAPTER FIVE
Woman the Provider

Morning began slowly in the Bushman camp. The nights were cold with the approach of winter, and figures lay huddled around the remains of fires, not stirring until the sun had risen high enough to warm them. The small children moved first, rubbing sleepy eyes as they tottered about from one inert body to another. Even /Gae≠tebe, usually a bundle of energy and merriment right through the day and half way through the night, was unrecognizably subdued.

After a while the stumblings and demands of the children roused their parents, and they too began the process of facing the day. Men prodded fires into renewed life, women put roots and knobbly gemsbok cucumbers (*Citrullus naudinianus*) onto the fires to cook [33] and, when they were ready, handed them round to be eaten — mostly to their own immediate family, but any child who happened to be around and hungry was always given something. In late April when we arrived, there were plenty of gemsbok cucumbers (a kind of melon), brought on by the heavy rain earlier in the month, but they were nearing the end of their season as winter approached. Curiously, when Laurens van der Post was in the Kalahari Desert in the early 1950s, these same melons were referred to as eland cucumbers. It seems you can pick your antelope.

/Gae≠tebe, more awake now, came to where the melons were piled, hot and tempting, and /Ganakadi (his aunt by our reckoning, and one of his mothers by his) cut the top off one of them, mashed the flesh inside the skin with a stick, and handed it to him. He sat down and dipped into the melon with his fingers, raising the soft, steaming, yellow pulp slowly to his mouth, keeping his fingers half inside his mouth as he chewed. It was an operation of the utmost seriousness [34].

Gathering gemsbok cucumbers, and all other varieties of plant food is women's work among the Bushmen. A group of three or four would go out every day, usually one or more carrying a small child, and they would walk through the veld, digging with their sticks for roots, or picking melons, berries or seedpods [32]. For much of the year there is an abundance and variety of plant food — over a hundred different species are used by the Bushmen — so there is no problem about finding sufficient to feed the whole band. So intimate and precise is their knowledge of the vegetation of the area in which they live, that the women know exactly where to go to collect each of the various plants available at that moment. Because of this there is no waste of energy. We were with them in a time of plenty, so the group of women that went out on any given day did not have to go far to gather enough food for the whole community. Each expedition that we witnessed took no longer than an hour and a half. But by the time spring has come, after several months without rain, the situation changes and more groups have to go out for considerably longer periods in order to gather enough to meet the needs of the band.

Richard Lee has estimated that among the !Kung Bushmen with whom he worked, a woman walked about 2,400 km (1,500 miles) every year. While this distance is not all covered in her search for food, quite a high proportion of it is. For most of the year this particular task is fairly undemanding and a woman may spend no more than five or six hours a week foraging; but in winter she may go out three or four days in the week, and walk for perhaps eight or nine hours at a stretch, gathering an increasing weight of vegetables as she goes. By the time she stops gathering and sets off back to camp, the load she carries can be considerable, sometimes as much as 15 kg (33 lbs).

Apart from the vegetable weight, a woman will very often have one child, and possibly two, who will need to be carried all or part of the time. On one gathering expedition that I accompanied, /Kwa-u/tee carried her young son Tshipi//xama with her all the time, slung in a kaross on her side, from which position he could reach for her breast for a feed whenever he felt like it. It was an accommodation he made full use of. He did not seem to affect her efficiency for a moment, but he was no lightweight and certainly increased the effort his mother had to put into gathering food. Small wonder that the women take every opportunity to sit and do nothing by the fire.

The women walked with a swift and easy stride in single file through the long Bushman grass which stretched away, shining in the sun, to the wide circle of the horizon. Very often the plants they were looking for revealed themselves by only the tiniest cluster of leaves above the surface, which most other people would not even notice. But they spotted everything, and the instant they saw something worth digging up they would stop and immediately set to work with rapid stabs of their digging sticks until the tuber was exposed; then they pulled it out, dusted it off, and popped it into the doubled-up kaross slung across their backs. For a small, easy plant, growing on the surface, they barely changed their gait but simply leaned down, stabbed the earth beside it, pulled it up and moved on, all in one fluid movement.

At times they would stop at a *Grewia* bush, pick the berries and suck the flesh, and then spit out the hard pip. The berries are about the size of a small grape, fibrous and not very juicy, but they have a pleasant flavour and are fairly sweet. They were rather wrinkled and past their best when we were there, so the women simply sucked them for refreshment on the way and did not bother to gather them.

One of the plants they gathered in considerable quantities was the *Bauhinia esculenta* which even I quickly learned to recognize by its long trailing creeper-like branches which ran at ground level, with pairs of flat, roundish leaves spaced at regular intervals. In late April the young tuber was at its best, and it remains good to eat for most of the winter. But by the end of August it gets hard and fibrous, and its water content, the main value of the tuber, becomes negligible. The *Bauhinia esculenta* also provides morama beans which are a much favoured food, rich in protein and oil. The whole pod is roasted in the fire, the beans taken out and either chewed as they are, or ground and mixed with other foods. A great advantage of these beans is that they can be dried and stored against a time when other foods are scarce.

The commonest root that we came across was a kind of wild turnip, *Raphion-acme burkei*, known as *bi* to these Bushmen. It flourishes all the year round and is a major source of water in the dry season to those Bushmen not within easy reach of a borehole. The *bi* tuber is shredded by rapid downward movements with a sharp-edged stick, while the person doing the work holds it steady with her feet [35]. The pulp is gathered on a piece of skin and, when there is enough, it is squeezed in one hand directly into the mouth [36]. Children stand around with their mouths open and are usually rewarded with a squeeze of *bi* water [37]. Then the dehydrated pulp, with what little moisture remains in it, is used to wash the face, arms and body, rather like a pulverized face cloth [38]. In the context of a ritual, such as the washing of a girl at the end of her menarcheal rite, it is the ever-present *bi* tuber that is used. But the tuber is rather fibrous and tastes somewhat bitter, so when alternative plant water sources are available, such as the various kinds of melon, they tend to be preferred. On one occasion Aa//xama and Uyokoe/teesa overcame the problem of bitterness by mixing the *bi* pulp with the chewed-up leaves of the *Boscia albitrunca* tree. They said that this made it sweeter; but it also required more effort on their part which would tend to put it fairly low on any list of Bushman priorities if simpler sources of sweet water were there for the taking.

Another abundant food was several species of *Scilla* which look like large spring onions. The women gathered them in quantity and, once back in their camp, roasted, peeled and ate them. Both the *Scillas* and the *bi* tuber were eaten with little discernible enthusiasm; as far as plant food was concerned, the greatest preference seemed to be for the luscious-looking green-fleshed tsama melons (*Citrullus lanatus*) that were constantly being cut open and eaten down to the skin. However, real gastronomic enthusiasm was reserved for meat alone.

Once the required root was located, it was sheer hard work to dig it out, for it was sometimes a metre (yard) or more beneath the surface. The only implement used is a digging stick, a simple straight branch of *Rhigozum brevispinosum*, a metre or more (three to four feet) in length, stripped of bark, thorns and subsidiary branches and sharpened at one end. This type of digging stick is employed throughout the Kalahari. It is fascinating, in some of the paintings of the now extinct southern Bushmen, to see that the women are carrying digging sticks of a different type, with a round knob part-way up the stick; this was a stone with a hole bored through it, which was used as a weighting device to help dig into the hard rocky ground of their terrain. The soft sand of the Kalahari demands no such refinement of design.

At Masetlheng, in the southwestern Kalahari, some of the !Xõ women showed us handfuls of what looked like large potatoes; they were truffles (*Terfezia pfeilli*), to us an expensive luxury, to them a source of vital nutrients. Truffles make a brief appearance in April to May, but they depend on rainfall and in dry years do not appear at all. At Masetlheng they were one of the very few plants available to the !Xõ for it was generally too dry for roots to survive, since the problem of water in that area is an acute one. These truffles had been brought on by a sudden downpour of rain about two weeks previously. I was astonished at the richness of their truffle harvest with no specially trained hounds (or pigs) whose help in locating these deeply hidden delicacies seems to be essential in other parts of the world. I was told it was quite simple to find them – all you have to do is to recognize a particular kind of crack in the ground, caused by the truffle growing deep down, and then dig for it. It also helps, of course, to have a Bushman's sophisticated understanding of the natural world.

The women's highly developed knowledge of plants was supplemented by their constant exchange of information as they walked along – here, perhaps, was a new cluster of plants, or there, the leaves of another plant seemed to be dying. The natural chattiness of the Bushman was channelled into a vital form of communication. In their gathering, as in everything else we saw them doing, they found an endless source of interest and amusement; with the Bushmen we found that nothing remained totally serious for very long.

It has always been the gathering of roots by the women that has provided the greatest part of the Bushman's diet. Meat may be their favourite food, and the only food to arouse real enthusiasm, but if the Bushmen had had nothing but the meat that the hunters provided, they would have disappeared without trace thousands of years ago. It is the prosaic unsung work of the women that has kept them alive. The roots, bulbs, tubers and fruits that they eat, with the vitamins and minerals in them, provide a well-balanced diet, especially when combined with the occasional supply of protein that comes in the form of meat as well as beans and, in some areas of the northern Kalahari, nuts. It is only recently with more and more Bushmen employed on farms and being paid with food such as mealie meal, that their balanced diet has been disturbed. With free rations, and with plant food becoming scarcer as the land is increasingly heavily grazed by cattle, the women no longer go out on gathering expeditions as frequently as they used to; but mealie meal does not have the vitamins that the vegetables provided. The effects of malnutrition – distended belly and stick-like arms and legs – are not uncommon sights. They are, however, relatively new ones. Milk would help, if it were available, but Bushmen have not normally been stock-keepers, and many of them still do not regard cattle as anything more than a meal.

Another thing that has changed fairly recently, as Bushmen have increasingly settled around boreholes, is the birth rate. Nomadic Bushwomen gave birth at an average interval of between four and five years, each child continuing to breast-feed until the mother became pregnant again. Breast-feeding in itself tends to suppress ovulation, added to which it appears that fertility may be lower among Bushmen than among many other groups of people. They themselves recognize this as a good thing, a natural protection against overloading the system, especially in years of drought. There seems to be some kind of connection between drought and reduced fertility.

In extreme conditions of drought, when there is simply not enough food and water to go around, and survival is a matter of concern, the birth of another child into a nomadic band can put an impossible extra burden on the band in general, and on the mother in particular. In such a situation the mother may never allow the new baby to breathe. For people who have such a patent love for, and enjoyment of their children, the anguish this must cause is unimaginable. It is a desperate necessity; fortunately a rare one.

Even when there is no drought, the situation of the band, or the health of the mother and her other children may be so precarious that if a woman conceives too soon after the birth of her previous child, she may decide she cannot keep the new baby. Lorna Marshall questioned some of the !Kung women among whom she worked for many years and gathered that although they did not regard such infanticide as morally or socially wrong, it was deeply distressing to them. They all claimed that they had never had to do it themselves: 'When they talked about it with me, they never once spoke concretely or directly of the act itself but had much to say about the necessity of it. . . . They spoke of the nourishment of the children as the primary reason; they spoke in explicit detail. They want children, all the children they can possibly have, but, they explained, they cannot feed babies that are born too close together. They said Bushman children must have strong legs, and it is mother's milk that makes them strong. A mother had not enough milk to sustain completely two infants at the same time. They believe a child needs milk until it is three or four years old at least.'

Such longterm breast-feeding is certainly a good idea where there are no alternative sources of milk available for a young child. To be weaned onto rough and indigestible veld foods at the age of two or under would jeopardize the child's chances of survival, or at least its chances of a reasonably healthy life.

In our band of Kua Bushmen in the southeastern Kalahari, the spacing of the children was generally closer together than four years. Since Bushmen do not count in years, and have only a hazy notion of the time that any event occurred (even a relatively recent one), it was difficult to assess the ages of the children. Also I reckoned that they were probably older than they appeared to my western eyes, partly because of their naturally smaller stature, but also because of their somewhat slower rate of development after weaning compared with the average western child. However, the guesstimate of children's ages that I arrived at is probably more or less equally inaccurate throughout, so that the resulting number of years between each child may roughly accord with reality.

When I asked Be/tee how many children he and Khangdu had, he first of all put up four fingers and then, after due deliberation, added the thumb. In fact, as each child was named and produced, the total mounted to eight. Counting is

not a common accomplishment among the parental generation. Their eldest
child, Aa//xama, I reckoned to be about eighteen, a lively girl, full of wit and
cheek, and with an exceptionally deep voice. She looked after her younger
siblings with great affection as a kind of secondary mother. The three children
next in age were at school an hour's drive away (or half a day's walk). We met
them when we went to film at the school one day. Tshipikan, a boy, was about
fifteen; his younger brother, Dyuogãe, about thirteen; their sister, Bia≠tebe,
about eleven. The four youngest, all boys, were with their parents. Noa-adigãe
was about eight; Iogãe, five; /Gae≠tebe, three and their new baby was less than
two weeks old. They said he had been born within the moon; and there had
been a new moon about ten days before we arrived.

    The intervals between these children range from two to three years, and this
seemed to be fairly typical throughout the band. It is now several years since
they were nomadic, and there is no doubt that this is a considerable factor in
the more frequent births. The women no longer have to expend as much effort
on gathering since almost every family has a son or daughter working on a
farm, and the rations with which they are paid are shared out among the various
members of the family in the traditional manner. The fact that these rations are
of less nutritional value than the vegetables the women collect is not immediately obvious, and the temptation to avoid the hard labour of gathering is a
powerful one, especially when they might have one or two small children to
carry around with them.

    To give birth to her new baby, Khangdu did as Bushman women have done
for thousands of years – she went out by herself into the veld when the labour
pains began, and produced her infant entirely alone, with no medical facilities of
any kind. Occasionally, especially for a first birth, the woman's mother, or
another close female relative, will accompany her. It is not considered necessary
to go far from the camp; usually the woman goes only a few hundred yards –
near enough for the baby's first cries to be heard by her family, or for them to
hear if anything is going wrong.

    Isaac Schapera, one of the first of the modern Bushman anthropologists, has
written of a number of different practices among the various groups of Bushmen:
the Heikum uprooted tufts of grass which they placed upside down on a tree as
a warning to the men, who may not be present when a child is born; an Auen
husband would tie his bowstring around his wife's body; a !Kung woman, when
her labour pains began, had to step over her husband's legs after he had made
incisions in his calves and rubbed medicine into them. These practices have
largely fallen into disuse today.

    The only group Schapera mentions where the women did not go out into the
veld to give birth, were the Bushmen of the Namib Desert: 'When labour is far
advanced the woman's husband makes a small fire outside the hut in which she
is confined, and carefully keeps it going. No pot may be placed on this fire, nor
may anything be cooked or roasted over it. It is believed that if this custom is
neglected both the mother and new-born child will go blind. After the birth

another larger fire is kindled alongside the previous one as a sign of rejoicing, irrespective of the sex of the child.'

Bushman women give birth in a squatting position which is now the favoured position among many 'advanced' people. The mother's attitude to childbirth is believed to affect the delivery; if she goes into the experience without fear then the delivery will be uncomplicated. In John Marshall's superb film, *N!ai, the Story of a !Kung Woman*, N!ai tells of her friend who resented and feared the forthcoming birth of her first child. When she dies in childbirth N!ai says it was because she had been so afraid. It is not that the Bushmen discount physical explanations, but among a deeply spiritual people the spiritual explanation has priority. For Khangdu, however, it was her eighth child, nothing had gone wrong with the previous seven births, and once again everything went as easily as she had expected. At ten days old her new son, rosy pink and with a halo of fine dark hair, was clearly doing well.

Khangdu was a quiet, unassuming woman with a ready smile and eyes that seemed to take in everything, especially anything to do with her children. When necessary she would speak in a very direct and forthright manner, and clearly expected to be listened to. If Be/tee were around she would always appear to defer to him, not expecting to assume the mantle of leadership.

There was one occasion when we inadvertently infringed one of the Bushmen's taboos concerning women. We had had a problem over filming a hunt in the area in which our three hunters lived which was severely lacking in game. After three days of fruitless searching for any kind of animal we decided, with the hunters' agreement, to move to Masetlheng, further to the west, where we had heard that game was more abundant. The Bushmen in that area were of the same language group – !Xõ – as our hunters, so that was not likely to cause undue difficulty. Our guide knew a group there to whom we could go, and he felt sure that they would understand what we wanted to do and would help us. This group did not hunt in the traditional manner any longer, so there was no question of using hunters from their own band. We arrived at Masetlheng and all went according to plan. We filmed a successful hunt, with a gemsbok as the quarry, and the hunters brought the meat back to the camp and distributed it.

The next day our interpreter came and told us that there was much distress and anger among the men of the village because their women had received meat from strange men. By some appalling oversight we had failed to explain the full details of what we wanted to do, and the men were justly incensed at this disregard for their tradition. Our film director went with the interpreter to where the main members of the group were gathered, sat down with them, apologized from his heart and told them how distressed we were to have caused this hurt – we had thought that everything had been explained beforehand. The generosity and warmth of their response touched us deeply. They said that no white man had ever apologized to them before, but because we had done so, and had explained how the mistake had happened, and had intended no wrong, we could come again. It was a humbling moment.

As far as we knew, this was the only occasion that we made such a mistake. We were all acutely aware of the possibility of offending through ignorance or insensitivity, and also of the fact that film crews are not famous for their perception of other people's sensibilities. For this reason we avoided reference to the enlarged buttocks, or steatopygia, of the women. Bushmen are extremely modest – they do not regard breasts as sexual objects but simply as a means of feeding their children; therefore they leave them uncovered. The buttocks, however, have considerable sexual significance and are consequently kept covered. The men are equally modest and always cover their unique portion of anatomy, the semi-erect penis. It was a feature that fascinated several early travellers who seemed to have no qualms about getting the Bushmen they met to undress and allow themselves to be inspected. I cannot see an old photograph or drawing of naked Bushmen, both men and women, without shame for the humiliation inflicted on them.

Steatopygia is caused by the accumulation of fat on the buttocks, and its existence has been the cause of some controversy. It was at one time maintained that it was a special adaptation to desert conditions. It is certainly true that this fat deposit does diminish in times of drought and food shortage, so it may indeed be an aid to survival. But paintings in the Drakensberg, and in other places that are very far from being deserts, show women with pronounced steatopygia. Also steatopygia is both more common, and of greater size, among the Hottentots (not exclusively a desert people) than among the Bushmen, so its connection with the desert must be ruled out. Phillip Tobias, Professor of Anatomy at the University of Witwatersand and an authority on early African peoples, has suggested that its evolution may be due to the occasional periods of deprivation inherent in the hunter-gatherer way of life regardless of environment.

The women's modest covering of their behinds either with western-style clothes or with their traditional clothes – a short skin hanging from the waist and a large kaross slung from the shoulders – made it difficult for us to gauge how widespread this feature was among the groups we were with. There was certainly no exaggerated steatopygia with any of them, though about half appeared to have fairly prominent behinds. There was only one occasion when the women lifted their karosses and aprons, or removed them altogether, and this was during the ritual that is performed on the occasion of a girl's first menstruation. This is very much a women's ritual, in which few men are allowed to take part, and it is a glorious celebration of a girl's passage from childhood to the beginning of womanhood.

There is a remarkable painting [44] at Fulton's Rock in the Drakensberg mountains of Natal, which David Lewis-Williams, in his research on Bushman art, has recently identified as depicting a girl's first menstruation ritual. By piecing together references to this ritual by Bleek's southern Bushman informants in the 1870s, and present-day practice among some !Kung in the northwestern Kalahari, Lewis-Williams became increasingly convinced that some previous interpretations of this painting were missing the point. He believes that the covered figure inside the incomplete circle is in fact a girl isolated inside a hut for the duration of her first menstruation, with one or two women to keep her company; that the female figures surrounding the hut and bending forward are women performing the ritual dance, and imitating the mating behaviour of female antelopes; and that the other figures (some definitely male, others probably so) represent the few men who join in the dance, some holding sticks which represent an antelope's horns.

Among the !Kung the dance that is performed around the hut in which the girl is isolated is the eland bull dance, and it is fascinating to see in the painting executed by the southern Bushmen, that there is the shadowy figure of an eland just below the main group of figures, a symbol of the supernatural potency (n/um) that the girl is believed to have at this time. As we have already seen, the eland had a unique place in the imagination of the southern Bushmen; it was not only the favourite creature of Mantis, but also the source of the most powerful n/um. Today in the Kalahari the eland is still regarded with the same kind of feeling, and it is the animal that hunters most desire to hunt.

With this painting clear in my mind, it was with a special interest that I watched the menarcheal rite that was performed by the group of !Xõ Bushmen with whom we spent some time. As one of the great rituals in the Bushmen's life, and one of the few that is still performed, we particularly wanted to film it; but the chances of our happening to be in the right place at the right time were negligible. We could hardly approach a group we did not know at all to film such a central and intimate ceremony. With the help of the school teacher at Lone Tree, Elizabeth Camm, I approached some of the women of the group we had already worked with and asked if they would perform this ritual for us to film, and I was astonished at the apparent enthusiasm with which they agreed. But first of all, they said, I must sit down and they would tell me what they were going to do.

Very often, they said, a girl would be out in the veld with her friends when she discovered that she had started to bleed. She would immediately sit down and keep very quiet, which would make the others realize what had happened. They chose a girl called !Kaekukhwe to play the main part; and what followed was exactly what the women had told me, so I could tell other people about it.

When !Kaekukhwe sat down, the game they had all been playing stopped at once and one of her friends, Zana/go, raced back to the hut where the women were sitting. With a whoop of joy, !Kaekukhwe's mother, /Kunago, leaped to her feet and ran to where her daughter was sitting, accompanied by several other women. Those who stayed back at the hut were already clapping and chanting. Zana/go ran back again to the hut to collect a kaross, and then returned like the wind to where !Kaekukhwe was surrounded by chanting and clapping women. Her mother bent down and took her daughter onto her back, while another woman covered her with the kaross so that even her face was lost to sight. Then she was carried back to the hut in which another kaross had been spread out for her to be laid on, with the original kaross covering her. Usually a special hut is quickly and roughly constructed for the girl, but on this occasion they simply used an existing one.

During the whole time of her menstruation the girl must not touch the earth, neither must the sun fall on her. She must wear no beads or clothes. Food is brought to her inside the hut where she remains alone for most of the time. For everyone else the ritual has something of a carnival atmosphere; for the girl herself this is far from true as she spends long hours entirely alone with her thoughts. Only when there is dancing around the hut do one or two women come inside and sit with her. No man may see her face, for if he does it is believed that ill luck will befall him. During her first menstruation a girl is believed to have great supernatural power which can be harnessed for the good of the community if rightly treated, but if not, can turn to the detriment of an individual or the whole group.

Every day the women dance around the hut, and on some occasions two or three of the older men join in [40]. Having only heard of the eland bull dance in connection with this ritual, I was surprised to be told that this group did the gemsbok dance. I asked why, and was told simply that this was the dance they always did. To my eyes it made little difference; and what seemed almost uncanny to me was how exact their performance was to the painting of those extinct Bushmen of the Drakensberg. Time and distance gave way to a common tradition.

As the women danced and clapped and shouted, they would tip forward with their bottoms in the air, uncovering them as they did so [41]. This occurred especially as they danced in front of the entrance to the hut (just as in the painting), and was always accompanied by gales of bawdy laughter. The men cut forked branches which they held to their heads as they danced, in imitation of gemsbok horns, and from time to time they jerked their pelvises forward in a manner that left little to the imagination, and was a source of voluble mirth to all [42]. At other times they would rub their horns in the bushes in the manner of rutting antelopes. The whole performance was full of earthy enjoyment, yet totally lacking the prurience that would accompany anything similar in a western 'civilized' culture.

At the end of her menstruation, the girl is washed inside the hut, with water squeezed from a *bi* tuber. Then she is scarified with a few short incisions on the back of each shoulder and in the middle of the chest above the breasts. I expressed concern for !Kaekukhwe being hurt just for our benefit, but the women regarded what I had said as a great joke. It was no problem for !Kaekukhwe, they assured me. Little girls are scarified at fairly frequent intervals from an early age in order to add to their beauty, and this would simply be another occasion for !Kaekukhwe to have her beauty enhanced. In any case, they said, she had agreed to it.

She sat there with not a flicker crossing her face as her mother made the required incisions and rubbed into them a mixture of fat and plant ash. This same mixture was then applied to her face, making a line down the centre of her

forehead, then from ear to ear under her chin, and large circles around her eyes
— all in imitation of the facial markings of the gemsbok [43]. Then they dressed
her with a skin over her behind, and a beaded apron covering her front, put
strings of beads around her neck and under her arms, crossing between her
breasts, and finally a beaded band around her head. Her mother and another
woman — one on either side of her — then led her out of the hut and into the
dance.

Throughout the dance she was serious and unsmiling, her eyes downcast.
This behaviour is also required of a girl among the !Kung, and Lewis-Williams's
informant told him it was because in her enhanced state of potency she can
affect the game that may be hunted in the coming days. If she keeps her eyes
down, so too will the animals when they are hunted; they will not look up and
see the hunter as he creeps up on them.

The dance continued into the evening, gathering momentum with the hypnotic rhythm of the clapping and chanting and the stamping of feet. Dust rose
from the earth and hung in the air like an evening mist, turning to red gold as
it was caught by the setting sun. By now everyone had joined in, young and old
alike, and the dancing figures whirled and leaped as they circled the hut and
wove their way through the bushes in a great figure of eight. The performance
that had been set up for our benefit had been transformed into a celebration for
the life of the whole band.

CHAPTER SIX

Children of the Desert

Bushmen do not usually display affection towards each other; all their affec-
tionate behaviour is reserved for children, and on them it is lavished with un-
abashed openness. Children are treated with great indulgence. At no stage in
our filming trips did we see a child being smacked (though I did not get the impression that this never happened – only rarely), and reprimands hardly sounded
like reprimands at all. The Bushmen's sense of fun, and their sense of the
ridiculous, nearly always turned what could have been a confrontation with a
child into an occasion when everyone, including the erring child, was reduced
to laughter. We did notice, though, that the required behaviour was not an
inevitable result.

There were children of all ages in the Kua group we were with, so we were
able to observe something of the relationships between the full range of age
groups, and between children and adults. Khangdu's tiny baby, about ten days
old when we arrived, was virtually never out of her arms, or lying close to her
side, so there was almost constant skin contact between them. As soon as her
baby cried, Khangdu would give him her breast. When sitting by the fire, she
would hold him across her lap and in the crook of her arm as he slept, and as
she moved around the encampment she carried him, often still asleep, slung in
a kaross at her side. At night, and at times during the day when Khangdu herself was lying down, the baby lay snugly in the curve of her body.

All Bushman children, until they can walk, have this almost permanent contact with their mothers. Once their eyes have focused and they have begun to
play with objects, the toys that are immediately available are the beads around
their mother's neck and in her hair or ears, or the bracelets around her wrists.
As babies are not usually carried on their mother's back, but at her side, and in
an upright position, it is only a short stretch to find either beads to play with, or
her breast to suckle.

There was one little girl of about four or five, called Masihagu (which means
'heavy rain'), whose mother had died when she was born. As her father /Wa/tee,
had two wives, Masihagu was immediately taken by the other wife, Namgãe,
whose youngest child was then being weaned, and she was cared for as though
she was Namgãe's own child, as also were the other four of the dead woman's
children, who in any case already regarded her as one of their mothers. This
special family situation was certainly fortunate for Masihagu; but Bushman

families do not seem to have the same clear distinctions in relationships as European families do, and any baby whose mother died in childbirth would certainly be taken by one of a choice of surrogate mothers, who would bring her up, and love her, as one of her own. And Masihagu certainly did not behave like a child who had been deprived of mother-love.

Bushman babies tend to learn to walk rather earlier than their European peers. Whether, as has been suggested, this is because they spend so much more time in an upright position during infancy, suspended in a kaross with arms and legs free to move, and also with an inexhaustible supply of adults and older children to support their first faltering footsteps, I am not qualified to judge. But as a theory, it does sound convincing. Certainly for every toddler (aspiring or actual) there seemed to be at least five children from the age of about four upwards, in constant though changing attendance.

Little girls in particular, from quite an early stage, take their toddler siblings under their wing. Even at the age of about four they seem to have a remarkably adult maternalism towards younger children, and are old enough to understand the necessity of not straying far from a group of adults — not that the mothers ever let their smaller children out of sight or sound. Boys, we found, were not such enthusiastic child-minders as girls.

Almost from the beginning boys and girls seem to segregate themselves in their playing. As each child begins to be weaned, and leaves its close connection with its mother, it attaches itself not to a group of children of its own age (Bushman bands are generally too small for there to be much possibility of peer groups) but to a group of children of its own sex, but of widely varying ages. Nearly every time we saw children playing (which was just about all the time), their sizes ranged dramatically from the very small to the almost adult. Presumably as a result of this, there seemed to be an almost complete lack of competitive spirit in their games, for competition would have given an unfair advantage to the older children.

However, my merry favourite, /Gae≠tebe, did have two friends of his own sex and age, and he was frequently to be seen playing with one or other of them. I only once saw all three of them playing together. There was one occasion when he and his friend, Khalgugãe, decided to have a boxing match. It was all very friendly and unaggressive, but the boys were right in the middle of a group of adults who were sitting and talking. When their elbows had made themselves felt to an unacceptable degree, two of the women — laughing, and with great, though firm, gentleness — guided the boys away to the edge of the group, where their elbows would beat only the thin air.

/Gae≠tebe was very much a father's boy, in the sense that he clearly regarded himself as one of the men (aged three or four), and the nearest available man for him to be with was generally his father. If Be/tee was not around, his uncle, Kangao, would do very well instead, and failing him, any of the other men of the group. He used to delight in trying to carry his father's skin bag [47], or one of his heavy wooden tools, sometimes with a wicked smile at his intentionally visible theft; sometimes with a very serious expression on his face, in perfect mimicry of the men of the band working out some deep problem. He was also a great dancer; from dawn till dusk, and usually well into the night, he danced his way through everything [55]. When the adults danced at night, he was always there, out in the front, dancing with all the energy in his little body. And during the day when no one was dancing at all, or doing anything very much, he would simply start to dance by himself, usually in front of a group of women whom he knew would very soon be unable to resist clapping and chanting specially to accompany his dancing [46]. Then, like the child that he was, he would get bored and run off to join a group of boys, or to start another boxing match with Khalgugãe.

We only once saw a child in a temper and behaving aggressively towards one of the adults. It was a little boy of two or three who had been carried by Hidikwa, one of the older women of the band, to where she wanted to sit with some other women. What the cause of the child's wrath was we never discovered – perhaps he had not wanted to be moved. In any case, he looked very petulant and on the verge of tears, and seemed undecided whether to stay or go. He had a stick in one hand, and he started to hit Hidikwa on the back. It could not have hurt her as the strokes were hardly forceful, and in any case fell on the kaross that was over her back. Hidikwa turned round, amusement written all over her face, caught hold of the stick and said something to the child. Then she resumed her conversation – and the child resumed hitting her with his stick. Still laughing, Hidikwa reached over and picked up a log, turned round and pointed it at him with gentle remonstration, put it down again and returned to her conversation. When the child started hitting her for the third time, she reached out and caught him in her arms, and tumbled him into her lap, laughing and remonstrating at the same time. In no time the child was laughing too, and then sat happily in front of Hidikwa, still clutching his stick with which he started beating the ground beside him with perfect equanimity. It was an exemplary lesson in how to convert anger into harmony through laughter.

Many of the games the children played were in mimicry of their parents' behaviour, or of the behaviour of wild animals. We often saw groups of boys playing at being animals, one – as a predator or a charging buffalo – chasing the others. They dodged each other around bushes or behind trees or, where the grass was thick and tall, by lying invisible until the chaser came so close that he was bound to see them. But they never strayed far from the encampment, having had it impressed upon them from a very early age that the greatest danger was to be alone in the desert.

The girls played in a more domesticated way, using their toddler brothers and sisters rather in the manner of dolls. They also made themselves toy dolls out of the superfluity of tubers that there was at the time; presumably in less abundant seasons such playthings are proscribed, as all available tubers would be required for eating or drinking. But when we were there the girls were allowed to make as many dolls as they wished, beautifully articulated with strong wire, and even with such intentionally comic features as two bulging buttocks, or a large European-style nose. Like little girls the world over, they would play with these dolls as though they were their babies, carrying them on their backs in miniature karosses which their mothers fixed up for them. The older girls turned the whole thing into a subject for mirth, prancing around in caricature of either their younger sisters or of their mothers. And the mothers too would sometimes join in the joke, holding the doll to a breast, which everyone found hilariously funny.

The boys were also gifted model-makers, making not dolls, but trucks [48]. Again they used tubers, and made several perfect models of the trucks we travelled in, complete with wheels which turned. Their masterpiece, however, was a model 35 mm stills camera, with every detail precisely observed and realized – revolving focusing and aperture rings, a hole right through the middle of the lens, carriage winder, shutter release button, and even a piece of transparent plastic picked up from somewhere to represent the lens [50]. The boys followed us about with their 'camera', delighting to take 'photographs' of us, twiddling the focusing ring, setting the stops, twisting themselves into awkward postures, and finally pressing the shutter release button – all in wickedly humorous imitation of us. It was suitably humbling to see ourselves so accurately parodied, but it was all done with the greatest good humour, and with no trace of malice. I am sure that if we had stayed longer, they would have made an equally exact movie camera and tape recorder, and would have caricatured the whole film crew at work.

Games are by no means the monopoly of children. Bushmen of all ages have a highly developed sense of play, and love to join in many of the ancient and traditional games that are still, though decreasingly, played in the Kalahari Desert. There is almost always a division of games by sex; men and boys participate in certain games, women and girls in others.

We asked the !Xõ Bushmen, with whom we spent a short time, to show us some of their games, and the extrovert old Dushe fell on the idea with enthusiasm. He detailed //Nao, a young man in his twenties, to make an *ahna* with which they would play a game which, once we had seen them at it, we decided was a kind of Bushman badminton. //Nao cut a short sappy stick, about 40 cms long (16 inches), and peeled it. Then he stuck into the pithy centre of the thinner end of the stick a soft round guinea fowl breast feather. About one third of the way down he then bound to the stick a guinea fowl wing feather about 15 cms long (6 inches). The binding was of sinew. Then some string, made from the fibres of the wild sansevieria plant, was used to make a thong with which to attach a weight (in this case a small stone, though in some areas nuts are used) to the thicker end of the stick. This done, all that was required was for a rather longer stick (about 75 cms/30 inches) to be cut for each player, and completely peeled except for a hand-grip. Then play commenced.

Dushe had the first go, throwing the *ahna* up into the air, and then, as it floated down vertically – the weighted end at the bottom, and the feather causing the whole thing to spin in the breeze – he tried to catch the thong with his stick and send the *ahna* whirling back upwards. That was the theory; the practice was rather less elegant and accomplished, and he confessed that it was many a long day since he had played the game. But he was determined to regain the skill that he claimed he had once had, and tried over and over again, with equal failure and increasing merriment both from him and from his audience. There was one boy there who was almost convulsed with giggles throughout the whole performance, but he would not try the game himself as he said he had never played it before and it was more fun to watch.

However //Nao agreed to test the *ahna* he had made, and he was certainly more competent at it than Dushe, though also somewhat out of practice. //Xolate (which means 'knee-caps'), Dushe's son-in-law, was about the same standard as //Nao, being equally out of practice. We felt sad that this game, once wide-spread throughout the Kalahari, is falling into oblivion. But such was the enthusiastic laughter of the young boys who had never played the game, that we hoped they would have a go at it once we had disappeared from the scene.

!Numani, another young !Xõ man, redeemed the honour of the group in another game which was clearly still current among them: //*kabi*, or stick throwing. He and three boys of varying heights and ages each cut sticks about 75 cms long (30 inches), and about 1.5 cms (half an inch) in diameter. They then took it in turns to throw – first running, and then, while still on the run, hurling the stick down as hard as they could onto the ground a few metres ahead of them. The stick bounced on the earth, and then soared off for a considerable distance, keeping fairly close to the ground. The aim was to get the stick to bounce for as great a distance as possible. Our performers were all rather accomplished (even the smallest one who could not have been more than eight years old), and usually managed to get their sticks to soar at least six metres (twenty feet) [49]. They were also very accurate in their aim. When the cameraman put the movie camera on the ground and asked them to make their stick bounce a short distance in front of it, all four were on target; and one of the sticks, as it bounced away, hit the lens hood, narrowing missing the lens itself.

Stick throwing is a game with obvious practical value in training boys in the coordination and accuracy they will need as hunters. The hunting of some small animals depends on running down the animal concerned and then, once within range, throwing a heavy stick hard enough and accurately enough to stun it until the hunter can reach it and finish it off. But despite this underlying serious purpose, the game of stick throwing that we watched was played with all the sense of fun that the Bushmen are capable of.

The girls and women of the !Xõ band played one of their own games – the melon game – and they were very expert at it. All ages took part, from the almost geriatric down to about seven or eight year olds, and there must have been about twenty of them in the end, as more and more joined in the fun. It is a game in which a small tsama melon (*Citrullus lanatus*) is used as a ball, and is tossed from one girl to the next according to strict rules, and accompanied by singing, clapping and dancing [51]. The rhythm is complex and changes according to the different stages of the game. The girl who first held the melon danced forward a few steps with very vigorous movements, and when a certain point in the rhythm was reached, she jumped on the spot with both feet, flicking sand into the air as she did so, and at the same time she flicked the melon behind her, to be caught by the next girl [52]. Some of the catches were very difficult, but this was all part of the game, and it was amazing to see how the girl whose catch it was would hurl herself forward in an instant, with her hand more often than not in exactly the right position. Misses, just as much as brilliant catches, were subjects of renewed merriment. All those awaiting their turn clapped and sang in accompaniment to the girl who was at that moment dancing with the melon.

In the melon game that we watched, the girls simply chanted rather than sang words. But when Laurens van der Post was in the Kalahari in the early 1950s, he was told some words for the song: 'We went out into the desert to look for blue wildebeest [or any other antelope], and we cried, "Oh wildebeest, wildebeest come to us!" But it simply flicked its heels and ran away.' And the dancing girls, as they threw the tsama melon behind them for the next girl to catch, simply flicked their heels and ran away.

The training for their adult roles, both for boys and girls, may – as with the stick throwing – begin inconspicuously in the form of games that develop necessary skills. But it may sometimes be continued in a more specific manner, though usually spasmodically. Children learn the skills they will need by some kind of osmosis – by accompanying their parents or other adults and observing what they do, even if they do not appear to be taking any notice. One of the things they seem to pick up most quickly is how to recognize the various plants that are good to eat. But only once did we see a young girl (Nwane/tee, aged about eight) go on a gathering expedition with her mother, /Wa-u/tee. She spent much of the time playing by herself, but from time to time she pounced on a sprig of leaves that she had spotted, dug up the root which the leaves had indicated to her was underneath, and ran to put it into her mother's kaross. By the time we all went back to the camp, she must have pulled up about ten roots or tubers of varying sizes. It was admittedly less than half the harvest that each of the women had gathered, but still not inconsiderable.

With the Kua Bushmen we saw two young boys being given a lesson in how to set a bird snare. It did not sound or look like a lesson; Kotuko/tee simply chatted away as he set the snare, and the two boys just sat around, the younger one, Iogãe, frankly bored, while Malehane took some occasional, short-lived interest. But when Kotuko/tee invited one of them to put the finishing touches to the snare, Malehane leaped to the fore with alacrity, and did the job with more skill than we would have guessed from his somewhat dilettante manner beforehand. Clearly more had penetrated than we had given him credit for.

The snare that Kotuko/tee set was intended to catch one or other of the medium-sized birds found in the Kalahari, in particular the Lesser Bustard, or black korhan which, we were assured, makes a very tasty meal. Unfortunately, the trap caught nothing during the time we were there, so we were unable to put the claim to the test. But we did have an unparalleled lesson in how to set the appropriate type of snare, though I doubt if any member of our film crew was as apt to learn as Malehane, despite the fact that we watched every move with rapt concentration as Kotuko/tee patiently repeated each stage several times for the camera to immortalize every detail. By contrast, Malehane's attention had appeared to be somewhere else for much of the time, but he had doubtless had the advantage of at least one previous occasion on which to take in the subtleties of the job.

The trap was a masterpiece of ingenuity and precision. First of all Kotuko/tee dug a deep hole with a stout stick, one end of which was sharpened for the job, and in it he put one end of a thinnish springy bough, about 185 cms long (6 feet). At the top of the bough he attached a length of string with a noose at the end, and just above the noose was a knot with a small loop in it, into which a wooden toggle was fitted. Next he took a strong and very sappy branch, about 45 cms long (18 inches), bent it into an arch, and buried both ends as deeply as possible in the ground as it was this stick that was going to have to take all the tension in the spring [56]. The bough was then bent right down until the wooden toggle could be put under the arched branch where it was held in place by another stick [57]. This formed the spring. Then some short sticks were stuck into the earth around the spring in a circle just big enough to hold the noose taut at the top of the circle [58].

The second time round Kotuko/tee invited one of the boys to set the noose around the sticks and to test the snare. Malehane bounded forward, triggered the spring with his right index finger, and in a trice his arm was trapped by the noose and lifted upward as the bough sprang back [59]. Any black korhan, pecking at the bait of acacia gum in the centre of the snare, would have to be swift indeed if its neck were to escape the noose.

This kind of spontaneous schooling in traditional Bushman life is gradually being eroded as the governments both of Botswana and Namibia are providing a growing number of schools in increasingly remote areas. Malehane will soon be exchanging his almost continuous play, interspersed with lessons in snare-setting and the like, for the schoolroom where he will join several of his cousins who are already receiving a primary education.

We drove for well over an hour one day to reach the school at Ngware, and asked for the classes in which three of Be/tee's and three of Kangao's children were being taught. In fact, it was all one big class of about forty children, sitting outside in the open air and being taught by a young Tswana man. In this school most of the children were Tswanas or Kgalagadi, with a few Bushman children among them. There were boarding facilities for those children who, like the ones we had come to see, lived too far away to go to school daily.

The languages used in class were both Tswana and English, the former already known to the Bushmen, the latter totally new to them. We watched them being put through a rather unsympathetic drilling in arithmetic and English language, and the whole atmosphere of the class was an unhappy one.

Compared with their brothers and sisters and cousins back at home, the Bushman children here seemed lacking in all *joie de vivre*. They answered their teacher's sarcastic questions as briefly as possible, their eyes downcast. We could hardly believe that they came from the same families as those merry imps who had caricatured us with their model camera. These children seemed to have had all the stuffing taken out of them.

We would have been very unhappy about the modern education of Bushman children if this had been our only experience of it. Fortunately a school of a very different character exists near Lone Tree pan, where the !Xõ group lives, so we were able to see something of the best as well as something of the worst. The Lone Tree school is run by Elizabeth Camm, who must be everyone's dream of a primary school teacher. Her first teaching job had been at Xanagas in the far west of Botswana, on the edge of the Kalahari Desert. There had been one or two Bushman children in her class there, and she became increasingly interested in them and their families. This interest was sharpened when a Bushman medicine man performed a healing ritual for her and the 'bad leg' that had been causing her considerable pain for several years, from then on ceased to trouble her.

She had already become concerned about Bushman education. She realized that many Bushmen felt that they were being left out of everything to do with Botswana, and she wanted them to feel part of what was, whether or not they knew it or liked it, their own country. Education seemed the first and obvious step towards involvement. For this reason she applied to teach in a school deeper in the Kalahari where most of her pupils would be Bushmen. She has learned the !Xõ language since her arrival at Lone Tree.

Her classes consist mainly of Bushman children, with a few Kgalagadi as well. She said that the Bushman children are very bright, and we were told the same at all four Bushman schools we visited, two in Botswana and two in Namibia. Also common to all these schools was the fact that in winter attendance drops dramatically – the mornings are so cold then that the Bushman children are loth to leave their fires. In summer Elizabeth Camm has between twenty-three and thirty children in her classes; in winter, about seven. We were there in the autumn, when the morning chill had not reached its worst, and there were nineteen children in school. There was such a vital sense of enjoyment in the class, with bright little faces positively bursting with enthusiasm to answer questions or volunteer information, that we reckoned the deterrent of the cold in winter must have been powerful indeed to keep the children away from school.

One of the schools in Namibia that we visited, run by the South African Defence Force, found another reason for non-attendance – the early marriage of the !Kung Bushman girls. This seemed curious to us, because in other respects marriage did not appear to change life much for a very young girl. Not all Bushman groups marry off their daughters early, but among the !Kung and the /Gwi, a little girl is frequently married at the age of about seven or eight to a young man at least twice her age. Among the /Gwi there is little in the way of marriage ceremony — simply the building of a new hut — but the !Kung go in for something rather more elaborate which includes the parents of the bride and groom exchanging presents and, on the evening of the day itself, when the bridal hut has been built, lighting a new fire in front of it.

But even when she is married, a little girl is usually still regarded as a child, and she may often continue to live with her parents. Nothing is really required of her (either economically or sexually) until after her first menstruation. This, far more than marriage, is the great turning point in a girl's life. The ritual which attends this landmark in her life, with all its abundant sense of celebration, also marks the change that is about to take place in her role in the band. From now on she is expected to take her share in the gathering of plant food, and in the other work that the women do. If the girl is married, she is now expected to make her home with her husband, if she has not already been doing so, and to sleep with him and care for him.

Before a boy may marry, he has to prove himself capable of providing for a family. Invariably in the past — but decreasingly in the present, thanks to the diminishing numbers of game animals — this meant that he had to prove himself as a hunter, and go through a special ritual which was performed when, for the first time, he killed one of the larger antelope alone. The traditional animal for a boy's first kill was the eland — the animal which, as we have seen, had the greatest significance for the Bushmen. But in areas where eland were rare, any other of the greater antelopes would do, and the most common was the wildebeest.

The boy had to be old enough and strong enough to endure what might turn out to be several days of hunting down his antelope, so he was rarely less than about fourteen years old. Once his arrow had pierced the antelope, he might not run in case, because of the supernatural link that was believed to exist between him and his quarry, the animal too would run, and would escape. On his return to the camp he must stay apart from everyone else, especially the women. The animal, once killed, must be cooked on a special fire which the women must avoid; and he himself must not partake of the meat. After this he was scarified by his male relatives with a series of short, vertical incisions on his face, arms, chest and back. If the animal he had killed was male, these incisions would be made on the right side, the side associated with masculinity; if female, on the feminine left side.

This ritual would be performed twice for each boy, once for the first male animal, and again for the first female. Thereafter the boy was regarded as a man and a hunter, and was ready for marriage. Today, with so few Bushmen still living as hunter-gatherers, hunting is less and less regarded as the way for a man to provide for his family. It is simply not a possibility that remains open to the vast majority. As we shall see, the new way to provide for your family is to have a job on one of the white- or black-owned farms that are encroaching ever more deeply into the Kalahari Desert.

CHAPTER SEVEN

Man the Hunter

Before the coming of the white man, the whole of southern Africa was a natural paradise, its mountains, valleys, deserts, plains and shores teeming with animals of all kinds. Predation of some species upon others maintained a natural population control in an area that was in any case large enough to support vast herds of all manner of creatures. The Bushmen, part of nature as they were, did nothing to upset the balance of this life. The number of animals that they shot or trapped for food was infinitesimal in the midst of such abundance.

As soon as white men appeared with their guns and ammunition, in whatever areas they occupied there began a sad decline in the population of wild animals. We have seen something of the wanton slaughter of 'sea cows' by some of the early Dutch settlers; but it was not until the nineteenth century, when a certain species of British gentleman turned its 'sporting' attention to southern Africa, and travelled widely there in pursuit of game, that the real destruction of wild animals began, and whole herds were decimated. The effect of such a loss on the Bushmen was incalculable.

The Bushmen rarely acquired guns, and their methods of hunting, whether with bows and arrows or with snares, were a source of fascination to the white travellers. A French traveller and writer, Emil Holub, in the late nineteenth century described how some Bushmen would cover themselves with animal skins in order to deceive their prey and get within bowshot of it; while others would uproot a small bush and use it as cover, imperceptibly getting closer to the animal they wanted to shoot. A number of other writers told how some of the Bushmen they came into contact with disguised themselves as ostriches so that they could approach more closely the game they were hunting.

Sir James Alexander, having seen two frames covered with ostrich feathers hanging in a tree, induced a Bushman with a present of tobacco to show him how he effected the disguise: 'He placed one of the feather frames on his shoulders and secured it about his neck, then taking from a bush the head and neck of an ostrich, through which a stick was thrust, he went out a little way from the huts with a bow and arrow in his left hand, and pretending to approach a Kaop [wildebeest], he pecked at the tops of the bushes in the manner of an ostrich, and occasionally rubbed the head against the false body, as the ostrich ever and anon does to get rid of flies. . . . Approaching sufficiently near the Kaop, which of course has nothing to fear from its feathered companion of the plains, the

Boschman slips the ostrich head between his neck and the frame, and cautiously taking aim, discharges his arrow at the deceived Kaop.'

This trick, though eminently successful, was occasionally fraught with perils. Alexander was told of one Bushman who, while disguised as an ostrich, was ripped open and killed by a genuine bird, presumably out of some misplaced territorial jealousy. On other occasions a black or white hunter had been known to shoot and wound, and sometime kill, a Bushman, thinking him to be a real ostrich.

One of the most delightful descriptions of the Bushmen's method of trapping animals comes from Francis Galton who watched them setting a snare. He did not go in for much detail, but was clearly impressed by their skill: 'Their spring is a very simple one. I admired the simplicity of the methods by which antelopes were induced to leap into the middle of it; an unpractised hand would have made a fence as though he were laying out a steeplechase course, but the Bushmen simply bend a twig across the pathway, which does not in the least frighten the animal, but which, in the gaiety of his heart, he overleaps. The pitfalls are neatly made.' Lest he should seem too admiring of the Bushmen, Galton adds that, 'there is, however, nothing in them which an English gamekeeper would not contrive as well.'

The Kua Bushmen we were with had lost the art of hunting with bows and arrows for there was no large game left for them to hunt; but their skill in setting snares for the smaller antelopes must have been up to the standard of Galton's nineteenth-century Bushmen. As usual in practical matters, it was Ramonne who took the lead, with /Wa/tee providing a strong supporting role. The other men, particularly Be/tee, talked a great deal, apparently offering advice and encouragement. They selected a place where the spoor of the antelope they were after – steenbok or duiker – was fresh, indicating that this track was in current use. Then Ramonne and /Wa/tee set to work.

The principle of this snare was virtually identical with that of the bird snare that Kotuko/tee had shown the two boys how to make two days earlier. But for this one it was necessary to dig a hole into which one leg of the hoped-for antelope would inadvertently step, thus triggering the spring to tighten the noose around the leg. The hole was astonishingly small, only about 12 to 15 cms across (5 to 6 inches), and roughly the same depth. Not far away from the hole a strong and sappy bough was planted deeply; a length of string was attached to the top end, with a small holding loop about half-way down, and beyond it the noose. The bough was bent down so that the holding loop just reached to the hole; a stick was put through the loop and wedged delicately across the hole which was then covered with pieces of bark, balancing on the edge of the earth and on the holding stick. These were completely covered by a light layer of sand, the noose was laid wide around the hole, and it too was covered with sand. The whole thing had become invisible. Finally thin twigs about 30 cms long (12 inches) were stuck in a circle round the snare, to direct the antelope's leg into the exact spot. As soon as this happened, the stick would snap out of the holding loop, the bough would flick upwards, the noose would tighten and the buck would be caught.

As it turned out, a steenbok was caught in the snare that very night. They had set a watch, and as soon as the steenbok stepped into the hole and its leg was firmly held by the noose, the watchman came running to tell us. They had lost too many snared animals to dogs or other predators for them to risk leaving it until the morning.

With the comfort of distance and freedom from hunger, it is easy for us to be unduly romantic about the Bushmen's attitude to animals. Western concepts of being kind to animals have little meaning in a society whose life has traditionally depended to a large extent on the killing of animals. You simply take the most efficient means at your disposal to achieve that end. When the Bushmen reached the snare that night they were armed with clubs and they used them. To us it was exceedingly unpleasant; to them it was simply practical, and they laughed with kindly indulgence at our squeamishness.

The following morning the steenbok was prepared for cooking, Ramonne again doing most of the work. So precise was his knowledge of the little buck's anatomy that he skinned it like a work of art, peeling the skin away from the underlying flesh as easily as if he were peeling an orange [72]. Later in the day he pegged the skin out for curing, and by the end of the following day it was as soft and supple as could be desired.

While Ramonne was skinning the steenbok and removing its stomach and intestines, /Wa/tee lit a fire and near it dug a hole about 30 cms deep (12 inches), roughly the same width, and rather over twice the length. When the buck was skinned and ready, and the fire had burned up well and produced good glowing coals, some of these were put into the bottom of the hole, the buck was laid on top of them, and the rest of the coals heaped over it [73]. Then it was left to cook. We asked when it would be ready, and they pointed to the sky and said, 'When the sun is there it will be cooked'.

Four hours later, when the sun was in the position they had indicated, we went back to the Bushmen's camp and they scraped aside the coals and took out the cooked buck [74]. First Ramonne cut through the rib cage and revealed the highly prized inner portions — the liver and kidneys. To us they looked un-appealingly undercooked, but Ramonne and /Wa/tee and their wives dipped into the dark red mess with their fingers and ate with evident relish. This was the hunters' portion, reserved for those who had been responsible for setting the snare and catching the animal. The rest was shared meticulously between the whole group, each family being given a portion in the initial distribution, and this they then divided among themselves. We too were given some of the meat to try — the better-cooked outside parts I am glad to say — and it was delicious, the taste somewhere between lamb and veal, and very tender.

There was a particularly charming moment when one of the very small boys, Tshipi//xama, came to collect his family's portion to take back to where they were sitting a short distance away from where the meat was being handed out.

He took the meat in both hands and clutched it firmly as he made his way carefully back to his family. But he encountered an obstacle; the path had a log across it, and beside it was a bush, one prickly twig of which barred the way. Tshipi//xama stopped, worked out the problem and then, with intense concentration written all over his face, secured the meat in his left hand while with his right he held aside the twig and stepped over the log. For one suspense-filled moment it looked as though he were going to lose his balance and drop the meat, but then he righted himself and negotiated the obstacle successfully. Nobody rushed to help, or even offered advice. They simply looked on, highly amused as always, while Tshipi//xama dealt with the problem by himself.

The following day we left the Kua Bushmen with considerable sadness as we felt we had got to know them a little and they had always made us feel welcome. But a couple of days earlier Be/tee had confessed to our interpreter that they would be glad when we left. 'It's not that we don't like you,' he said. 'We do — but we are so tired.' Never in their lives, it seemed, had they done so much every day; for us they had concentrated into less than two weeks what they might normally have done in more than twice the time. With us gone, and with the food and tobacco we had given them, they were looking forward to some well-earned leisure.

Our main reasons for moving on were that this group did not perform a healing ritual with a trance dance, and they no longer hunted large game with bows and arrows — both essential ingredients for our films. So we drove westwards and spent the rest of that particular filming trip with two groups of !Xõ Bushmen, one of which still hunted with bows and arrows, though not to the same extent that they used to a few years ago. This was partly because of the reduced numbers of game, and partly because many of them have attached themselves to Tswana-owned cattle farms, on which they work in return for food. Since this food is shared, Bushman-like, among the whole family, there is less incentive to go out hunting. But some of the men still have bows and arrows, and indeed they still make them, though now most are made for sale to the gradually increasing numbers of tourists to the Kalahari, with the result that much of the care and skill has gone out of the job.

A Bushman bow is made from the wood of the raisin bush (*Grewia flava*). It is about one metre long (39 inches), lightly curved, and tapering almost to a point at both ends. The stress points are bound with sinew for extra strength, and this also provides a hand grip in the middle of the bow. The bowstring is generally made of two thin pieces of sinew taken from the long back muscles of a large antelope (eland or gemsbok are preferred), twisted together into a single cord of enormous strength. The tension is very important, and the bowstring is tightened until it produces the musical note that indicates the correct tension — the bow is also used as a musical instrument.

The arrows are more complicated to make, being composed of four separate sections: the arrowhead, the link shaft (about 5 cms/2 inches long), and the main shaft (45 cms/18 inches), with a short sleeve of hollow reed to join the arrowhead to the link shaft. Arrowheads used to be made exclusively of bone (the shin bone of an ostrich) and consisted of a single unbarbed point. Now the most common variety is made of metal and is barbed. This is fitted into one end of the sleeve whose other end fits over the bone or hard wood link shaft, and the whole join is tightly bound about with sinew. The link shaft is fitted into the reed main shaft and is only lightly bound to enable the main shaft to fall away once the arrow is embedded in the flesh of the animal. If the main shaft were to remain attached, the animal could more easily remove the whole arrow by rubbing itself against the branches or trunk of a tree. Bushmen have been known to shoot up to about 100 metres (110 yards), but as the arrows are not flighted, and are therefore less accurate, they are only likely to hit their target up to about a quarter of that distance.

Bushman hunters keep their arrows in round quivers the same length as their arrows, made from the root bark of one or other of the various acacia trees that grow in the Kalahari. The quiver is carried in a leather hunting bag, together with lengths of corded sinew for instant repairs, a pair of fire sticks (or nowadays a box of matches) and a stout throwing stick in case he runs down a small antelope or other animal of manageable proportions. When the hunter is not in imminent need of his bow, it too is carried in the bag, which also has a special sheath for carrying safely his long, iron-headed spear.

The bows and arrows of the Bushman hunters are so puny by contrast with the size of many of the animals they have always hunted, and the Bushmen themselves are so small and slight in stature, that at first glance it seems improbable that they could ever have made the slightest impression on them. Their solution to this fundamental dilemma of size was in the use of poison. It was the effectiveness of the Bushmen's poisoned arrows that so awed the Bantu-speaking neighbours of the now extinct southern Bushmen. Today in the Kalahari the same poisons are used as have been used by Bushmen from time immemorial. Their intimate knowledge of the plants and insects and reptiles of their environment enables them to know and find poisons that are deadly in their effect on even the largest animals, but which leave the meat untainted. Juice from various species of *Euphorbia*, venom from such snakes as the puff-adder and the cobra, as well as that of the trap-door spider and the scorpion, are used either separately or in a mixture.

Perhaps the most common source of poison, and the one that we saw both being collected and later used to doctor the arrows, is the larva of the chrysomelid beetle (*Diamphydia simplex*). This beetle, which is spotted rather like a ladybird but with a longer body, feeds on the leaves of a small tree or shrub of the *Commifora* species. The larvae, wrapped in hard, dark-brown cocoons about the size of large peas, are found in the roots of the shrub [61]. It is the grub itself that is a poison of a lethal kind which, when it enters the bloodstream, attacks the nervous system of the animal, leading to a general paralysis and inevitable death. Yet taken orally, we were told, it is not a poison at all, and it in no way affects the meat of the animal it has killed.

We watched and filmed while our three hunters, /Tade, ≠Kabe/twa and //Kaeki, doctored their arrows with the poison, in preparation for the hunt. They sat under a tree which threw a dappled shade over them and the inevitable fire around which they were sitting. /Tade picked up a piece of wood with a shallow depression in it, and into this they put the grubs as they extracted them from their cocoons. With a piece of stick /Tade pounded the grubs to liquid, and then chewed some bark of *Boscia albitrunca* and spat the resulting fluid into the wooden dish with the grubs. This acts as a kind of glue to keep the poison plastic; otherwise it tends to dry to a very brittle consistency, and would flake off the arrow too easily.

They put the poison onto their arrows with a small stick, not onto the tip of the arrow as we had expected, but soaking it into the sinew binding that runs from immediately behind the arrowhead to the link shaft [62, 63]. To have it on the sharp edge of the arrow would be dangerous – the slightest scratch on a finger could be fatal – and provided the arrowhead enters deep into the animal's flesh, the poison behind the tip will be just as effective. ≠Kabe/twa, the eldest of the three, also applied the poison direct from a grub onto the arrow; he rolled the grub lightly between his thumb and forefinger, breaking down its insides to a liquid but being careful not to burst the skin. Then he flicked off the head and gradually squeezed the insides out and onto the sinew binding.

Having poisoned about eight arrows each, they packed them away into their quivers, put the quivers and other necessary paraphernalia into their bags, fitted the spears into their sheaths, picked up their bows and set off on the hunt [64]. For the rest of that day they cast about in the bush, looking for spoor that was fresh enough to indicate that the animals concerned might be close by. It was a long hard walk through the heat of the day, and the only game to be seen was a small herd of springbok on Matlo-a-phuduhudu pan, just too far away for the hunters to shoot, and too open to view for them to get close enough. As soon as the springbok saw their crouched figures moving across the pan in their direction, they flicked up their tails and started to pronk – leaping vertically into the air with stiff legs, and bouncing up again as soon as they had touched the earth. Convincing each other of danger by these preliminary warning signals, the whole herd of springbok were soon streaming away into the distance, ever further from the range of the Bushmen's bows and arrows [65].

Towards the evening, as the air was becoming cooler and the light warmer with the setting of the sun, the hunters returned to camp; the cameraman and two assistants – the maximum number allowed to follow the hunt, lest a crowd should frighten off the game – followed wearily behind. They reckoned they had covered about thirty kilometres (nineteen miles), carrying considerably heavier equipment than the Bushmen. In fact the Bushmen had started the hunt by telling them that they would never keep up. By the end of the second and longer day, when they covered about thirty-five kilometres (twenty-two miles), /Tade conceded that the three from our team were indeed men, and not the boys they had originally judged them to be. It was a good moment.

That evening we sat around the fire discussing with the hunters what we should do in view of what seemed to be an almost total lack of game, and the rapidly approaching time when we should have to stop filming and head out of the Kalahari. It was decided that we should spend one more day looking for game around Matlo-a-phuduhudu, and if that also failed we should be ready to leave the following morning to drive, together with the three hunters, south and west to Masetlheng pan where we had been told there was game. The problems of taking the hunters into the territory of another Bushman band could be overcome without difficulty, we were told, because our guide knew the group there well, they no longer hunted with bows and arrows themselves, and would be happy to help us.

With a relaxation induced by decisions made, rest and good food after hard physical exertion, and also doubtless by the hunters' new and unexpected respect for these soft-looking white men, the three Bushmen talked for the first time about their hunting. They said that the animal they most like to kill is the eland, because it is big and can feed the whole band; and also because, of all the antelopes, it has the most fat. It has a great deal of fat in its chest around the heart, and this is mixed with the rest of the meat when it is cooked to give extra value to the lean meat. Fat, they said, is good; it makes you fat, and to be fat is a good thing. Yet they said that the eland is also the most stupid animal, because even when it catches the scent of the hunters, it will continue to move in the same direction in which it was already travelling, which makes it easy to track.

They told us that when they come upon their quarry dead or dying, the animal belongs to the hunter whose arrow had pierced the flesh, and whose poison had caused the animal to fall. And when the animal is dead, even before they send word to the rest of the band back at their camp, the hunters will make a fire and cook and eat the best portions. They take out the tongue and the liver, the parts that have the most fat in them, roast them on the open fire, and eat them before anyone else gets there, because after a long time spent on the hunt they are tired and hungry and in need of strength.

When any animal other than an eland is killed, they take the meat home to their camp. But when they kill an eland the whole band will come from the camp to the place of the kill. Not only is the eland too big to carry what might be a great distance back to camp, but also, they said, it brings bad luck to take an eland home; better for the band to come from home, and divide the meat up at the place of the kill, and stay till every morsel is finished. They will have a great feast and a great celebration.

Although the animal belongs to the hunter whose arrow killed it, it is always shared between all members of the band. The owner's family will receive the meat at the top of the shoulder, for this is regarded as the best part (besides the liver and the tongue), and also the fat around the brain and at the base of the horns. His various relatives will receive the portions established by tradition as correct for that particular relative. It is very precise and very fair. In this concept and practice of sharing the Bushmen have changed not one iota from the end

of the eighteenth century (and indeed long before) when Sir John Barrow wrote
that 'universal equality prevails. . . . When one feasts they all partake, and when
one hungers they all suffer'.

The following day they again found no game, so we carried out our decision
of the night before and left early the next morning for Masetlheng. We took the
precaution – of which the hunters took a somewhat dim view – of stopping in
Hukuntsi to hire a man with a gun who, as a Botswana citizen, had the right to
shoot game. We none of us looked forward to the end of the hunt with a
wounded, half-paralysed animal dying a slow death. If we had the chance, we
would ask Aharob to finish it off quickly. As it turned out it was a worthwhile
provision.

After a day and a half of rough driving, we reached Masetlheng, a huge pan
whose light grey, parched and encrusted surface was surrounded by a wide
circle of low scrubby bushes. Beyond this there was the most astonishingly
beautiful parklike scenery. The grass here, unlike the Bushman grass we had
seen almost everywhere else, reached only to about mid-calf, was stouter and
greener and looked like wild wheat. Dotted about in this grassland were some
yellowwood trees (*Terminalia sericia*), two species of acacia (*erioloba* and *luderizii*)
and *Boscia albitrunca*. The whole feeling was of a more verdant land than we had
experienced so far in the Kalahari; but the appearance was deceptive. The local
Bushman band, with whom we made almost immediate contact, told us that
there was virtually no water there. The greenness was the result of an unexpected rainfall about two weeks earlier.

They told us that they had lived before at Bohela-batho, the place whose
name means 'where the people end', and where we had stopped to film the sipwell. Then they had moved to Hukuntsi because the borehole would give them
plenty of water. But there was no game there, and the Kgalagadi had treated
them badly, taking away from them what food they had. Here at Masetlheng
they had only just enough water to drink; but the great advantage was that the
Kgalagadi left them alone and so they had enough to eat. They had no objection
to our hunting in their area, for they no longer hunted themselves. Gemsbok in
particular, they said, were in fairly good supply, and we should concentrate our
hunt on them.

After the eland, the next most favoured animal for the Bushman hunter is
the gemsbok, to me the most dazzling antelope of all with the black stripes on its
face and its four white socks. Its capacity to survive in the most unpromising
desert conditions is astonishing: for both the gemsbok and the eland, like the
Bushmen themselves, can survive in times of drought on water-storing tubers
which they dig out of the earth.

There at Masetlheng, our Bushman hunters set off once again. In what was
left of the day they saw several gemsbok and some springbok, but they could not
get within bowshot. But the following day was another story.

They started early in the morning, and before long, in an area of long grass
and occasional bushes, they saw a group of three female gemsbok grazing quite

32. Gathering plant food is the task of the women. Whenever they spot a likely leaf, they stab the earth with their digging sticks and pull up the roots. Here they discover a clump of scillas.

33, 34. (*below*) Bushman women cook gemsbok cucumbers in the fire. When cooked, the tops are cut off, the flesh mashed with a stick, and /Gae≠tebe settles down to eat.

35△   36△   37▽

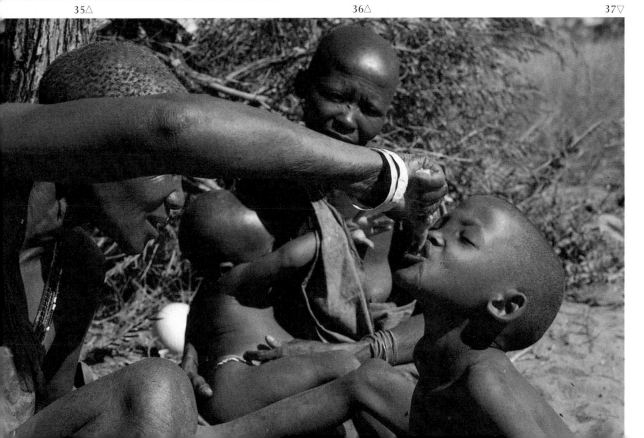

35. //Koe/tee scrapes a turnip-like *bi* tuber, reducing it to pulp by rapid downward movements with a sharp stick.
36. She squeezes some of the pulp in her hand, and the white, bitter liquid travels down her thumb and into her mouth.
37. Khalgugãe nudges //Koe/tee, and is rewarded with a drink of *bi* water.
38. All drinking water extracted, //Koe/tee uses the moist pulp to wash her face.

39. Ramonne throws the bones. He shakes them – two pieces of rib, two vertebrae and one odd-shaped bone – in his cupped hands, then throws them down. He and others discuss the message they seem to hold.

38△

39▽

40△

41▽

42▽

On the occasion of her first menstruation, a Bushman girl is isolated in a special hut where she must remain until it is over.

40, 41. Outside, women dance around the hut, exposing their buttocks as part of the sexual symbolism of the dance. For this ritual the !Xo Bushmen perform the gemsbok dance.

42. Older men cut branches to represent the horns of gemsbok whose mating behaviour they mimic.

43. (*above*) Her menstruation over, the girl is washed, scarified, painted, and adorned with beads.

44. This painting at Fulton's Rock in the Drakensberg is probably of a first menstruation ritual. The figure in the circle represents the girl in her hut, while women dance around her. The ritual seems little changed today.

45. (*opposite*) Malepae, one of the women of the Kua band, with her son. Like many Bushmen today, she shows a strong admixture of black blood.

46. An indefatigable dancer, /Gae≠tebe is egged on by the clapping and chanting of the women.

47. Dancing over, /Gae≠tebe walks off with his father's heavy skin bag.

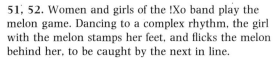

48. Bushman children are ingenious toy-makers — here Bodi/awa makes a model of our truck from a tuber and some wire.

49. Stick-throwing is a popular game with boys. At a run, they throw the stick onto the ground in front of them as hard as they can; the stick bounces and then flies on as far as possible.

50. One boy in the Kua band made a model of our 35 mm stills cameras, exact in every detail.

51, 52. Women and girls of the !Xo band play the melon game. Dancing to a complex rhythm, the girl with the melon stamps her feet, and flicks the melon behind her, to be caught by the next in line.

51△   52▽

53. The Kalahari does not look like a desert. Tall Bushman grass catches the late afternoon sun.

54. Malehane and Iogãe often play together despite their age difference.

55. (*opposite*) /Gae≠tebe as usual at the centre of a dance, joined by some friends and by his big sister, Aa//xama.

53△

54▽

(*opposite*) Kotuko/tee teaches Malehane how to set a bird snare.

56, 57. Kotuko/tee puts one end of a springy branch in a hole he has dug in the ground, and attaches a length of string to the top of it. He makes a noose at the other end of the string and ties a wooden toggle above the noose. Another stick is bent in an arc, and its ends buried deeply in the ground. The toggle is put under this arched stick, and this forms the spring.

58, 59. Malehane tests the snare with his finger, and his arm is caught in the noose.

60. (*above*) A silent but eloquent witness to the vanished Bushmen of the Drakensberg, this hunter steps out alone on the rocks at Giant's Castle to follow the game, armed only with his spear.

61. Korakoradue digs for poison grubs with which to doctor the arrows. Larvae of the chrysomelid beetle are a common source of poison; but they also use the venom of snakes, spiders and scorpions.

62, 63. (*below*) //Kaeki prepares arrows before the poison is applied. The poison grubs are pounded to liquid and a binding fluid is added; the poison is soaked into the arrowhead's sinew binding.

peacefully. Immediately they bent over at the waist and, the closer they approached downwind of the gemsbok the lower they crouched to hide their movements [66]. When they could, they took cover behind bushes, completely disappearing from sight as they did so. At about twenty metres (twenty-two yards), they let fire their arrows in quick succession – /Tade first, then ≠Kabe-/twa, and last //Kaeki [67]. One of the three arrows (≠Kabe/twa reckoned it was his) hit one of the three gemsbok who all immediately took flight. The Bushmen ran up to the place where the gemsbok had been and identified the spoor of the wounded animal. Each animal, even of the same species, has a spoor that is completely individual – to the Bushmen, though certainly not to us Europeans, uneducated as we were in the finer points of the ways of the wild.

Then began the long hard process of tracking. It can take several hours before the poison begins to affect a wounded animal, especially one as large as a gemsbok, and slows it down so that it becomes separated from its companions to face death alone. Sometimes the tracking of a large animal can take several days in all. On this occasion we were lucky, and what could have been a two-day marathon was accomplished within the day.

It was astonishing how swiftly the Bushmen moved as they followed the spoor in pursuit of the wounded gemsbok, picking out its individual footprints from the others, and passing swift messages to each other with their hands, without so much as hesitating in their stride [68]. To begin with they communicated not only with hand gestures, but in low, scarcely audible whispers; but as they came nearer to the animal they were tracking, so they moved in utter silence. A broken twig, stems of grass bent in a particular direction, the call of a bird, and the spoor itself, everything is an immediate message to the Bushmen about the direction in which the animal was heading, how long ago it was there, the speed with which it was moving, whether it was beginning to tire or was near to collapse. Every message is passed on to the other hunters in the complex and effective hand language evolved by their ancestors thousands of years ago.

At last the Bushmen had the wounded gemsbok in view. She had collapsed and could no longer get up, though she made several attempts to do so. She had retreated with her hind quarters in a thick bush so that the only way the hunters could approach was facing those lethal horns, which she still knew well how to use. At one moment, when /Tade approached almost within range, she made a last desperate attempt to get up and impale him on her horns [69]. But /Tade was on the alert, and skipped away almost as if he was engaged in a dance of death with the gemsbok. Laurens van der Post told us that he had twice in the Kalahari seen the skeletons of a lion and a gemsbok together, with the lion impaled on the horns of the gemsbok. And several of those nineteenth-century travellers reported the same extraordinary sight.

The final part of the hunt, the *coup de grâce*, is always accomplished with spears, each hunter driving his spear into the heart. On this occasion the Bushmen's aim was not so effective, and Aharob was asked to shoot the gemsbok with his gun to put her out of her agony. The skill with which the Bushmen had tracked their quarry had been astonishing and beautiful, but for us the end of the hunt was another matter. With the gemsbok dead, and with nothing more to fear from her horns, ≠Kabe/twa went up and pulled out the arrowhead, and with a pleased smile confirmed that it was indeed his. The gemsbok, and the honour of the hunt, belonged to him; the meat was to be shared with all.

As soon as the gemsbok was skinned, the three men cut out, cooked and ate their hunters' portions [70]. Then ≠Kabe/twa stayed with the carcass and cut it up into large joints, while /Tade and //Kaeki went to the camp to fetch help for carrying the meat back. When they returned, each of them took a load of meat which they carried either open on their shoulders, or wrapped in a kaross and suspended from their foreheads [71]. ≠Kabe/twa loaded so much meat into his kaross that he had the utmost difficulty in getting up from the ground. But once up, the weight hardly seemed to bother him at all. They walked in single file, //Kaeki leading the way carrying the great head of the gemsbok on his shoulder like a figurehead on a ship. And as they approached the camp a chant went up – a celebration of the prospect of meat.

As the evening wore on, and appetites had been satisfied, the celebration became increasingly vital. However weary the hunters might have felt, all that was forgotten in a timeless hunt ball of the desert. The women clapped and chanted, while the hunters danced around the fire with all their remaining energy, dancing their thanks to the gemsbok that had fed them. And even their stomachs, inflating out and being drawn back in again, performed their own individual dances in gratitude to the animal that had taken away their hunger. A Bushman hunter once told Laurens van der Post, 'Ever since there have been Bushmen in the world, we have never killed one of these great animals without saying thank you to it with a dance for allowing itself to be killed so that we could live.'

CHAPTER EIGHT

The Business of Leisure

It would be wrong to give the impression that the Bushmen are constantly and arduously at work. At any given moment in a Bushman camp you will see about half the members of the band sitting around a fire, doing nothing at all except smoking their pipes and pursuing their non-stop conversations. At times they tell each other stories: sometimes tales of remarkable personal experiences; sometimes the old stories handed down for countless generations and acquiring individual variations and new perceptions with the passage of time.

Old Dushe at Lone Tree [81] was an enthusiastic exponent of the former kind of storytelling, and filled in hours of otherwise empty time with tales of the astounding hunting exploits of his youth. His wife, //Kae//kae, listened with an expression of amused scepticism, while the rest of his audience punctuated his narrative with exclamations and comments in a suitably fervent tone of voice, accompanied by howls of laughter at appropriate moments.

In these long moments of leisure, when they talk and listen to stories, they often do nothing more strenuous than delousing each other's heads. But many of them occupy their hands making things that are either useful or decorative – men make or mend their bows and arrows, make string, carve bowls and spoons out of wood, or incise pictures or geometrical designs on ostrich eggshells; women spend hours making the tiny ostrich eggshell beads which they string together into long necklaces, or sew onto bags and items of clothing.

The Bushmen love to decorate themselves and their clothing. In the past ostrich eggshell beads were the only material available for their ornaments, but for many years now they have been acquiring tiny coloured glass beads by trade with their black neighbours, and they use these with great delight. More recently larger, plastic beads have come into their lives, and these too are strung around their necks, arms and ankles, along with all the rest. Women certainly decorate themselves more than men, but the men are far from averse to clusters of beads sewn or pinned onto the skins that they wear or onto their hunting bags.

Among the !Kung Bushmen at Tsumkwe in particular, we found an almost passionate dedication to beaded decoration which, combined with the brightly coloured western-style clothes that most of them now wear, produces a dazzling effect. Yet among the group at Lone Tree which, of all the Bushmen we met, was the most industrious at making ostrich eggshell beads, the everyday wearing of beads was minimal; and the western clothes they wore were much more

subdued in tone than those at Tsumkwe. But one thing that was immediately
evident in all the groups was that they regarded western-style clothes as things
of beauty in themselves. However tattered their clothes were – and many consisted more of holes than of material – they felt themselves tremendously well
turned out in western styles. I began to understand this apparent aesthetic lapse
when I compared it with my own attitude when I bought a beaded bag – for me
its holes and other irregularities simply added to its attractiveness.

Another thing that is regarded as a great enhancement of personal beauty is
scarification. We were told that the incisions made on !Kaekukhwe's shoulders
and chest at the end of her menarcheal ritual would add to her beauty. She, in
common with other little girls, had already had several experiences of scarification since the age of about seven, with incisions made on the arms and
shoulders in particular. Among some groups the buttocks are a much favoured
place for this decoration – unlike the breasts which are merely functional, buttocks are regarded as extremely sexual, and the greater the degree of fat, and the
greater the number of scarifications, the more attractive they are deemed to be.

There is also an element of adornment in the scarification of hunters – the
visible sign of their prowess and consequently a work of art. Besides this, men
take some pride in the shaving of their heads, which not only serves as a means
of disinfestation, but is also regarded as a reinforcement of their personal charms.
The design of the hair that is left on the head is carefully thought out, whether
it should be a thick tuft on the top of the head, or a few very narrow bands to
form an outline to the crown, or something quite new and original. When
Be/tee's thick crop of hair was shaved off by his wife, Khangdu, he opted for a
single narrow band from ear to ear, closely following the hairline at the top of
his forehead, with another line going back from the centre point to the crown of
his head. It was a very close shave, apart from the design, and was entirely
accomplished with a hand-held safety razor.

One of the Bushmen's most favoured leisure activities is smoking; and it
would seem, from the frequent references to it by even the earliest European
travellers, to be a long-established habit. In fact it almost certainly goes back
several centuries before the first Europeans set foot in southern Africa. The Bushmen have never grown tobacco themselves – or *dagga* (the local name for marijuana) which they have had for even longer than tobacco, and which is very
popular with them – but they have obtained both by trade with neighbouring
Africans. They generally smoke it in short hollow bones (a piece of a small antelope's shin bone is ideal), but we also saw a few old cartridge cases with the ends
taken off, and even the occasional mass-manufactured pipe [81].

There was one form of smoking that we had heard about, but which we did
not see in operation for some time. But on the last day of our stay with the Kua
group, after their appetites for meat had been satisfied by the roasted steenbok,
the men made a kind of pipe in the ground. The artist, Thomas Baines, had seen
the same thing about one hundred and twenty years before, and it has evidently
not gone out of fashion. Baines described very much what we also saw; they

'make two holes in the ground and connect them by a rather scientific mode of tunnelling. Water is then poured in, and above its surface, in one hole, is placed a little burning tobacco; the man kneels down, applies his mouth to the other, and enjoys the luxury of an unportable hubble-bubble.'

As we watched and filmed, each of the men in turn took a mouthful of water from an ostrich eggshell, knelt down and sucked on the end of the tube that had been inserted into one of the holes in the ground. The inhaled smoke bubbled through the water in his mouth, and then the man whose turn it was at the time, sat up on his heels and, with a contented smile, slowly let the smoke escape from his lips.

As far as the more traditional pipes were concerned, women seemed to smoke just as much as men, and they all took snuff, but the 'unportable hubble-bubble' seemed to be mainly a male preserve. Only one of the women joined in the session. They used a mixture of standard tobacco and *dagga*, and were evidently well satisfied with the result. Indeed Kangao was so satisfied that he specifically asked our interpreter to translate for us his apologia for *dagga*. 'It's nice', he said, 'and it makes me forget my hunger. It also makes me want a woman. It brightens my vision and makes me see more sharply. I never get a hangover from smoking *dagga*; neither do we have any quarrels after we have smoked. Dancing and *dagga* are equal in making us feel happy; and they are equally calming when we are upset. We don't grow it ourselves. We buy it from people who come to us [Kgalagadi], and we pay for it with animal skins. We have smoked it for a long time − it was introduced before my time.'

Just as with their work, the leisure occupations of the Bushmen are almost invariably divided by sex. Men traditionally do certain things, women others. Many of these occupations are rather difficult to distinguish from work, and they should probably be classified as such since they contribute to activities that are clearly work; the only difference is that they are done sitting down around a fire, surrounded by the full flow of chatter or stories.

Making string is one such activity, done pre-eminently by Ramonne, but also by one or two of the other men of the Kua group. While walking through the veld they would pick some of the tall spiky leaves of the wild sansevieria plant and bring them back to camp. Then, sitting down with a smooth piece of wood in front of him, and a strong stick with a sharpened edge, Ramonne scraped the green flesh from both sides of the leaves, leaving a small handful of white fibres which he set aside carefully, the top ends together [76]. Once he had enough of these he picked up a cluster of fibres, divided them into two equal bunches, still held together at the top, and then rolled each one separately on his thigh until it was tightly corded [77]. Next he rolled both cords together, making a two-ply string. As each bunch of fibres began to run out he would introduce new lengths into the loose ends, and again roll the join against his thigh until it was corded with no visible sign of a join at all.

When the right length of string had been made, Ramonne made a small noose at the end of it, and fastened it around a big toe. Then, with a stone, he rubbed off all the protruding fibres, leaving the string smooth enough for the noose to operate with no fear of snagging [78]. Having tested the noose on his arm for smoothness, it was set aside, ready to use the next time they set a snare. The string is incredibly strong, even the thinnest variety – it certainly needs to be to survive the strongest resistance of an antelope struggling to free itself. Several visitors to the Kalahari, either sceptical of the strength of the string, or simply wanting to see its strength for themselves, have persuaded the Bushmen to have a tug of war with it. No one, as far as I know, has reported that it broke.

Another exclusively male occupation is the carving of wood. Bowls and spoons are the most common artefacts, with geometric designs burned into them. These are both objects that the Bushmen use in their daily lives, though increasingly they are acquiring by trade or purchase enamel, plastic and light metal goods instead of using wood. The wooden bowls and spoons are now made mainly for trading purposes, or to sell to passing tourists.

The men also make spear blades and arrowheads as they sit around a fire in their camp – the former from iron rods, the latter from fencing wire, both of which are obtained by trade from neighbouring black Africans. They also make knife blades, which they set in wooden handles and use for a multitude of purposes such as skinning animals.

Another occupation of the men, which produces something that is both useful to the Bushmen themselves, but is even more valuable as an exchange medium, is the tanning of animal skins. Having skinned an antelope, the Bushmen peg out the skin, hair side downwards, using a large number of short thin sticks of *Grewia flava*. These are placed at intervals of about 12 cms (5 inches), and about 1 cm ($\frac{1}{2}$ inch) from the edge of the skin, and are pushed firmly into the earth so that the skin is smooth and taut [83]. As soon as it has dried – only about a day in hot sun and dry weather – the pegs are taken out and the skin is scraped free of any fat or other subcutaneous tissue, using a very sharp blade. In the past, sharp-edged stones were used, and these can often be found in old Bushman shelters in the Drakensberg and elsewhere. If the skin is to be made into clothes, the hair is also scraped off from the other side.

Once the scraping is completed, the curing begins. They rub in the juice of a *Crinum* bulb until the skin is quite wet, and then pound and knead and rub it together. Once this juice has dried off, the skin is again kneaded and, with the small antelopes, is then soft enough to be used. With the large antelope hides, *Crinum* juice has to be applied up to three or four times before the desired flexibility and softness is achieved.

The skins are used to make traditional clothes of all kinds, loincloths for men, front and back aprons for women, and karosses for both, using thread made of sinew, and home-made needles of bone or metal. They also make carrying bags and hunting bags, and frequently decorate them with beads, especially the smaller carrying bags or pouches. Otherwise, skins are one of the Bushmen's most important mediums of exchange; with them they acquire tobacco, *dagga*, iron rods, fencing wire, glass and plastic beads. Within the past few years, with their increasing contact with the outside world, the range of goods acquired in exchange for skins and other traditional Bushman artefacts has increased enormously, and now includes cooking and eating utensils of various kinds, western-style clothes, safety pins (often used as earrings), blankets, matches, lighters and even, occasionally, transistor radios.

Not for trade purposes at all, but strictly for their own use, is the making of dance-rattles — the essential equipment of every man when he takes part in the frequent dances of the Bushmen. So important are these dances, as we shall see, and so vital a role do the rattles play in underlining the rhythm of the music, that the making of them is an occupation of almost religious significance. However, this does not imply an attitude of heavy solemnity which is far from the Bushman's nature.

The rattles are made from the cocoons of a moth or butterfly (the Bushmen use the same word for both) which lives on *Acacia mellifera* trees. The cocoons are found and gathered from the trees during the winter months (June to August), and are slit down one side to remove the larvae. Broken ostrich egg-shells are pounded down into very small pieces, and several of these are put inside the cocoon. Then the cocoons are secured at each end by a leather thong, and attached to each other side by side until they form an extended string, about 150 cms (5 feet) long [82]. Each man has two strings of rattles, one for each leg, and he winds them around his ankles and ties them firmly with the loose ends of the thongs. And then he dances, stamping his feet on the ground in time with the clapping and chanting of the women.

In the one trading store at Hukuntsi we found a large number of ostrich egg-shells for sale, each one engraved with representations of animals, or with geometric designs — another spare-time occupation of Bushman men. Apart from those ancient Bushmen of the Tsodilo Hills, there were no painters among the Bushmen of the Kalahari. No one could claim that the engraving of ostrich egg-shell water-containers is a high form of art, but it is a charming one, and it is the only form of visual art practised by the Bushmen in the Kalahari Desert.

Ramonne, as we had come to expect, was the main exponent of the art among the Kua group. He was certainly the best, though Koto used to practise most assiduously [75], and was doubtless young enough to improve. First Ramonne incised his design onto the surface of the shell, using a sharp knife. Since the eggshell is creamy white all through, it was almost impossible to see what was being done; but he worked on steadily, and when the design was complete, though still quite invisible, he took a piece of charcoal from the edge of the fire and rubbed it into the incisions. Gradually the picture grew, black on white, before our eyes — a design of ostriches, small antelope, and various decorative shapes. Then he blew off the dust, rubbed it over with his hands, and the job was finished.

Tough as these ostrich eggshells are, they are far from indestructible; but when they do break, they are never wasted. The women gather up the sherds and use them for making beads. At Lone Tree the women seemed to be making beads all the time, sitting in sociable groups and working not in the manner of a production line, but each one executing every stage of the process herself and making her own strings of beads. The various tools were passed from one to the other as they were needed.

First they would break up the eggshell sherds into suitably sized pieces — little squares or triangles about 1 cm ($\frac{1}{2}$ inch) across. Then they drilled a hole in the centre of each piece, using a home-made awl — a needle-sharp piece of metal fitted into a long wooden handle — which they rolled between their palms. This caused it to rotate at high speed, and in a few seconds it had drilled a hole through the shell. When they had a fair-sized heap of drilled pieces, they strung them onto a fine sinew thread, made in much the same way as string. Then, taking a small curved antelope horn and resting the beads on a stone base, they chipped away delicately around the edges of each piece of shell until it was circular in shape and about $\frac{1}{2}$ cm ($\frac{1}{4}$ inch) in diameter. The final process was to lay a length of trimmed beads along a grooved piece of wood and rub a notched soft stone up and down to smooth off any rough edges.

By joining pieces of sinew thread together, they make strings of enormous length which hang in swags of six or seven rows either just around their necks, or else passing under their arms as well. And apart from making necklaces, they use the beads to make headbands and to decorate their carrying bags with simple, and often very lovely designs.

Most of these objects are now used not by the !Xõ Bushmen themselves, but for trade. The making of beads is a laborious process, each bead being individually shaped so that a whole string takes a long time to produce. Sadly, when it comes to trading, the odds have always been against the Bushmen; they are easily intimidated by the larger, more powerful Africans who claimed the land as their own and who dictated what the Bushmen might have in exchange for their beads and their cured hides. More recently an organization called Botswanacraft has been set up, a semi-government concern which sends people out into the various administrative districts of the Kalahari to buy beadwork and other artefacts from the Bushmen. The price (which is paid in cash, not kind) is determined by the quality of each individual article. The goods are then either sold in the Botswanacraft shop in the capital, Gabarone, or exported. This does protect the Bushmen from some degree of the exploitation they were subject to before — but not all of it.

While Dyirohã, !Kabakakũ and !Humka sat and made beads during one afternoon, they were joined by Kwa!kae and her young son. The child alternated between tottering around from one woman to the next, and returning to his mother, snuggling into her lap and reaching for her breast, while Kwa!kae joined in the ceaseless chatter and occupied her hands with playing a hunting bow. With a stick she tapped the string at regular intervals, creating a low, hollow note and a hypnotic rhythm as a background to their work and conversation. At one moment, thanks partly to some extra-energetic activity of her son, the bowstring became unfastened at one end, and Kwa!kae let out a yelp of vexation and immediately set to work to repair the damage [79]. Once that was completed, she returned to her rhythmic, monotonous music.

The hunting bow is the original Bushman musical instrument, and is doubtless the one from which their other stringed instruments derived. Kwa!kae was not a particularly gifted player, or perhaps she was just not giving it her full attention. Certainly to have played it properly would have prevented her from talking, for one end of the bow is normally held between the lips with the mouth acting as a resonator. By changing the opening of the mouth, so the notes are altered; and the repetition of a short period of different notes is the basis of all Bushman music.

We frequently saw !Humka playing a more complex, four-stringed instrument, the //gwashi. Like most of the Bushmen's instruments, apart from the hunting bow, the //gwashi came to them from one of the black African peoples – in this case probably the Ovambo of northern Namibia – but it has become very much the possession of the Bushmen themselves, and the vehicle of their own individual and intricate form of music. The old //gwashi were made of a block of wood of the mangetti nut tree (*Ricinodendron rautanenii*), hollowed out in the centre and with four (or sometimes five) curved sticks sunk into one end, to which the sinew strings were attached. Nowadays, in place of the wooden resonator, it is much more common to see an empty food can, of the kind used in foreign aid programmes, and still usually with the donor's name visibly printed on the outside.

!Humka used to wander round with her four-stringed //gwashi in her hands, plucking the strings with her thumbs and index fingers. Occasionally she would sing as she played, but more often than not she would get caught up in some conversation and would stop singing while continuing to pluck out the tune on her //gwashi as she talked.

We did not come across any particularly gifted musicians on our filming trips, perhaps because we were too concerned to film specific activities. But with all three Bushman groups that we were with for varying lengths of time, there was an almost constant background of instrumental music of some kind. At Lone Tree it was the hunting bow and the //gwashi; with the Kua Bushmen we saw neither of these instruments. Instead the only instrument they seemed to play (apart from a crude guitar made from a tin can) was the thumb piano – another borrowing from the black African repertoire of instruments [82].

The men used to make these thumb pianos when there were no other more pressing tasks. On a small wooden base they attached a number of metal keys, made from short lengths of fencing-wire beaten flat, and held in place by two bands of metal, one running under the keys and one over to give them tension and resonance. The sound is produced by plucking the ends of the metal keys, each of which produces a different note. Only the men seemed to play them, and whenever a group of people gathered round a fire, you could be sure that the haunting, tinkling music of at least one thumb piano would accompany their talk and their work.

Sometimes the playing of musical instruments is accompanied by songs, for the Bushmen have always set to music their thoughts and feelings about every aspect of their lives. They have songs about plants, birds, animals and insects, songs about items of clothing and food, about marriage and love, about hunting and gathering. Some groups even have a song about the dance-rattles and the deliciousness of the larvae they find inside the cocoons. In the European tradition a song generally implies the existence of words; but not so with the Bushmen. Many of their songs have no words at all, yet they will tell you that they are about specific subjects – a bird, a feeling of loneliness, success or failure in hunting. Instead of words they use vowel or humming sounds which they chant to the melody they are playing on the instrument – short, intricate musical phrases endlessly repeated – or simply to the accompaniment of their clapping. But many of the songs do have words – brief, simple expressions repeated over and over again to the hypnotic, complex rhythm of the music.

Some are healing songs, named after 'strong' things like the eland, giraffe, honey, rain and mamba. Some are old, and others quite new, for the Bushmen are natural musicians and innovate all the time. But two of these healing songs, those of the eland and the rain, are very old indeed, the words coming from an unremembered past, the music from a very ancient scale, now not in use except for these two songs alone. All healing songs are believed to possess n/um, the supernatural power that can be transformed for the good of the community in healing sickness or social tension. The singing and clapping of the women, and the dancing of the men, are essential ingredients for the release of n/um in the central religious ritual of all Bushmen – the healing dance.

CHAPTER NINE

Dance, Trance and Medicine Men

Dances seemed to begin quite casually among the Kua Bushmen. On one occasion, late in the afternoon, when the sun was low and red in the west, it all began with /Gae≠tebe who was dancing by himself, as he often did, quite oblivious of anyone else. After a while his big sister, Aa//xama, came along and laughed her deep throaty laugh at the sight of the diminutive lone dancer. /Gae≠tebe looked up and joined in the laughter, entirely correct in his apparent assumption that he was not being laughed *at* but *with*. Aa//xama joined in his dancing, and gradually more children of varying sizes did the same [55].

One small boy, //Guikwa, found the whole thing too much to cope with on his own two feet, so he stood and howled with misery until his mother came to rescue him. /Ganakadi swung him up onto her shoulders and joined in the dance with her son riding piggy-back. From then on contentment reigned, not to say something of a carnival atmosphere which the Bushmen seem to have a genius for evoking. One of the older girls, in joking imitation of /Ganakadi carrying //Guikwa, carried a doll in a kaross on her back, a source of great amusement to all. Not to be outdone, /Ganakadi — having persuaded //Guikwa that he did not, after all, need to be carried — found another doll and danced about with it held to her breast. The general hilarity that this provoked seemed to convince /Gae≠tebe that this was not the place for serious dancers like himself, so he stalked off to join the men, and the dance gradually fizzled out.

Of the seven or eight dances that we saw in the Kalahari, there was not one that did not have this element of joyous ribaldry. Even in the healing dance, when several men went into trance, bawdy insults and the resulting laughter were woven like vivid threads through the fabric of the ritual. They were part of it, not separate from it. The men danced, and the women clapped and chanted, with an almost tangible sense of enjoyment; and the onlookers, too, were involved in the whole experience, and added to it with their jokes and comments.

Apart from /Gae≠tebe's dance, the Kua Bushmen danced on two occasions while we were there. Some time after sunset, when the sky still held a soft orange glow, one or two of the women began to sing casually; a few more came over to their fire and joined in; then the clapping began. Gradually the rhythm became more insistent and the men could no longer resist the call of the music. One by one they put their dance-rattles around their ankles, and with a shout leaped into the firelight and began to dance — short rhythmic steps, sometimes with both feet together, sometimes with one foot performing a complicated counter-point to the main theme of the other. Every ounce of energy went into the dance, their bodies leaning forward from the hips, their arms held out sideways and waving to the rhythm of the music. The combination of repeated phrases of chant, complex rhythmic clapping, the stamping of the dancers' feet, and the eerie swish, swish of the dance-rattles, built up into a powerful cosmos of hypnotic sound.

Suddenly old Korakoradue leaped into the circle of dancers, complete with ancient, battered straw hat which he raised and replaced on his head to roars of approval from everyone. By now there were deep grooves in the sand, forming a circle around the fire where the men were dancing, following each other round and round in the flickering light of the fire. They danced first the blue wildebeest dance, followed by the ostrich and then the ostrich wings dances. These, es-pecially the ostrich dance, were their favourites. In between the dances they stopped and smoked and chatted. Then, once again, the women would begin to sing in a desultory manner, gradually picking up intensity, and the men would be impelled back into the dance.

At another fire nearby, some of the children were having their own dance. Not so /Gae≠tebe. He, as usual, was with the men, bouncing up and down and stamping his feet, his arms waving about in imitation of his father, his face split from ear to ear with a grin of pure ecstasy. This was where the real action was, and nothing would induce him to leave it and join the children.

On no occasion when they danced, did any of the Kua Bushmen go into trance. The dance remained on a level of simple enjoyment; yet there was, in the broadest sense, an element of healing in it for, as Kangao had explained when extolling the virtues of *dagga*, '*dagga* and dancing are equal in making us feel happy; and they are equally calming when we are upset'. There was certainly a great sense of sharing, of opening themselves to each other in a way that could only be beneficial. They did have a medicine man in their group, they said, but he was away at the time. And old Korakoradue had told me that although he and the others were not able to see the Great God, Bise, this medicine man did, on occasion, see him. It was through medicine men, he said, that Bise spoke to them and cared for them. 'Such a one is Mudumo.'

But they did, like all Bushmen, practise other methods of healing. On one occasion Be/tee told us that he was feeling rotten. For several days now, he said, his head had felt as though the blood was boiling inside it, and his wife was therefore going to make incisions on his face to let some of the bad blood out. Khangdu took an old safety razor and quickly made two incisions on either side near the ears, and a few on his forehead as well, and followed this up with a complete head-shave, using the same razor. Then Be/tee washed his face, by now dripping with blood, and announced that he felt much better [84]. But the most powerful medicine is that which comes in the great healing dance.

There is an awful fascination in reading the accounts of some of those nineteenth-century travellers, and being repeatedly astonished at the gulf between their attitudes and those of our own twentieth century which we are pleased to think are more enlightened. John Chapman, just over one hundred years ago, came upon a group of Bushmen performing a healing ritual in broad daylight. Clearly he had not the remotest idea what it was all about, and he tried hard to remain aloofly unimpressed by such strange goings-on; but occasionally something akin to involvement begins to peep through before being smothered again by worldly-wise superiority:

> About sixty women, decorated with all the beads and trinkets at their command, and formed into a semicircle, were clapping their hands and singing to the time and tune of a quick waltz; while about thirty young men, adorned with plumes of black ostrich and eagle feathers on their heads, a few ancient beads on their bodies, a fan (the tail of a gnu) in their hands, and the fruit of the moana tied to the calves of their legs, bore them company. The shells of the moana fruit, being perforated with holes, and the pulp sifted out, made a rattling noise as the men kept time to the monotonous music performed by the women, in front of whom the men were tramping and marching to and fro, grunting and singing, and describing all sorts of gymnastic evolutions and contortions, with occasionally a graceful movement, the result of accident rather than design. Now and then a wild peal burst from the chief dancers, and the females, bowing low in acknowledgement of the compliment, responded with thrilling yells. The principal dancer, who seemed to command general admiration, commenced like a reasonable being, but ended like a man in a frenzy, gesticulating with hands and feet while he lay on the ground with his face to the sun. At these contortions, made by severe muscular exertion, he laboured for a long time. . . . These savage gestures and capers over, the company turned their attention to some dishes of bulbs, and the insect deposits of the mopani trees, which they greedily devoured.

Chapman's reference to the dancers wearing feathers on their heads is particularly interesting because in several Bushman paintings, dancers can be seen with caps on their heads, to which feathers are attached. This headgear seems to be associated only with dancers (though not with all of them), and some are in a state of trance. Whether the feathers were purely decorative, or had some symbolic significance in the ritual, is unknown. Today Bushmen do not wear feathers on their heads for the healing ritual.

From the number of people involved, it would seem that Chapman's group may have consisted of more than one band, for when Bushman bands are encamped within easy reach of each other, they frequently come together for a healing dance. Neighbouring bands usually have relatives among their numbers, so that each band is a natural extension of the other; and there may be a particularly highly regarded medicine man in one band who can handle more difficult cases and his power needs to be shared with other bands.

Nowadays Bushman medicine men in the Kalahari are involved only in healing, though this embraces not only physical ills, but spiritual and social ones as well. To them they are all seen as products of the same evil. But in the past, among the extinct /Xam Bushmen of the south, there was a wider range of categories of medicine men. We have already seen, from a brief look at some paintings and stories, that there used to be medicine men specifically associated with rain who, in a state of trance, would tie a cord around the (conceptual) rain-bull's horns and lead it over the area where rain was desired. There were also medicine men of game who were believed to be able, while in trance, to lead game to the band's area so that they would have greater success in hunting. The southern Bushmen, like their present-day Kalahari counterparts, also had medicine men of healing; and the descriptions of their rituals, and what they believed themselves to be involved in, are very similar to the healing rituals still performed today in the Kalahari Desert.

J. M. Orpen was given a description of a healing dance by his guide, Qing, who was attempting to explain to him the symbolism of trance in some Bushman paintings. Qing told Orpen, 'It is a circular dance of men and women, following each other, and it is danced all night. Some fall down; some become as if mad and sick; blood runs from the noses of others whose charms are weak, and they eat charm medicine in which there is burnt snake powder. When a man is sick, this dance is danced around him, and the dancers put both hands under their armpits, and press their hands on him, and when he coughs the initiated put out their hands and receive what has injured him — secret things.'

At the same time as Orpen collected and published his material, Wilhelm Bleek and his sister-in-law Lucy Lloyd were collecting stories, legends and personal histories from Bushman convicts in the Cape. Among these various accounts there is a considerable amount of information about medicine men — or 'sorcerors', as they rather misleadingly translated the Bushman word. Since they had never seen a healing ritual themselves, and since much of this unknown experience had to be described by the Bushmen in metaphorical language which was impossible to translate with precision, Bleek and Lloyd must have been mystified and tantalized by much of what they were told. The fascinating thing for us, as we watched a Bushman group perform this ritual in the Kalahari Desert, was how exact were the descriptions they recorded to what is still performed today, one thousand miles to the north of where the /Xam Bushmen lived.

/Han≠kasso told Bleek and Lloyd that a medicine man, when healing a sick person, would sniff out the thing that was causing the sickness, and then sneeze it out through his nostrils, causing his nose to bleed; hence nose-bleeds in the paintings being such a clear indication of trance.

Various creatures were seen as the immediate cause of the sickness. He mentioned a lion, an owl and butterflies; and the sound that the medicine man made as it was sneezed out was said to be the cry of the creature concerned. Once this had been done, then the medicine man could take out the 'harm's things. . . . They call them bits of wood, for the things are like sticks. . . . These he sneezes out nicely. When the person recovers in consequence, he goes quietly to hunt, if the springbok are there.'

We were told by the Bushmen we met that the noises that the medicine men made were caused, not by animals, but by the pain they felt as the supernatural energy, or *n/um*, began to invade their whole bodies as they went into trance. But the 'harm's things' are seen in very much the same way — sometimes as little sticks, sometimes as pieces of metal, or a whole Pandora's box of foreign bodies which have to be extracted from the sick person.

While healing is the supreme purpose of trance, it is not the only thing a medicine man finds himself capable of while in a state of trance, particularly in the deep trance which they call 'death'. He can handle fire and burning coals and not be burned; he can see right through every part of a person's body to know where the damage or illness lies; he can see great distances and know what is happening even in the dark; he can go on out-of-body travel, either to another Bushman camp to find out how friends and relatives are, or to the Great God's home to argue and plead for the life of a sick person.

An old and very powerful healer called K"xau gave Megan Biesele an extraordinarily graphic account of an out-of-body visit he made to the Great God's home. He described his journey there, through a river, and through the earth itself, and finally climbing 'the thread of the sky' to the place where God himself was, and where the spirits were dancing:

> My friend, when you visit God, you sit this way [in an attitude of respect, with arms folded across the knees]. People sit this way when they go to God, the great, great God, the master. . . . They dance the giraffe dance. What you do there, where God is, is to dance like this. . . . And the women sing like this [K"xau sings]. They sing and they sing. . . . When God sits on his chair he watches all around. And when people come from somewhere else and see him, they tremble with fear. . . . When you go there, friend, you make yourself small like this. Friend, when you go there, you don't go standing up straight. You make yourself small so that you are a mamba. That's how you go to him. Because if you do that, he'll let you live. If you go to him like a regular person, you'll die. . . . You won't come back. When you've gone back there, you have died and you aren't going to come back. But if you're a snake, friend, you'll stay alive. . . .
>
> Then you return to where everyone is, and you hide your face. You hide your face so you won't see anything. You come and come and come and finally you enter your body again. All the people, the *zhu/twãsi* [!Kung] who have stayed behind waiting for you — they fear you. Friend, they are afraid of you. You enter, enter, enter the earth, and then you return to enter . . . the skin of your body. . . . Friend this is what it does, this medicine [*n/um*] that I do, this *n/um* here that I dance.

The healing ritual is regarded by the Bushmen as of paramount importance in their lives, the central religious ritual of a people for whom life holds no divisions between the religious and the secular, the sacred and the profane. Everything is part of the Great God's ordering of all things, and he has given to his people the ability to appropriate for themselves something of his own divine energy, through the dance and trance. But the appropriation of this *n/um* is no absolute guarantee of success; healing involves entering into a battle with the Lesser God and with the spirits of the dead, or even with the Great God himself, who are trying to take away an individual, or to cause dissension in the band.

Sometimes the battle is lost and the sick person dies and goes to join the spirits; perhaps, they say, that person's time had come and no power could then bring him back. But in its wider healing purpose — dealing with social tensions and bitterness within the band — the trance dance is almost always successful.

It was a group of !Xõ Bushmen near Lone Tree Pan whose healing ritual we were able to film. The group itself was somewhat disparate, being composed of people from various different local bands whose men had taken jobs with a company making another new road through the Kalahari. Most of them came from the band near Lone Tree with whom we had already done some filming; but one, a man called !Kase, was a /Gwi Bushman from the central desert. He seemed to fit in happily with the !Xõ in what was for all of them a new context — doing a daily (if temporary) job in return for money. They had no regular pattern in their healing rituals, they told us; they usually did it only when someone was actually sick, or if they were particularly happy — for example, they had danced a few days before for the birth of a child.

On this occasion one of the men in their group, !Koga, was sick. He did not have any definable symptoms, but had had a fever for several days and was feeling very ill and weak. There was also a young boy of about eight or nine who they said needed healing, though they did not consider that his sickness was so deep; to us he was a classic case of malnutrition, with distended belly, stick-like arms and legs, and a gaunt face that seemed all eyes. For these two, but especially for !Koga, they had decided to have a healing dance that night, and we were invited to come and film.

We drove at evening for miles along just the kind of road these Bushmen were making by day — two ruts of sand piercing the surrounding bush. Then we turned off and lurched even more uncomfortably along a less defined track, and ended up crashing through virgin bush. We arrived just after sunset when the sky still held the last remnants of the day, but it was dark enough for the fire to create its own circle of warm light around it.

The fire, like every other element in the ritual, is important, for it contains its own *n/um* which contributes to the whole accumulation of divine energy among the dancers. Its light and warmth embrace every person participating in the ritual — the dancers, the women who chant and clap, the onlookers who shout encouragement or insults or both. The surrounding darkness shuts off the rest of the world so that the *n/um* can grow and work in the charmed circle of the firelight. For the fire, with its own *n/um*, plays a vital role in heating up and expanding the *n/um* inside the healers. Sometimes, while in trance, a healer may feel such an affinity with, and compulsion towards, the fire that he will pick up burning coals, or throw his body or his head into the fire, and yet remain unburned. They say that the *n/um* inside them is itself so hot that it is not surprising that the fire does not burn them. To those of us with western scepticisms it was astonishing.

When we arrived the Bushmen had already gathered a large pile of wood to keep the fire going and another pile to feed the subsidiary fire around which anyone who wished to sit out could do so and still keep warm. Bushmen are always economical with their fires, putting on only enough wood to maintain a low but steady fire; anything bigger would be wasteful, and in any case would be too hot as the dance gained in intensity.

It was the women who tended the fire throughout the dance, for they sat in a circle around it as they sang and clapped, keeping the rhythm and vitality of the music to the required level. The songs that the women sang – almost always songs without words – themselves contain n/um, endowed by the Great God and given to man who in the dance can release it and use it for healing. The clapping of the women and the rattling of the ankle rattles enhance the power of the n/um and help to heat it up to the point at which the healer goes into trance. Various medicine songs have enjoyed a particular popularity for the purposes of the healing ritual. Among some !Kung groups the gemsbok song was the one most commonly used, but in recent years it has been superseded by the giraffe song, and its accompanying dance.

But the !Xõ group that we were with still favoured the gemsbok song which the women sang, while the men danced its visual counterpart, the gemsbok dance [87]. To begin with, however, the women sang a variety of different medicine songs, starting off in an almost haphazard manner and then becoming more concentrated as the evening wore on, and as more men joined the dance. Some danced for a short time only, and then went and stood and watched the others, or sat by the second fire nearby. In the end, four men remained, healers all, who between them, and in varying stages of trance, were going to do battle with the spirits who had caused !Koga's sickness.

Their dancing became ever more intense as it too acquired n/um from the singing of the medicine songs. As each dancer moved to the insistent rhythm of the music, so the n/um which lives in his stomach became hotter, rose up his spine and finally boiled, at which point he was in trance. The sweat which poured off their bodies was evidence of the increasing heat of the n/um inside them. The heat and pain which the boiling create are intense and require considerable courage to pass through, and to cope with throughout trance. As an expression of this pain, the healers let out chilling yelps and shrieks at various stages of the ritual. 'Qai! qai!', they shrieked which means, 'pain! pain!'.

From time to time, either an individual or any number of the four healers together, would come and lean over !Koga, pressing him and rubbing him with their hands. They would wipe sweat from their own bodies, especially from under their arms (as Qing had described to Orpen), and would rub it onto !Koga's body, for the sweat, emanating directly from the boiling n/um inside them, is itself a bearer of n/um. Occasionally a healer would lie down beside !Koga so that there should be as much contact as possible between his skin and that of the sick man, so that the n/um could flow directly from one body into the other [85].

Sometimes, when all four healers were bending over !Koga together, they seemed to rise up from him in a human pyramid, held together by their hands on each other's bodies. As they laid their hands on him either directly, or indirectly through the body of another healer, so the deity would explain to them the secrets of the illness. Then they pulled from !Koga's body the evil things that had caused his illness [86].

Every so often one or other of the healers would run off, away from the circle of the fire, and would stand there with his hands on his head, gazing into space as he chanted and let out the occasional wailing shriek. Sometimes on these occasions they hurled abuse at God and the spirits of the dead, and told them to go away and leave the sick person alone, and not to be so greedy as to want him for themselves. It is a crucial point in the battle. We were told that these were times when the *n/um* inside the healer had become particularly fierce, and he would become unsteady and his actions jerky; to control it he had to go away by himself until it had cooled sufficiently for him to return to the dance, and could lay hands steadily on those he was healing.

Although !Koga received the lion's share of the healing activity, the healers in fact laid hands on everyone there, paying particular attention to the mal-nourished boy. The expenditure of energy was enormous; and the sense of involvement and compassion of the whole little community was powerful and we felt that it embraced even those of us who were filming. We were all in the experience together, encapsulated by the firelight against the surrounding night.

Suddenly !Kase, the /Gwi Bushman from the central Kalahari, crashed down on the ground, groaning and wailing, his limbs jerking uncontrollably. All the attention of the other healers – themselves in a lighter state of trance – now turned to him, for he had gone into the deepest trance, or 'death'. It is a danger-ous state which needs all the caring and protection that the others can give him; otherwise his soul might leave his body completely and death, instead of being temporary, might become permanent.

One of the symptoms of !Kase's state was that he felt cold; so they pulled him near to the fire and poured warm sand onto his limbs. They rubbed his body all over to relax his muscles which the *n/um* had tautened; and they brought a tiny tortoise shell, filled with powdered aromatic herbs, medicine whose smell helped to cool down the heated *n/um*. Apart from the other healers who came to care for !Kase, a woman also came from among the singers and massaged his body with strong rhythmic movements of her hands, while one of the healers held him from behind in a sitting position. They told us that the work of this woman was to deflect all possible visitations of the spirits at this dangerous moment, and to take out of the healer's body all the evil things that he had taken out of !Koga – the 'harm's things' that had caused his sickness. These things she takes into herself, to be lost again at her next menstruation. Therefore only a woman who is near menstruation may do this work, otherwise the evil things would stay with her, and they would also stay with the sick man.

They told us that on that night they had had to struggle particularly hard to revive !Kase, for he had gone into such a deep trance that they had become very anxious for him. They didn't know why this had happened but, having dis-cussed the matter at some length among themselves, they thought that it might have been because, as a /Gwi, the medicine songs that he was used to at home were different. Therefore the songs that had been sung that night, and the *n/um* that had emanated from them, had affected him differently from the songs of his own people. They were not entirely satisfied with this conclusion, but felt it might have something of the truth. !Kase had taken part in this healing dance because he was a very powerful dancer, and because he was a particular friend of !Koga. He felt a deep sympathy for him and gave of his best, for his will to heal was even greater than that of the other healers.

A healing dance will often last right through the night and into the new day, for dawn is believed to be a time when the *n/um* is especially potent. But the group we were with stopped dancing not long after midnight. Whether this was because of the exigencies of their road-making work we did not find out, but it seems a likely explanation. Among those Bushmen who still live, at least in part, by hunting and gathering, the day after a night-long healing dance can usually be spent in maximum idleness. With our group, all the men except the sick !Koga had to be at work the next day.

Highly regarded as medicine men are, especially those known to be particularly powerful, it is only in the context of the dance and trance that they are so regarded. To be a medicine man or woman does not absolve anyone from the normal day to day activities of the band — that person hunts or gathers plant food with the rest. But medicine men do have a responsibility to share the *n/um* that they have with the rest of their community, just as everything else in Bushman life is shared. This sharing is expressed not just in healing, but also in teaching younger people who have not yet achieved trance, how to heat up and control their *n/um*, and how to overcome their fear of the pain that it brings. In return the medicine man usually receives some kind of gift as 'payment' for the healing he has accomplished.

Today, as more Bushmen come into contact with a cash economy, the concept of payment has in many cases gone further than the giving of a gift in return for a successful cure. Some medicine men are now turning professional, expecting cash payment for services rendered, and refusing the service if the payment is not agreed in advance. It is one of the deepest erosions of the traditional Bushman ethos, perhaps the most telling barometer of the change that is taking place in every area of their life and thought.

CHAPTER TEN

The Beginning of the End

'We who were made first, have come to be last. And those who were created last, have come to be first. Even though they arrived later than we did, Europeans and Bantus have come to be ahead of us.'

This is the beginning of a story told by !Kun/obe, a !Kung Bushman woman, to Megan Biesele. It tells how the people of the world came to be divided into the two groups – the more powerful cattle-owners and farmers, and the poor hunter-gatherers. It was all because of an old Bushman called Karã/tuma who lived long, long ago. He was the firstborn of his parents, who later gave birth to a black man, and finally to a white man. He had the first chance at everything, but invariably he did the wrong thing.

One day when he was out hunting, Karã/tuma came across a cow and wondered what this strange-looking creature could be. Even more strange than its looks was the fact that it was not afraid of him, and did not run away. With delight at the ease of the job, Karã/tuma shot the cow and his whole band feasted on the meat. Later he told a black man about this strange animal, and when the black man came across some of them in the bush, he too was amazed that they showed no fear and did not run away like other animals. But instead of killing them for immediate feasting as Karã/tuma had done, he and his friends built a kraal, and drove some of the cows into it. These in due course gave birth to calves, and then the black man discovered how to milk the cows.

When offered some of the cows' milk to drink, Karã/tuma refused, and said that he would only lick the pot after the black man had drunk from it. Then he lost a tug-of-war with the black man for the use of a leather thong, and was told that from now on he would have to use string instead; with this string he snared small animals to eat. Karã/tuma walked through a field of sorghum, not knowing it was good food, and because the rough husks irritated his skin, he burned down the whole field. When the black man saw what Karã/tuma had done he said, 'Are you crazy? This is sorghum; it's food, you fool, I'm going to take what's left home with me.'

'Thus', said the Bushman storyteller, 'Karã/tuma ruined us; that day he spoiled the chances of our people for all time. . . . I fear this thing. It gives me pain. And I despise that old man of long ago who caused it to happen. I think that if I saw him today I would beat him. But he's dead and there's just nothing that can be done.'

The most tragic thing about the Bushmen is the clear sense they have of their own inferior status; they know that in the eyes of almost all whites and blacks they count for nothing. And when such attitudes have prevailed for centuries, perpetuated by the greater power of those who hold them, those who are so regarded have no option but to acknowledge their truth. The story of Karã/tuma reflects not only the acknowledgment of their inferiority, but also their sense of anguish and utter helplessness in the face of it. Their blaming of Karã/tuma is a blaming of themselves for something they were never in any position to counteract.

There is little that the Bushmen of today can do about their situation for themselves; a person can only pull himself up by his bootstraps if he has bootstraps. If the Bushmen are to survive into the next century with a positive sense of their own dignity and value, it can only be, at this stage in history, if we – black and white alike – do whatever is in our power to reverse the process we have both started and continued, and restore to the Bushmen their sense of dignity, and also their economic viability; for it is we who have taken both away. We have unremittingly taken their land and their livelihood away from them in the past, and we are still doing so today. We have failed to recognize that in their own context their values have as much validity as our own. We have also failed to recognize that until we came to southern Africa they had a way of life that worked. We did not. Now neither they nor we have a way of life that truly works.

Reversion to the old life is no longer the answer – clocks tend to be incapable of being turned back, and in any case most Bushmen no longer want, neither do they have the necessary skills, to return to the life of the hunter-gatherer. These people who were once the sole occupants of the whole of southern Africa have no rights at all, and in many areas land which they occupy is officially deemed to be 'uninhabited'. Today, just as much as ever before, they are a non-people; they are a tattered remnant clinging to the edges of the industrialized world with its armies, its mines and factories, and its high-tech agriculture, all of them encroaching ever more deeply into the Bushmen's last and only home – the Kalahari Desert.

In some parts of the Kalahari, incursions by outsiders have been going on for a long time. Small numbers of Kgalagadi people, with their cattle, have been living on remote pans in southwest Botswana for a century or more; but today the process has accelerated alarmingly. All over the Kalahari, boreholes have been sunk which have brought in their wake Bantu-speaking pastoralists and their cattle and goats [94]. Unable to compete for the available food with these newcomers, the larger game animals have all but vanished from some areas, leaving only the small antelopes – steenbok and duiker – whose natural foods are not eliminated by the cattle. In some areas the cattle are over-grazing the grass, with the effect that the bushes there are becoming dominant, and are encroaching on what was once good pasture. So the process is self-defeating. Not only that: the plethora of boreholes, increasingly heavily used, tends in the long term to lower the water-table, and could eventually reduce the Kalahari to a vast bowl of waterless sand.

Even more important to the lives of the Bushmen than the loss of their traditional game is the loss of the plant food, their staple for survival, which has also been reduced by the coming of the cattle and goats, but even more by the increased numbers of people. With their main sources of food increasingly denied them, more and more Bushmen have had to attach themselves to one of these black pastoralists for whom they work as cattle-herds, and in other unskilled capacities, in return very often for food and water only. Where wages are paid at all they are invariably negligible. The Bushmen are held in very low esteem, and are generally regarded as parasites; though they are 'allowed' to remain living on the lands of which their ancestors were the sole inhabitants for thousands of years, the new pastoralists have now taken over these lands as their own.

At least these Bushmen have not been turned out of their ancient lands as they have been in some areas, mostly by white farmers, and by the proclamation of game reserves which benefit a small fraction of the white community. While these black-owned cattle-raising ventures remain of low intensity and marginal profitability, the possibility remains of a kind of symbiosis — albeit not particularly satisfactory to either side — between the Bantu-speaking farmer-patrons and the Bushmen who work for them. But when, in the course of time, new methods and increased efficiency become the order of the day, it seems inevitable that it will be the Bushmen who are squeezed out. It is a pattern that has recurred with monotonous regularity throughout the centuries; and it occurs still.

At Tsetseng, not far from the little trading post of Kang, we stopped at a large, dried-out pan, into which a herd of cattle was streaming to drink at the borehole. Most of the herdsmen were black, but there was one young Bushman, dressed in ragged long trousers, shirt and sleeveless pullover (in the midday sun), who herded the cattle and drew water from the well in a bucket to pour into a trough for the cattle. We were told that there were no 'wild' Bushmen left in the area; all of them are now sedentary, living within reach of the borehole, and most of them work for a black farmer.

A few kilometres away from the pan we came across a young Bushman woman also doing farm work. She was carrying bunches of dried grass from a trailer, and dumping them beside the framework of a new hut, to be used for thatching. After we had been watching for a few minutes her baby, lying in a heap of grass nearby, started crying, and she picked him up and carried on with her work, with him tucked under one arm. We were told that she 'belonged' to a Kgalagadi farmer who did not pay her wages in return for her work, but instead gave her food (mealie meal and meat), water and tobacco. Shocked as we were by the word 'belonged', it was evidently used in a looser and less exclusive sense than it might immediately suggest. But it was bad enough, for it reflects an attitude of mind that holds few prospects for the Bushmen. Bushmen in the position of this woman have no real alternative open to them – if they give up the work they lose the food, and they can no longer hunt and gather in the over-grazed cattle lands. You work or you starve.

Bushman women have had their traditional economic status as the major providers of food in the family taken away by the lack of plant food left for them to gather. They either work for a farmer themselves, as this woman was doing, or they become totally dependent on what their men can provide in the same way. As non-providers the women have lost respect within their society and this, more than anything else, is leading to dissensions within families, and the gradual erosion of family mores. Increasingly, Bushman women cohabit with Bantu-speaking men, not least because the resulting children will have a better chance in life with a black father.

A few days after these two encounters we came across some Bushmen involved in a different type of agricultural work. They were driving a fine herd of about six hundred head of cattle from the rich cattle-raising area of Ghanzi in the west, right across the Kalahari Desert to the abattoir at Lobatsi in the south-east. It is a job for which the Bushmen seem eminently well suited for they are good with animals, ride horses as if they were born on them, and know the Kalahari. The following morning we got up before daylight in order to film the cattle setting off after their night's stop at the borehole at Lone Tree pan. Then we drove ahead of them for some distance, and stopped and waited for them to catch up with us. The first we saw of them was a small cloud of black dust in the distance, gradually coming closer and growing larger, then accompanied by the regular pounding of hundreds of hooves and the insistent lowing of the cattle, and the occasional shrill communications of the herdsmen. Then they were all around us – a sea of fat rumps, swishing tails and heads with great curved horns – the dust and noise filling our eyes and ears as they thundered past.

In the past when the Kalahari had few roads or boreholes, the cattle drives took five or six weeks, during which time all the Bushmen's knowledge of the desert, and where to find water, was taxed to the utmost. Inevitably the cattle lost a lot of condition on the way, and many were taken by lions. Today, with reasonable roads and with boreholes liberally scattered along the route, survival is not a problem and the journey is accomplished in two weeks. Then the Bushmen return to Ghanzi – usually to renewed unemployment, for most of them are hired only for the drives. When these took up to six weeks each, the Bushmen could be assured of several months' employment per year. Now they can be sure of only a very few weeks.

We met two sons of the white owner of this herd, rushing through their supervisory duties before returning as quickly as possible to Ghanzi for a football match the following day. They seemed friendly, likeable lads; but our guide told us with pent-up fury that these same two young men had once strung up a Bushman in a tree for some minor irritation, and would probably have left him there all night had not the local police happened to come by, whereupon they had hastily cut him down. He said he knew this to be true because the Bushman concerned was the gentle, humorous Kangao of the Kua group we had just recently been with.

The Bushmen of the Ghanzi area have already gone through a further stage of development than those we encountered at Tsetseng, and the development has been all negative. In the last year of the nineteenth century a group of white settlers, mainly Boers wanting to get away from British rule in Cape Province, came to the Ghanzi area. They were far from rich, and had relatively few cattle. They settled on the land, though with no official title to it, built houses, sank wells, but did not put up fences. Their cattle roamed freely, in the care of Bushman cattle-herds who, despite a certain unreliability, were essential to the farmers as there was no other non-white labour in the area.

With the security of work, and the food and water that it brought, these Bushmen settled into a more sedentary pattern of life, attaching themselves to the Boer farmer who had taken over their particular hunting and gathering territory. The cattle were few enough in number not to eliminate either the game or the plant food, and these traditional sources of food were supplemented by the rations the farmers gave them in return for their work. For both the Bushmen and the Boers this provided a mutually satisfactory symbiotic arrangement. Both regarded the land as their own, but neither had an officially recognized title to it.

In the 1950s, however, everything began to change. New white settlers arrived, mostly British from South Africa who were more affluent, and were intent on introducing modern and profitable farming methods. The land was systematically surveyed, and freehold titles were granted. The farms were fenced, which meant not only that the cattle-herds ceased to be needed since the cattle no longer ranged freely through the veld, but also that the game could not move across the land. To maximize the profitability of the farms, intensive farming methods and improved breeds of cattle have been introduced, and the stock-per-acre ratio vastly increased.

Those Bushmen who have jobs are paid wages and have the right to live, together with their extended families, on the white man's farm. The rest — about ninety per cent of them — have no work, no possibility of hunting game or gathering plant food, no right to remain on any farm if the farmer tells them they must leave, and nowhere to go to, for there is no block of land that has been allocated to them. Even such jobs as there are, are being given increasingly to Bantu-speaking Africans who, after a considerably longer period of contact with, and education by, Europeans are regarded as more reliable, more in tune with the requirements of the white farmers.

The majority of the Bushmen are unemployed, underfed, and are squatting illegally on land that 'belongs' to a white farmer. Demoralization is extreme. Many have taken to stock theft as the only means they have of keeping starvation at bay for themselves and their families. Many more have fallen victim to at least one of the three classic 'gifts' that civilized society has always tended to inflict on primitive people — alcoholism, tuberculosis and venereal disease.

The Central Kalahari Game Reserve, a short distance to the east of the Ghanzi farms, is open to any Bushmen who wish to go and live there. Bushmen alone are allowed to hunt there (on foot, and with bows and arrows only), and it is occupied by those few Bushmen (probably under a thousand) who still live something like the ancient hunter-gatherer life. While there are still Bushmen who can, and wish to, pursue the old life, it is vital that the Central Kalahari Game Reserve is preserved, not just to protect the wild animal and plant life, but to protect the Bushmen too. However, this situation is unlikely to last much longer. A report of June 1980, produced for the Remote Areas Development Office of the Ghanzi District Council, states that 'the most consistently expressed desire of the residents of the game reserve was that they should begin to live like other Batswana [people of Botswana]'. Many Bushmen from the Central Kalahari Reserve make occasional visits to trading posts such as Kang to acquire goods not obtainable in their traditional life; and in times of drought increasing numbers of them are driven to squat at boreholes outside the reserve, where they come into contact with a cash economy. Some never go back. Furthermore, boreholes are being sunk even in the heart of the desert. The traditional Bushmen of the central Kalahari are indeed an endangered species. As their old life becomes obsolete, what these Bushmen need is not so much protection, but rights to water, and to land on which to develop themselves.

The Bushmen of the Ghanzi farms, and all others who have already become dependent on a black or white agricultural/pastoral economy, no longer have the skills to enable them to return to the old life. Also they regard themselves as a cut above the 'wild' Bushmen through their contact with another way of life, even though they are at the bottom of that way of life. Yet some of them do pay periodic visits to the Central Reserve to gather plant food and to hunt, for there is nowhere else where they can do either.

Some of the more vocal Bushmen of the farms have complained about the lack of land of their own. They point out that they cannot any longer live permanently in the Central Reserve, which in any case is not large enough, nor does it have enough water, to provide a living for many more Bushmen than already live there. These Bushmen too need land where they can live and where they can be allowed the means to develop a viable economic base. In multiracial Botswana this would not mean separate ethnic areas; but it would mean a revolution in the attitudes of the majority of Botswanan citizens to enable the existing partial integration of the Bushmen to be completed without the humiliation and indignity that affect it now.

There have been a number of projects in Botswana which have attempted to help individual groups to find some way of supporting themselves, and to restore their self-respect. Some projects have been organized by religious groups; others have been started by individuals, and occasionally continued with government help and funds.

One such development project was started at Lone Tree, one of the places where we visited and filmed. It was initiated by Dr Tony Traill, of the department of linguistics at the University of the Witwatersrand, at the Veterinary Department's borehole at Lone Tree pan on the Ghanzi-Lobatsi cattle-drive route. On behalf of the Bushmen that lived there, Tony Traill applied to the government for permission to divert water from the borehole for an agricultural project. When this was granted he took six men of the band to Serowe in eastern Botswana for a six-week government-sponsored course in vegetable gardening and small livestock husbandry, run by the Serowe Farmers' Brigade. On their return to Lone Tree they fenced an area about 50 metres (164 feet) square, tilled it and planted it with various types of vegetables, and also tobacco.

The purpose of the garden was to supplement the Bushmen's diet which was following the all too common trend towards vitamin deficiency as mealie meal replaced wild plant food. However, Bushman bands have always consisted of a group of individuals with little communal vision, and the success of the garden at Lone Tree was jeopardized almost from the start by lack of agreement and squabbling. One tobacco crop was harvested. None of the Bushmen was able, or prepared, to act in a supervisory capacity, and Tony Traill was only able to visit during the university vacations.

On one of these visits, Tony and a friend built a shack at the site of the garden; in this an ex-student of his lived for nine months, acting as teacher for the children, supervisor of the garden and purchaser of beadwork and other artefacts. During this time the garden flourished; at the same time Tony sold the handicrafts in Johannesburg for high prices, and on his visits to Lone Tree he brought back clothing and hardware as well as cash. Unfortunately, stricter tax laws soon put an end to that, and now the artefacts have to be sold within Botswana through Botswanacraft.

The authorities increasingly regarded the Bushmen at the Lone Tree borehole as undesirable squatters; so when, through Tony's mediation, the mining company, de Beers, provided the money for a borehole away from the cattle-drive route, the Bushmen were moved a few kilometres away to Kagcae where water had been found. With a borehole of their own, they were able to keep more cattle and goats, which they are somewhat better at than they are at gardening. They have built a cattle kraal of sorts, but there is little concept of herd management – again because of their endemically non-communal outlook.

A school was built at Kagcae, and also accommodation for a teacher. The government at first employed a German couple as teachers and supervisors; then four years ago Elizabeth Camm arrived, a Coloured Botswanan girl, deeply concerned that the Bushmen were being left out of what Botswana had to offer. The children at Kagcae can get a primary education there, but for anything more advanced they have to go as far away as Xanagas in the far western corner of Botswana. There are, as yet, virtually no jobs in which they could use this education.

The Kagcae settlement was created as an exclusive Bushman scheme, on the principle that the Bushmen are the most underprivileged group in Botswana.

But Tony Traill is quick to point out that it was impossible to maintain exclusivity in the school, for example, without discriminating against underprivileged Kgalagadi children who also need education. Besides this, in the desert a water supply is the greatest means of breaking down social and ethnic barriers, for everyone settles within reach of the borehole, and everyone's need of water is the same. Thus Bushmen and Kgalagadi inevitably meet in the school, in the store and at the cattle post.

It is, in any case, government policy in Botswana to integrate the Bushmen into the wider society of the country. The problem is that the Bushmen have the least say in how that integration should happen; other people may express highminded opinions on the subject, but the only opinion that is not canvassed is the Bushmen's own. It is all too possible that they could lose their identity and still remain at the bottom of the heap.

The government has a very real problem over the individualistic attitudes of the Bushmen, with each group wanting its own development scheme, for small rural schemes cost a great deal of money, and the government simply does not have the resources to go round. Therefore they are trying to encourage Bushman bands to settle at points where facilities already exist, such as Kagcae. Disparate groups who, in Bushman terms, have nothing in common congregate in unusually large clusters, and many social problems arise.

A band at Lokalane, 24 km (15 miles) south of Lone Tree, resisted being moved to Kagcae because they did not want to live in such close proximity with a band with whom they had only slight ties, and because they wanted their own scheme. This has left them with no development prospects as far as the government is concerned. The only hope in cases such as this is for the money to come from private sources, and for someone with considerable energy and persistence to help the Bushmen to run it in its initial stages.

In Namibia a different situation exists for the Bushmen for integration is not yet the order of the day. In the 1950s the South African Government, on the initiative of Dr Hendrik Verwoerd, the architect of apartheid, set aside an area in the northeast of the country (the western edge of the Kalahari) exclusively for the Bushmen. Other areas were set aside for other ethnic groups, though most of the country was reserved for whites. Many whites settled in the Gobabis area which was ancient Nharo Bushman territory. The dispossessed Nharo either went across the border into Botswana, or north into the newly designated Bushmanland, part of which had always been inhabited by !Kung Bushmen. As the Kalahari goes, the eastern third of Bushmanland is a reasonably fertile area, with adequate water, and one of the objectives of the territory was to encourage Bushmen to settle and to till the earth. It also gave them a certain protection against the incursions of the more dominant African population groups, who still want to move in with their cattle, and who regard the land as wasted in the hands of Bushmen.

One of the bad things about this arrangement is that all Bushmen not already living in Bushmanland, or who did not move there, became guests on sufferance in all other areas. To the west of Tsumkwe, on the edge of the Kalahari, lies the great Etosha Pan, imaginatively proclaimed a game reserve to create privileged conditions for animals. Less imaginative was the treatment of the Bushmen who had lived in the area for thousands of years. The beginning was reasonably promising, for the Bushmen (and only the Bushmen) were allowed to hunt in the traditional manner within the reserve. This sensible arrangement was brought to a sudden end in the mid-1950s when a law was passed prohibiting hunting inside the reserve in any manner whatsoever. Overnight, from being legal hunters the Bushmen became poachers, and there were several occasions when the white game rangers rounded up hunting groups of Bushmen and locked them up for a while as punishment.

We met one of these Bushmen, Simon Tsam, who is still working in the reserve as a tracker and labourer. He told us that after the time when hunting was banned, one of his main jobs was to track zebra for the white rangers to slaughter in their culling programmes. The Bushmen are given zebra meat to eat. It is hard to imagine what difference it would have made to the zebra population of Etosha if the Bushmen had been allowed to hunt a few for themselves. They would not have had to depend (in an ultimately demoralizing manner) on the hand-outs of their bosses; furthermore, it would have been a way of recognizing that they lived on the land of their fathers not by favour but by right. As it is, they are made fully aware that they are employed (if they are lucky) on white man's land, doing things the white man's way.

We accompanied Simon Tsam and a group of other Bushmen employed on the reserve as they went about their normal work. First we went to an old water pump, driven by a windmill which had broken. Two Bushmen climbed up the rigging to the top, stopped the sails and locked them still, and then proceeded to repair the damage. Next we drove about 30 kilometres (18.5 miles) to the northern fence which was tall and said to be elephant-proof, but it did not look so strong to us. We drove slowly beside the fence looking for breaks in the wires, and as soon as one was spotted the van would stop, the Bushmen piled out, and immediately set about their task. They worked with great dispatch, exchanging only the words necessary for the job; then, when it was finished, they threw their tools into the back of the van with a clatter, and climbed in after them. Then the chatter broke loose – reassuringly for us, since it showed that despite their changed lives, some Bushman characteristics survived.

In the clinic at Namutoni, one of the three tourist centres of the Etosha game reserve, three young Bushmen lads had come for treatment for influenza. There had been an epidemic of gastric 'flu among the little Bushman community, and two people had died. Their resistance is low because of wrong nutrition; their previous well-balanced diet of meat and wild plant foods has been replaced by meat and mealie meal, and is badly deficient in vitamins. June Owen-Smith, the nurse at Etosha, sees her main role as dispensing health education, vaccinations and vitamin pills; but it is only a holding operation. She reckons that the Bushmen there will die out from tuberculosis and venereal disease.

Apart from Etosha, the farms and, as we shall see, the army, tracking down Bushmen in any other regular employment in Namibia was like looking for the proverbial needle in a haystack. The police only employ Bushmen in Bushmanland; the courts only employ Bushman interpreters on an occasional basis in Bushmanland; the mining companies do not employ any at all; nor do the shops or the electricity board. But the railways produced two names.

About 120 kilometres (75 miles) west of Namutoni is the copper-mining town of Tsumeb, where the railways employ one Bushman among their otherwise all-African labourers. Philip Ameb – a name he was given relatively recently – was born not far from Tsumeb which he has seen grow from a small village to a considerable industrial complex. He grew up on a farm owned by a white man, and when he was a child his people used to hunt with bows and arrows. At the age of about thirteen he shot his first large antelope (a gemsbok), and went through the first kill ritual. He also shot kudu and eland, and told us with some pride that he had been a good hunter. He said there was still plenty of game about, but now he and his people are not allowed to hunt. But they still dance, and still perform healing rituals about once a week.

Philip Ameb had started work with the railways in February 1980 because he needed to earn money to pay to live on the farm where he had grown up. He said he liked his job as a labourer with the permanent way gang, but his children were going to school and he hoped they would be able to get better jobs than his. His wife was a Damara woman (one of the African peoples of Namibia) and he thought this would be a help to his children in finding a better life.

The other railways' employee was the most uprooted Bushman we came across. He was a classical Bushman type, short and slight and with high cheekbones, and he worked as a packer and sorter in the staff dispensary in Windhoek, the capital of Namibia. Specially for us to film him, he had put on his best clothes, a smart denim-type suit and a collar and tie. He was also wearing a pair of steel-rimmed spectacles which his supervisor said he had never worn before. It was a charming expression of self-image.

His name, Petrus Hamatenja, is an Ovambo name, for he came from Ovamboland, northwest of Etosha, and had been brought up there by an Ovambo family. While he was still a baby his parents, on account of drought, attached themselves temporarily to a cattle-owning Ovambo family who had access to a well. After a while his parents left and went back to their band, leaving their baby behind, presumably thinking that he had a better chance of survival there than with them in the parched desert. Petrus said he had had no contact with Bushmen since then, and could remember nothing of his parents. He had been told the story by his Ovambo 'parents'. They had been good to him and brought him up together with their own children, with whom he had played and helped to herd the cattle. He said he had been to school for two months. He spoke Afrikaans, Herero and Ovambo, but no Bushman language.

We took him back to Katutura, the black township on the edge of Windhoek (though Namibia is officially multiracial), where he shares a house with some young African men. Although he smiled and greeted his friends, and they returned his greeting cheerfully, there was something extraordinarily lonely about him. He has spent a lifetime as the odd man out, and will probably continue to do so.

By far the largest single employer of Bushmen in Namibia is the South African Defence Force. Its Bushman battalion is at Camp Omega, situated in the middle of a nature reserve in the Caprivi Strip. It is a heterogeneous collection of Bushmen from basically two different groups – the Va'sekela, who are a sub-group of the !Kung, and the Mbarakwengo. Most of them came from Angola, and escaped across the border during the troubles that surrounded independence in 1975. Many had served in the Portuguese army which scarcely endeared them to the new rulers of the country.

The SADF took these Bushmen over, and established the beginnings of a Bushman unit. To start with there were forty-five Bushman families and six whites (officers and NCOs). Today there are rather over two hundred whites and about one thousand Bushmen (NCOs and other ranks). Yet the total Bushman population of Omega is about 6,000, which includes families as well as other hangers-on attracted by the high rates of pay (about R500/£270 per month) that the soldiers receive, the benefits of which tend to trickle down to everyone else thanks to the Bushman habit of sharing. Thus the operation that the SADF has committed itself to is not just a military one, but a social one as well, and of considerable proportions. So much so that only about ten to fifteen per cent of the time is spent on military operations and training, while eighty-five to ninety per cent of the time is spent on community development. The army is trying to establish Camp Omega as a town in its own right, and to train the Bushmen to run it as such.

To do this, they have established a Community Board – a kind of town council – consisting of a number of the leading Bushmen who act as a direct link between the Commandant and his officers and the rest of the Bushmen at Omega. Through this Board the army is trying to foster a new attitude to community relations, inevitably based on a western model. The first stage in this is school education (in Afrikaans), not just for the children, but for young adults as well. There are 450 pupils, being taught by eleven white soldiers, two of whom are fully trained teachers. So far the education is only up to a fairly elementary level, but plans are under way, between the Defence Force and the South African Department of Education, to provide facilities for extending schooling further for those who want it and have the capacity for it. What they will be able to do with that education once they have it, remains imponderable.

The Dutch Reformed Bushman Church, with a congregation of 184 baptized members, was established at Camp Omega in April 1982. It shares the church building with the whites, but they have services at different times. The Bushman lay preacher, Sergeant Mario Mohongo, is a charming and serious young man. He had been in the Portuguese army in Angola and had come under the influence first of Catholics and then of Protestants. Now he runs the Bushman church services, preaches and counsels. He feels it is important to teach his people about Christ, for while the old beliefs might have been adequate for their traditional life, he does not believe that they are adequate for their new and changed way of life. He believes that the only way to help the Bushmen retain what was good in their old lives in their new situation is through Christ.

The Commandant wanted us to see as much as possible of every aspect of the Bushmen's life at Omega, both civil and military, and he organized for us a tight programme which was followed with military efficiency. First we went to see some of the living quarters – pleasant wood-built houses, some of them with trim little gardens around them which seemed astonishing to us as the Bushmen we had come across in Botswana and Namibia had never grown plants even for food, let alone for decoration. But these Bushmen were from Angola where some of them had grown crops. Groups of people sat around, chatting and listening to western music on large transistor radios, and the women knitted or made crochet-work quilts. They seemed to have been metamorphosed into a completely different type of human being from the Bushmen we had met elsewhere.

The camp bakery is staffed by Bushman women in a perceptive move to give back to the women something of their lost status as providers. Just as their cousins, who are associated with African pastoralists in the Kalahari, are no longer able to gather the staple plant foods, and have to depend on what the men earn, so too with these women – though they are considerably higher up the income ladder so long as the army remains in Namibia. Another way of keeping some of the women usefully and gainfully employed was started by the Commandant's wife as part of a whole programme of adult education. She and some of the other white women have started sewing classes. A room, complete with serried ranks of modern electric sewing machines, has been made available for the purpose, and considerable numbers of Bushman women are making western-style clothes; to my eyes the clothes were of a quite remarkable ugliness, but we were assured that they were just what every Bushman wants to wear; and they sell like hot cakes in the camp shop.

There is also a brand new hospital with forty beds which was opened in February 1982. Before then there had been a somewhat makeshift arrangement with only eighteen beds; even this small number to begin with was above re-quirements, since there was a marked resistance among the Bushmen against going anywhere near the place. Now, with permanent staff, including eleven Bushmen, some of that resistance is breaking down. One of the patients whom we saw was a young woman who had given birth to a son during the night before. Her two previous children, for whose births she had flatly refused to go into hospital, had been stillborn. Because of this she had been persuaded to try the hospital this time, and her healthy son was the happy result. She had given him an Afrikaans name, Liewens, which means 'life'.

In another ward was a little girl of about five or six, suffering from mal-nutrition and an acute gastric condition. With the unaccustomed diet that they are now having to adapt to, and a lack of knowledge of the principles of nutrition, the major problems that the hospital has to deal with among children are related to wrong nutrition. It may be one of the biggest killers but as its effects are usually indirect, by lowering resistance to other diseases, this is hard to quantify. Children with malnutrition are not usually brought to the hospital, and it is only when there is a complication like this child's acute gastro-enteritis, that the parents will bring it for treatment. In many cases this is too late.

Our social visiting over, we were taken off to follow the soldiers going through wargames for our benefit, using live ammunition. All the weapons they used, and the ammunition that went with them, were of Russian origin, captured while on operations in Angola. 'Oh yes', the Commandant remarked breezily, 'the Angolans are very generous with firearms. All we have to do is to go in and collect them.'

We had come to Camp Omega believing what seemed to be the generally accepted opinion that the Bushmen were used exclusively as trackers, following the spoor of the enemy through even the most unpromising terrain – a military adaptation of one of their age-old skills. We found this assumption to be very far from the truth, for the Bushmen who come from Angola have long since lost such skills. Instead, they are trained in every aspect of warfare and are, we were told, the doughtiest of fighters. Stories abound of the Bushmen's acts of daring and valour, and of their astonishing powers of perception, and were told with great relish and pride (and certainly some hyperbole) by the white officers. The Bushmen seem to arouse the same feelings of respect and affection as the Ghurkas.

The first battle exercise that they laid on for us was a mock ambush with three armoured cars, the first of which was 'blown up'. As soon as this happened, all the Bushmen manning the vehicles piled off and went into action with their machine guns, rocket launchers, AK47s and every other imaginable weapon of destruction. It was all very efficient, very noisy and (at least for those, like me, uninitiated in warfare) very realistic, except that there were no bullets coming back in the opposite direction.

Then they started tracking, following the spoor of the imaginary enemy with something of the speed and dexterity that we had seen with our three hunters as they had tracked the wounded gemsbok. It was a somewhat spine-chilling conversion of an ancient skill.

Next came a session in weapon training, with a white NCO putting a group of Bushmen through their paces, either individually or together, with a mind-blowing range of weapons, including RPGs, machine guns, M79s and mortars [93]. On the way back to camp at the end of the day we saw another anomalous occupation for Bushmen – washing up.

The following morning we were out on the parade ground early to see the soldiers being lined up and marched about to establish the discipline of the day [92]. An important part of the parade was the Bible-reading. The white pastor had chosen that well-known passage from St John's Gospel: 'In my Father's house are many mansions . . .' It seemed an odd choice for a people whose homes

64. Hunters scan the horizon for game. The animal they most desire to kill is the eland, not only because it is big and has the most fat, but also because of their spiritual identification with it.

65. As the hunters come closer to the game they are following, they crouch down to hide their human stature, and approach downwind of the animals.

66△   67▽   68▽

66. Hunters move silently as they approach the game, crouching low and taking cover behind bushes when possible.

67. Within about 20 metres of their prey, the hunters fire their arrows.

68. Once an animal has been hit, hours of tracking ensue. The hunters follow the spoor of the wounded animal, and use hand gestures to communicate with each other.

69. Unable to go any further, the gemsbok retreats into a thick bush for protection; but she is still able to use her lethal horns. The end comes when the hunters drive their spears into the heart of their quarry.

69△   70▽

70. Having skinned the dead gemsbok, the hunters cook the portion they are entitled to.

71. (*above*) The carcass is cut up into large joints and carried back to the village where it is shared out among the band with strict equality.

72. Ramonne skins the steenbok which had been caught in a snare. Later the skin is pegged out for curing, and once cured will be used to trade for mealie meal, tobacco and – increasingly – manufactured goods.
73. Ramonne puts the steenbok in the 'oven' – a hole in the ground. Red hot wood coals are put in, the steenbok laid over them, and the rest of the coals piled on top.
74. Four hours later, Ramonne and /Wa/tee uncover the steenbok which has been cooked to their taste.

72△

73△

74▽

75. Koto engraves an ostrich eggshell. The design is scratched onto the white surface with a sharp knife. Charcoal is then rubbed into the incisions to reveal the design.

76. As //Koe/tee scrapes a *bi* tuber, Ramonne scrapes the flesh from leaves of wild sansevieria plants, exposing the fibres with which he will make string.

75△   76▽

77. Ramonne rolls the white sansevieria fibres on his thigh until they are corded, then rolls two of these cords together to make a strong length of string.

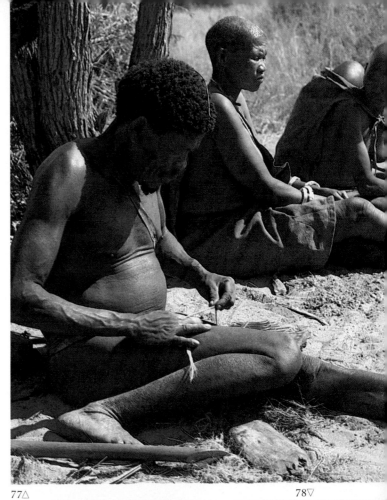

78. Ramonne tests the string for strength, and smooths it with a sharp stone.

77△   78▽

79
80

81∇

79. Kwa!kae mends a bow. Made from the wood of a raisin bush, with a bowstring of corded sinew, it is used as a musical instrument as well as a hunting weapon.
80. Maisakhwe and !Wanaka listen to a story.
81. Smoking is a long-established Bushman habit. Tobacco, either alone or mixed with *dagga* (marijuana), is often smoked in a short hollow bone but sometimes, as here, an old cartridge case is used, with the end taken off.

82. Ramonne makes ankle rattles from the cocoons of a moth while Be/tee plays a thumb piano.
83. Tanning a hartebeest skin. Once pegged out, scraped clean and dried, the juice of a *crinum* bulb is rubbed in. Then the skin is worked until it is soft and flexible.

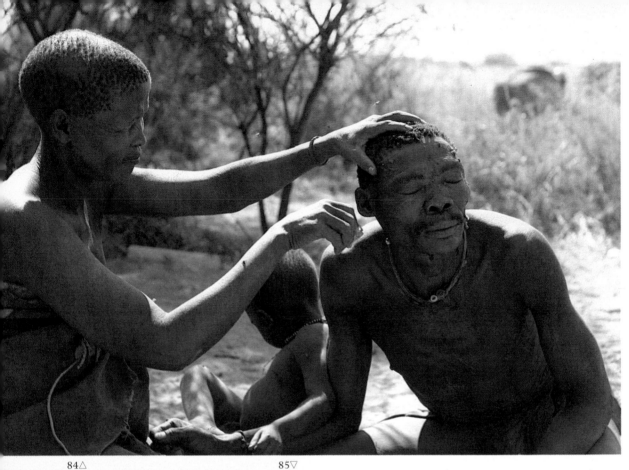

84. When Be/tee complained that he felt unwell, Khangdu, his wife, made incisions on his forehead with a safety razor to let out some of the bad blood.

85. The healing ritual is of paramount importance to the Bushmen. The healers dance round the fire, accompanied by the chanting and clapping of the women, and draw aside to tend the sick. Here a healer lies by !Koga so that his healing power can flow into the sick man.

86. The healers lay hands on !Koga to learn the secrets of his illness and to draw out its evil cause.

87. (*opposite*) On the verge of trance, the healers dance on.

88. A semi-traditional village at Tsumkwe, Namibia, where many Bushmen were encouraged to settle. Army pay enables them to buy modern goods, but their diet has become dangerously unbalanced.

89. A modern Bushman home at Tsumkwe, built to western and not Bushman concepts of living. At first many Bushmen lived in traditional huts outside the buildings, and kept stores and chickens inside.

90. At the Bushman school at Tsumkwe, the children are first taught Afrikaans and then given basic tuition in reading, writing and arithmetic. There are few jobs available when they leave school.
91. A Bushman prayer meeting at an army camp near Tsumkwe. The pastor, Dominee Ferdie Weich, though much loved by the Bushmen, could report no permanent conversion to Christ in 21 years.

92. Bushman soldiers at morning parade at Camp Omega, Namibia. The South African Defence Force is the largest single employer of Bushmen in Namibia, but most are refugees from Angola.

93. Members of the Bushman battalion at Camp Omega are given weapon training. The camp is situated in the middle of a nature reserve in the Caprivi Strip.

94. A herd of cattle on a pan in Botswana. As more boreholes are sunk, the increased numbers of cattle and people reduce both plants and game – the Bushmen's traditional foods.
95. Milking time at /Gautsha, Namibia. Under an enlightened scheme to help Bushmen acquire and care for their own cows, a better diet and way of life has been made possible for some Bushmen.

96. A Bushman working on the railway in Namibia, his ancestors' exclusive hunting territory.

97. Dam came home after a cataract operation wearing glasses, and with the miracle of sight.

98. John Marshall with Bushmen in Tsumkwe. His family has spent long periods there since 1951.

99. A Bushman woman on a black-owned farm in Botswana. She is given no wages — only food.

have been taken away from them everywhere in southern Africa. We wondered
if all our mistakes had to be left for God to sort out in the next world.

In fact, the army is fully aware of the problems involved in the very existence
of their Bushman battalion. They recognize the fact that these people, uprooted
from their ancient environment, and trained only as soldiers in the western
tradition, have no alternatives in life. What happens when the South African
army has to pull out of Namibia? Most of the soldiers are from Angola, and have
worked since they left for the South African army. They have no affiliations
with Namibia in whose territory they have lived since leaving Angola. With the
army gone, they would suddenly be deprived of an income and a way of life;
and even if they still had the skills to provide for themselves as hunter-gatherers
(which they do not), they live in the middle of a nature reserve where neither
hunting nor gathering is a possibility. To move 6,000 people to another part of
Namibia would pose an overwhelming problem for whatever area they were
sent to, not only in terms of sheer numbers, but also in terms of the conflict that
would arise between them and their new neighbours.

The Commandant, devoted as he clearly is to the Bushmen, said that he would
like to take them back to South Africa — yes, even the hangers-on as well. One
wonders where in South Africa they could now be accommodated. However,
the General who commands the forces in Namibia has said that they are pressing ahead with their plans for the development of Camp Omega as a town in its
own right, where the Bushmen could continue to live should the army have to
withdraw. What is not immediately clear is what kind of productive base could
possibly exist for them, in the middle of a nature reserve, to replace their present
army employment and income, life insurance schemes and pensions. It is a
massive responsibility that the South African Defence Force has taken on.

The Bushmen at Camp Omega are completely isolated from the other Bushmen of Namibia, coming as they do from another country and other clans, and
working for yet another country. For its own Bushmen, as for the ten other
ethnic groups that make up the total population of Namibia, a form of repre-
sentative government, in the shape of a Council of Ministers, was established in
1978 and lasted until January 1983. The Bushman Minister — known as Chief
Kashe, though the Bushmen have never had Chiefs — went through a process of
change and adaptation to an alien and sophisticated political system that would
have been cataclysmic even for someone already attuned to the complexities of
western-style politics and bureaucracy. For Kashe it was a change from the
Stone Age to the atomic age in four years.

During the time that he was a Minister, Chief Kashe lived in a pleasant house
in a mainly white suburb of Windhoek, had his own Mercedes car as well as one
supplied by the government, a Herero chauffeur and other staff, and a sub-
stantial ministerial salary. He was fortunate in that he had a very sympathetic
white adviser who spoke his language perfectly, for although Chief Kashe can
understand a certain amount of Afrikaans, he does not speak it. His main communication with his fellow Ministers was through his adviser.

At the same time his new role estranged him from his own people. He still had a home in Tsumkwe — a modest mud-and-wattle hut with a thatched roof — and his wife and children lived there while he spent most of his time in Windhoek. With many more material things than his fellow Bushmen, and finding himself no longer able to share what he had in the traditional Bushman manner, he was not regarded by the people of Bushmanland as any longer one of them, or in any way able to speak for them. Now he has no job, no house in Windhoek, and no salary. He has returned to Tsumkwe to live again among his own people, and is trying to revert to his old way of life. It is a process that must be as traumatic as the change that was required of him in his four years as a Minister.

Bushmanland is surrounded by a high wire fence, with a gate across the one road that leads to Tsumkwe. The man at the gate — an African — wrote down our car number while we sat outside the closed gates and read the notice warning us that there was no petrol in Bushmanland. The road is a dirt road, fairly unstable and pot-holed in places, and part of it was being re-made as we drove along, which only added to the uncertainties of the drive.

After the proclamation of Bushmanland as the Bushman homeland in the 1950s, the authorities decided to establish an administrative centre at its heart. A Commissioner was appointed, Claud McIntyre, and he and his wife set up their tents under a great baobab tree in the middle of nowhere on Christmas Day 1959 — the beginnings of Tsumkwe. The plan was to encourage the Bushmen to settle in permanent communities, and to till the earth to provide food for themselves. Since the government provided no money, McIntyre went to all the farmers in the surrounding areas and was finally given a pump; he made the borehole himself. But for the first four months that the McIntyres were there, drinking water had to be brought in containers from Grootfontein, some 299 km away (186 miles).

Under the supervision of the McIntyres, several patches of land were put under cultivation, worked on by some of the Bushmen, and on these were grown such foods as ground nuts, melons, pumpkins, marrows, maize and sorghum. Up to 1972 about sixty per cent of these gardens were still in operation; by 1978 only one remained. In that year the army moved into Bushmanland — a unit of the SADF which employs about 160 local Bushmen — and they introduced some cultivation projects, some of which are still in operation. In 1964 goats had been introduced, and the Bushmen were encouraged to buy them and milk them. Between 1973 and 1981 at least eight hundred goats were bought by the Bushmen; when we were there in June 1982, there were four left. The Bushmen tend to regard goats as instant meals rather than as sources of milk; and they are, in any case, susceptible to predation by jackals and hyenas.

The white pastor at Tsumkwe, Dominee Ferdie Weich, believes that the reason for the lack of success of the gardens (in which he too was involved), and also of some other projects, is that the Bushmen themselves have never felt part of them. As far as they were concerned, they worked on a garden, built a fence or a clinic, in return for money; but it was never seen as *their* garden, fence or clinic. Even though it was explained that any given project had been designed specifically for them, it was not something they could see as part of their way of life. It was the white man's project, but they were perfectly happy to help.

One of the most unfortunate examples of this was in the building of new permanent villages for three of the Bushman groups at Tsumkwe [89]. The concrete dwellings with corrugated iron roofs were not regarded by the Bushmen as anything to do with them. Built according to western concepts of privacy, they took no account of the Bushman manner of living in the open, with everyone overlooking everyone else. Yet the Bushmen had to live there. To begin with, many of them simply continued to live outside, perhaps putting up a hut in the space in front of their new shelter, and they kept their bags of mealie meal and their chickens inside. Now some people are sleeping inside, but most of the shelters that we saw were a jumble of clothes, bags, bottles and cooking utensils, with hardly room for a human being.

Dominee Weich arrived in Tsumkwe in 1961, about fifteen months after the McIntyres. Of the various white officials appointed to Bushmanland – the Commissioner, a conservationist, two educationists and the Dominee – he is the only one who visits the Bushmen in their villages and talks to them in their own language.

We had the opportunity of going with Dominee Weich on a visit to one of the army camps in the area, and it was moving to see the warmth of the welcome he received. Yet, by contrast with the apparently flourishing Christian community of Bushmen at Camp Omega, all attempts to preach the Gospel to the Bushmen here have universally failed to produce real results. There was one occasion in 1973 when Dominee Weich brought in an evangelist for a three-day mission, and several Bushmen said they wanted to be cleansed from their old ways and turn to Christ. One of these was a young man called Bo; but during a period of four-and-a-half years when Dominee Weich was away from Tsumkwe, Bo took to drinking, got involved in a fight and killed a man, and spent some time in prison. Now, the Dominee says, although Bo is still nominally a believer, his behaviour is no different from what it was before. All the other converts have similarly fallen away.

Bo was among the group that Dominee Weich visited; he read them a passage from the Bible, and then they all prayed together – or rather, the Dominee prayed and the Bushmen sat in polite and awkward silence. The occasion seemed to characterize the traumatic transition that is taking place in the lives of the Bushmen of Tsumkwe – they are no longer at one with their old traditions, but neither are they part of those traditions that others try to bring to them, however good their intentions. The Bushmen are, as it were, moving house; they have left the old house, but have still not found a suitable new one. In the meantime all their goods, both physical and spiritual, are in a state of utter disarray.

In August 1981 a bottle store was opened in Tsumkwe. Chief Kashe was one of the supporters of the scheme, and many people said that this was simply an attempt to win popularity and votes. On the last Friday of every month, when the army pays its soldiers, the bottle store does brisk business; and the clinic does brisk business over the weekend that follows, coping with the effects of the fighting and acts of neglect that invariably occur. The nurse who runs the clinic, wife of the conservationist, told us some horrifying stories. On one occasion a young, unmarried Bushman mother wanted to go to bed with a man, but her toddler was getting in the way. To keep him quiet she emptied down his throat the remaining half of a half bottle of brandy. The child died.

That story, the nurse told us, could be repeated many times over, with variations in detail. It is, perhaps, the inevitable result for people who have never had a tradition of drinking alcohol, and who find themselves, because of the break-up of their traditional life, with too much leisure and nothing new to fill it with. With the demoralization and apathy that this brings, and with access to cash through some of the men's employment (in the case of those employed by the army, a great deal of cash) drinking is bound to follow. And when people eat so poorly, their resistance is too low to cope with the effects of alcohol.

Another problem that the clinic has, similar to that of the hospital at Camp Omega, is the Bushmen's resistance to coming with an ailment until the symptoms have become acute. Quite often it is left too late for anything to be done. Just before we arrived, a man had come in to the clinic whose head had been deeply wounded by an axe in a drunken brawl two weeks before. The man had complained of headaches, but only went to get treatment when he saw maggots dropping from his head. He had to be taken to the hospital at Grootfontein – a thing most Bushmen flatly refuse to accept because they fear that the hospital means inevitable death.

In 1981 a team of ophthalmologists from Cape Town visited Tsumkwe to inspect and treat the eyes of as many Bushmen as would come. Almost to a man they refused. However, a sprightly old man called Dam, who had been blind for about ten years, plucked up his courage and went to see the ophthalmologists. His blindness had been caused by cataracts, and they told him that they could do something for him, but that he would have to go with them to Cape Town – even more terrifying than going to Grootfontein. Dam agreed, much to the dismay of his friends who thought they would never see him again. When he came back a few weeks later, sporting a pair of spectacles and ecstatic with the miracle of new sight [97], the other Bushmen went in droves to the clinic to have their eyes inspected, only to be told that the ophthalmologists were no longer there, and the thing could not be done. They would have to wait until next time. At least one barrier may have been broken down which could pay dividends in the future. But in the meantime the general attitude to the clinic is one of apathy; they simply can't be bothered to go. At the same time, the clinic does not have enough staff with the inclination to visit Bushmen at home, or to follow up existing patients, or run health education programmes.

Perhaps the most important development at Tsumkwe is the Bushman School, run by the educationist and his wife whose little daughter attends the school along with the Bushman children. The first thing that is done is to teach the children Afrikaans, and then they are given a very basic education in reading, writing and arithmetic [90]. We visited the two classes – one for older and one for younger children – and in both a cheerful atmosphere prevailed. Bright little faces watched the teacher intently, then puckered with concentration at the task of writing down arithmetical symbols in an exercise book.

At the moment the education that the children receive seems to hold as many drawbacks as benefits. Some of the children with their newly won knowledge feel superior to their parents' generation. Yet there are few jobs that can make use of this education, which is in any case very limited. And despite the fact – as we were told in every school we visited, whether in Namibia or Botswana – that the Bushman children are of above-average intelligence, there is no opportunity for them to take their schooling further than a very rudimentary level.

During the time that we were at Tsumkwe, Chief Kashe and his adviser, François Stroh, came there to hold a meeting with the Bushmen to discuss a persistent rumour that a large part of eastern Bushmanland, the only part with reasonable soil and water, was going to be turned into a nature reserve. The fact that there are already over one hundred such reserves in Namibia did not seem to enter the debate. Where facts are few, rumour and fear take over. Many Bushmen have moved out of Tsumkwe to escape the demoralization and apathy that seem to have become endemic in the place, and have started a more viable way of life of their own. If this proposed game reserve were to go ahead, these people would be forced to move back to Tsumkwe. It was the last thing they wanted.

When the news went round that Kashe and François Stroh were coming on a specific day to talk to them, several Bushmen from these outlying villages walked or rode into Tsumkwe. The meeting was held in what has become the traditional place for such gatherings, under the great baobab tree where the McIntyres had established the first administrative centre. Kashe spoke first, assuring the Bushmen that no decision would ever be made without the consent of the Bushmen. Then François Stroh spoke, underlining what Kashe had said.

Next the Bushmen themselves told these two representatives of the government what they felt. ≠Toma, the leader of the Bushmen of /Gautsha, and a man of impressive dignity and wisdom, told them that he, like many others, had left Tsumkwe because it was not a happy place, and they had been able to make a better life at /Gautsha, raising cattle and milking them. Was it right, just to preserve wild animals, for people to be forced back to live in a place which offered no life, but a living death? At /Gautsha they had built a kraal for their cattle, they had learned to care for them by working on the Administration's farm at Tsumkwe, they had good grazing for them near the village, and adequate water from the waterhole. The cows were providing good milk, and as a result their children were healthy. Furthermore, because the land was not over-grazed, and the human population not excessive, as it was at Tsumkwe, there was enough wild plant food for the women to gather, and game for the men to hunt. If the game reserve were established they would have to give up the only opportunity they had had of a viable way of life of their own.

With reassurances all round that there were no plans for a game reserve, and there would never be any without the Bushmen's agreement, the meeting disbanded. Nobody seemed quite sure whether to believe what they had been told.

The following morning, quite early, we drove out to /Gautsha to see for ourselves what was happening there. On the way we passed ≠Toma and his wife !U, together with some other people from /Gautsha who had been at the meeting. They had stayed overnight at Tsumkwe and left at dawn for their two-hour walk. In the Land Rover, in four-wheel drive, low ratio all the way, it took us three-quarters of an hour. We took some of the Bushmen on board and lurched the remaining twenty minutes' drive in acutely crowded discomfort.

We arrived towards the end of milking time. Inside the cattle kraal – a great circle of densely packed branches – those men who owned cows sat on old tin cans and milked their animals [95], most of which just stood placidly and needed no tethering. Children ran in and out between the legs of the cattle, occasionally stopping and squirting some milk from an udder straight into their mouths. Then the barriers across the entrance to the kraal were lifted, and the cattle streamed out and away to their pastures, accompanied by one or two men and a gaggle of children.

To look at, there was nothing very remarkable about /Gautsha; but by contrast with Tsumkwe it was buzzing with life and cheerfulness, with the exception of one woman who was conducting an argument with her husband at screaming pitch. No one seemed to take very much notice of her, including her husband, which only added fuel to her fury. In the middle of this argument ≠Toma arrived, and as he walked through the village he stopped and talked to little groups, telling them what had happened at the meeting the day before. As he passed on to the next group, those he had been with remained earnestly discussing the implications of what they had been told.

One man, more than anyone else, is responsible for the change that has taken place at /Gautsha and some other villages in the past few years. John Marshall [98] first came to Bushmanland in 1951 with his parents and sister. His father, Laurence Marshall, an American businessman, had recently retired and wanted to do something with his family. He had heard about 'wild Bushmen who hide behind bushes and shoot you with their poisoned arrows', and decided that the family would go in search of them.

For their great expedition Laurence Marshall assigned specific tasks to each member of the family: his wife, Lorna, was to write an anthropological work; his daughter, Elizabeth, was to write a general book; and John was to make movies. He himself, he said, would be the Field Marshall. Lorna Marshall has become the doyenne of Bushman anthropologists; Elizabeth Marshall Thomas's book is a classic; and John has made many outstanding films on the Bushmen and their way of life.

The Marshalls never really believed that the Bushmen were as unfriendly as they were sometimes reported to be; but when they found such an open, fair and competent society of people, they were captivated. At the outset the Bushmen gave them some of their own names, and John was named after ≠Toma, the leader of the /Gautsha band. Every member of the family has returned to the Tsumkwe area several times since 1951. In 1978 after an absence of many years, John Marshall returned.

'I knew there would be a lot of changes. I think I expected to see people still gathering and hunting, but probably also doing things like planting a little garden now and then, and raising goats, or even cattle. And I was astonished to find that that wasn't happening; people had given up the gathering and hunting life but hadn't replaced it with any productive economy that would give them a decent diet and a decent living.'

John set out to discover the problems that were besetting people there, and the reasons why they were not doing well. Together with Claire Ritchie, he started to do genealogies in order to establish a bottom line of population dynamics: numbers of people, death rate, birth rate, how many children were being born, how many children were dying. Those kind of actuarial figures would be the basis on which to begin thinking about development.

'We finally got most of the people in this area dated and named, and it turned out that the population had dropped slightly, it was barely holding its own, and that trend seemed to have gone back for about fifteen years. We wondered if it was a low birth rate or a high death rate; and it turns out that it is a high death rate. Then, when we did our surveys of what people were eating, what their economic life was like, we discovered that they had a very poor diet, a much worse diet than, for example, what Bushmen in Botswana are eating today'.

Malnutrition has been one of the biggest contributory causes of the increased death rate at Tsumkwe, for it has lowered the people's resistance to disease. Since the bottle store was opened in 1981 the situation has been exacerbated, not only because of increased violence, but also because in many cases people are drinking rather than eating; and people are neglecting their children because they are drinking.

Side by side with this demographic survey, John has encouraged some of the Bushmen to help themselves to become cattle owners. With a small annual income, left by Laurence Marshall in his will for the purpose, John has established a Cattle Fund to help those Bushmen who have the motivation, and will learn the know-how, to acquire their own cattle. Instead of the kind of institutional development that there has been at Tsumkwe — building a school, clinic, houses, etc. — which would in any case be too costly for the means at his disposal, he has tried to help people with basic tools; to help a collaborating group of Bushmen who are willing to put the effort into making a kraal, milking their cows regularly, and doing occasional work on the Administration farm.

John is adamant that a Bushman must work to fulfil these basic qualifications, and prove his serious desire to keep and care for an animal, before the Fund will give him help to buy a cow. In this way, John points out, 'self-help doesn't need very much money. You don't have to keep pouring money into self-development if self-development is working. If it isn't working then there is something wrong with your idea and your plan, and you had better think of something else. But in this case it seems to be working at /Gautsha. People are building responsible kraals, they're milking, they're using milk products, their kids are eating better, and they are beginning to develop an economy that could see them through the next twenty years.'

John Marshall's scheme is helping a relatively small group of Bushmen in Namibia to become self-sufficient. Depending on the political outcome in that country, it may be that in the future, just as now in Botswana, what will be needed is help in integrating the Bushmen into a wider Namibian society. Meanwhile, both in Botswana and Namibia, projects remain small-scale, local, dependent on the energy of a few individuals, and are of fluctuating success.

!Kun/obe told Megan Biesele at the end of her story of Karã/tuma, 'People should cry out for themselves. People should protest. Black people cry for themselves, and they stay alive. The Afrikaaners cried for themselves, and they are alive. These people over there went about crying and crying, and they were lifted up. We who are Zhu/twãsi (!Kung), let us cry out, so that we will be lifted up. Unless we do, we are just going to ruin.'

If the Bushmen will indeed cry out for themselves; if more and more of them throughout the Kalahari are helped to become motivated towards self-development; then, after all, there might be some hope for their future. Then perhaps the story of Karã/tuma might be reversed, and the Bushmen might no longer be God's last people. But the signs are not encouraging. In March 1984, I was told that the nature reserve was, after all, very likely to be imposed in eastern Bushmanland. If it is, that flourishing little community at /Gautsha will have to move back to the apathy and demoralization of Tsumkwe. The Bushmen need other people to cry out on their behalf.

Laurens van der Post

WITNESS TO
A LAST WILL
OF MAN

O, man remember.
UPANISHADS

Witness to a Last Will of Man

I have told the story of the Bushman of southern Africa in books and films and talks to people in many parts of the world. I should have done more and done it better; but I have the melancholy justification that I did all I could do in my time and place. The Chinese have an ancient saying that the wise man speaks but once. I cannot claim the wisdom that this saying presupposes: but I have a feeling that it applies even to the not-so-wise, and perhaps most of all to the foolish. I have no temptation, therefore, to go back on my tracks. Unfinished as this history remains, its completion is best left to those whose business is history, and who have the relevant dedication, the love of the subject and the training, all of which are possessed by the author of the main book which precedes this essay. All that I can and should still do, perhaps, is to add to this tragic story of the Bushmen more of my experience of his being, and the role he has played in my imagination so that the horror of his elimination over the gruesome millennia behind us can be fully understood. I do not intend to write about it as a piece of historicity but as a profoundly significant event which points unerringly to a cruel imperviousness in our so-called civilization.

One of the most deceptive of popular half-truths is the saying that history repeats itself. Only unredeemed, unrecognized, misunderstood history, I believe, repeats itself, and remains a dark, negative and dangerous dominant on the scene of human affairs. Although the Bushman has gone, what he personified, the patterns of spirit made flesh and blood in him and all he evoked or provoked in us, lives on as a ghost within ourselves. This is no subjective illusion of mine evoked by the special relationship I have always had with him. Something like him, a first man, is dynamic in the underworld of the spirit of man, no matter of what race, creed or culture. I know this as an empiric fact because of all the books I have written and films I have made about the Bushman; his story has been translated into all languages except Chinese, travelled the world and been taken into the hearts of millions as if it were food in a universal famine of spirit. What this means for our own time depends in the first instance on our rediscovery of these patterns in ourselves and our readiness to cease being accessories after the fact of diminished consciousness, of which murder is the ultimate symbol. As Hamlet in his haunted fortress had it, when the time is out of joint, as ours certainly is, the readiness is all.

It has seemed increasingly urgent to me, therefore, to look into the causes of this imperviousness and reinterpret the Bushman's story in the light of my own day. Not only the present but the future depends on a constant reinterpretation of history and a re-examination of the state and nature of human consciousness. Both these processes are profoundly and mysteriously interdependent and doomed to failure without a continuous search after self-knowledge, since we and our awareness are inevitably the main instruments of the interpretation.

This for me is not as simple as it may sound. The obstacles encountered by all who try to serve the Word, whole as it was in the beginning, are always formidable but never more so than when they seek to throw light on areas of our aboriginal darkness where consciousness has left an infinity of meaning, unchosen and untransfigured like ghosts of the unborn in a night without moon, stars or end. Once launched on this voyage of exploration, it is significant how much easier it is to confine oneself to studying the external and visible reality, the mechanistics of archaic communities and the behaviour of man. There is a great deal of self-satisfaction and an almost tangible sense of achievement to be found in a demonstrable approach to life. I imagine this has a great deal to do with the absorption of anthropologists in the outward pattern of 'primitive' societies and their dutiful recording of aboriginal behaviour and ritual. This recording can hardly be done without condescension, and it is diminishing to both observer and observed when the latter is almost exclusively regarded as an object of study and the theme of yet another PhD thesis.

The real trouble began for me, as it has done for countless others, when I sought to understand imaginatively the primitive in ourselves, and in this search the Bushman has always been for me a kind of frontier guide. Imagination shifts and passes, as it were, through a strange customs post on the fateful frontier between being and unrealized self, between what is and what is to come. The questions that have to be answered before the imagination is allowed through are not new but have to be redefined because of their long neglect and the need for answers to be provided in the idiom of our own day. For instance, in what does man now find his greatest meaning? Indeed, what is meaning itself for him and where its source? What are the incentives and motivations of his life when they clearly have nothing to do with his struggle for physical survival? What is it in him that compels him, against all reason and all the prescriptions of law, order and morality, still to do repeatedly what he does not consciously want to do? What is this dark need in the life of the individual and society for tragedy and disaster? Since the two World Wars that have occurred in my own lifetime, disorder and violence have become increasingly common on the world scene. Surely these things are rooted in some undiscovered breach of cosmic law or they would be eminently resistible and would not be allowed to occur? Where indeed does one propose to find an explanation for the long history of human failure? How can one hope to understand this aspect of man and his societies, and comprehend a scene littered with ruins and piled high with dunes of time which mark the places where countless cultures have vanished because men would not look honestly, wholly and steadily into the face of their inadequacies? The answers to none of these questions are available unless one is prepared through profound self-knowledge to re-learn the grammar of a forgotten language of self-betrayal, and in so doing the meaning of tragedy and disaster. It is the ineluctable preliminary to our emancipation, especially for those priests and artists who have been subverting themselves and the societies which they are dedicated to preserve. Unless one is honestly prepared to do so, one is warned at this crepuscular immigration post that one had better not cross the frontier.

For the English-speaking world the most significant example of such an imagination shift is to be found, of course, in Shakespeare's *Hamlet*. It was preceded by works in which Shakespeare celebrates the beauty, the potentials for happiness, the plausible attractions and surface patterns of the outer world. But suddenly it is as if the wind of time from some absolute frontier of the universe brings him a scent of the existence of a denied meaning that is far more than surface beauty, and so much greater than either the happiness or unhappiness encountered on the worldly scene. And at once it is as if, with Hamlet, man crosses not only for himself but for all men, this long shunned frontier of the spirit, and from there begins years of journeying of a new kind. The journey this time inevitably goes down into an underworld of mind and time, where man is confronted not only with all the inadequacies and consequences of his worldly consciousness but also faces alone and unsupported by a familiar pattern of living the stark necessity of making his own choice between good and evil, truth and untruth, before he is free to move on towards the wholeness that their opposition so paradoxically serves. Shakespeare, I believe, becomes, in his great phrase, one of 'God's spies' and takes on himself 'the mystery of things' so '*utterly*' (as the Bushmen would have it), that he could come to rest in the conclusion: 'Men are such stuff as dreams are made on'. But even as dream material Shakespeare in *The Tempest* is still faced with an ending that would be despair, 'unless I be relieved by prayer'. Why prayer? Because it is the symbol both of man's recognition of the existence of, and his dependence on, a power of creation beyond his conscious understanding, and greater than life and time, that time which Einstein described not as a condition in which life exists so much as a state of mind. In prayer, there is an image of certain promise that through this recognition and this remembrance and surrender of the part to a sense of the whole, Shakespeare could summon help from the heart of the universe to live the final portion of the overall dream with which his art was invested and to which his flesh and blood was entrusted.

All this may seem as remote from the Bushmen and Stone-age culture as to be irrelevant. Yet in reality it has an *a priori* significance not only for understanding the nature of primitive being but for preventing the contraction of individual consciousness which is such an alarming symptom of our collectivist day and promoting the enlargement of individual consciousness into an expanding awareness on which the renewal of our societies depends. The collectivist and intellectual turned 'intellectualist', the promoter of 'isms' of the intellect that are to the sanity of being and spirit what viruses are to the body, will no doubt find it absurd but it is precisely because the Bushman has been a scout and frontier guide to me from infancy in the same dark labyrinthine underworld of human nature which Shakespeare entered precipitately with *Hamlet*, that I have been compelled to tell the world about him. From time to time during my life I try to reappraise what the Bushman has done for me and here I do so probably for the last time. I cannot disguise that for many years I lost conscious sight of him as I went my own wilful way but instinctively he was always there and bound never to mislead or fail. He could not fail, as I realized looking back on to the vortex of the movement which he started in my imagination, because I recognized with the clarity and precision of instinct of the child that he was still charged with magic and wonder. He was an example of a 'spy of God', to follow beyond the well-dug trenches of the aggressive Calvinist consciousness of our community into some no-man's land of the spirit where he had taken upon him the mystery of things. He, too, was from the beginning 'such stuff as dreams are made on' and had soldiered on in the field where the prophetic soul of the wide world also dreamed of things to come.

The essence of this is self-evident, I believe, and confirmed by the elements in the matter which first forced their way into my conscious imagination. I do not know how old I was when the first grit of external fact was placed in position and the pearl within began to form. All I know is that it was before the age of five when I first began to read by myself with an acceleration and absorption which surprised as well as somewhat alarmed the extrovert pioneering world into which I was born. It came in a way I still find significant, very soon after the visitation of the great comet in our star-sown sky, with months of earthquakes and great tremors of rock and ground and a terrible drought which still presides in my recollection as the greatest fear my being has ever encountered. Though the exact time cannot be determined, the moment itself is definite and clear.

I was being read to by my mother in the evening of one of the rare occasions she was at home. My father was still alive and a lawyer much in demand. As a politician and statesman he was away a great deal and she never failed to accompany him, because great and natural mother though she was, she knew that for all the assurance and authority with which he moved in the world, there was a neglected child in him that needed mothering, even more than her own children did. But when at home she gave us unendingly and impartially of herself with an unfailing abundance that still seems miraculous to me. One of her most precious ways of giving was through her love of stories and her gift of telling them with the capacity of total recall cultivated in her by the Hottentot and Bushman fragments of humanity who found asylum in my grandfather's home – 'Bushman's Spring'. She read superbly – so much so that the reading of the first of several books by Dickens, *Nicholas Nickleby*, lives on so clearly in my mind that I have never been tempted to re-read the book or see vamped-up versions of it on stage and television because my memory holds an experience that cannot be bettered and in a sense is sacred. But on this first occasion she was reading a story particularly chosen for me because she knew that I shared her own love of the aboriginal people of Africa and their stories in a way that none of her other children did. She knew especially that through the presence and influence of my first Bushman nurse, who went under the European name 'Klara' because her own was too difficult for ordinary pioneering tongues, my imagination was involved as much with the world of the Bushman as of the European.

It is worth pausing to note how early the coincidences came to crowd in on the imagination of the child that I was, perhaps as the signs of confirmation that the classical age of China held them to be. They came as unsolicited messengers bearing the wonder so necessary for the enlargement of the human spirit, and a sense of a reality too strange, as T. S. Eliot had it, for misunderstanding. First of all, there was 'Bushman's Spring'. It was built in the heart of great Bushman earth and within sight of what was once a precious source of unfailing Bushman water. On the hills beyond the spring there were the circles of stone walls raised by that great branch of Stone-age civilization, the Bushman of the plains, to protect them against the frost and thin winds of ice from the Basuto Mountains of the Night. The stone shelters were unroofed because rain was never abundant or regular, and was always welcome. My grandfather who had built 'Bushman's Spring' had frequently fought against the Bushman. He had helped to organize the raid that eliminated the last of the Bushmen in the southern Free State, except for two little boys, whom he took back to his home and, as little old men, were to be my companions when I was a child. Above all, there was my Bushman nurse, Klara. She said her name meant 'light', and, for me, she was bathed in wonder: the light of rainbow morning, a crystal day and magic lantern evening, playing on the bright blue beads of glass of a heavy necklace around the smooth apricot skin of her throat. I remember her face as one of the most beautiful I have ever known; oval, with a slightly pointed chin, high cheek bones, wide, large and rather slanted eyes full of a dark, glowing light as of the amber of the first glow on earth shining through the brown of evening on man's first day. These features gave her an oddly Chinese appearance especially as I never saw the thick, short, matted hair which was always wrapped in cottons of the brightest colours. No one ever shone more brightly in my emotions. She remained at the deep centre of the love of the feminine which has given me so much. Not even my mother meant so much to me although I loved and admired my mother so that all she gave me can be measured only by imponderables. Although she died more than twenty years ago, not a day goes by without its outstanding events compelling the thought, 'I must write and tell mother about it.'

As a result, this still, high-veld evening when Klara had put me to bed and held my hand while she listened as intently as I to my mother's reading, is near and alive, in spite of the more than seventy years that separates me from it. This shrill, brittle, self-important life of today is by comparison a graveyard where the living are dead and the dead are alive and talking in the still, small, clear voice of a love and trust in life that we have for the moment lost. She was reading to me the Wilhelm Bleek and Lucy Lloyd account of one of the greatest Bushman stories, 'The Lynx, the Hyena and the Morning Star'. This story had appeared in some learned journal in the Cape and I think it is so much a key Bushman story that I have retold it and assayed some of the riches it holds for me in *The Heart of the Hunter*. No detailed retelling of it is therefore necessary now. All I need as a frame for the portrait of the occasion is to define its theme as one of primordial jealousy. It is a story of the irresistible envy the ignoble are compelled always to have for the noble, the deprived for the enriched, the evil for the good and all that results from what my French grandmother called *nostalgie de la boue*. As such it is an orchestration in its own primitive counterpoint of the same pattern which sees Iago undo all that is brave in Othello and extinguish the beauty and innocence that is Desdemona.

The shape of the story is from beginning to end pure and true. It is of a perfect proportion of beauty that is for me always as alarming as it is enchanting. The Morning Star, the 'Foot of the Day' as Klara also called it, has chosen a female lynx as a bride. It was still the time before the coming of Mantis and his fire that frightened all natural things away and left man for the first time alone in the dark by his glowing coal. All on earth and in the universe were still members and family of the early race seeking comfort and warmth through the long, cold night before the dawning of individual consciousness in a togetherness which still gnaws like an unappeasable homesickness at the base of the human heart. No match of the masculine and feminine could have been more precise, or have a greater potential of harmony. Just as the Morning Star was the brightest and greatest hunter among the hunting stars of that hemisphere, the lynx, for the Bushman as for me, was the most star-like of animals on earth. The temptations for the Morning Star to make the wrong choice in the animal kingdom of Africa must have been almost overwhelming. There has never been another such kingdom to equal it in the numbers, wealth, variety, power, glory, beauty, tenderness and forcefulness of its natural subjects. Among the aristocratic cat families of Africa alone competition for the Morning Star's hand must have been formidable, and one considers the claims of the cats first because they walked alone in the forests of the night of Africa as the Morning Star hunted alone in the great plain of heaven on the rim between night and day. In such a position, with his experience of the power of the night and privileged vision into the heart of the light, the Morning Star caught the imagination of the first people of Africa in the meaningful and precise way which all the world's star-conscious mythologies have had a knack of doing.

Such an exalted element of heaven inevitably demanded to be joined to an equal and opposite life on earth. Only a cat who walked alone could be suitable for so fateful a joining of the most illuminated masculine transfiguration in heaven to the love of creation instinctive in the feminine earth. The claims of the lion in this regard must have been most powerful, plausible and eloquent because it too was a cat that went a way of its own and tended to be individual and specific among the crowds and herds of natural life in Africa. Moreover the lion combined such a formidable complex of talents, spirit and energies that he was universally accepted as the King of beasts of Africa and no feminine being could have ever been more fierce, urgent and triumphant in the cause of procreation of the natural life in Africa than the lioness.

But somehow such a marriage would have been disproportionate. The lion was too big, too physical, proud, domineering and self-sufficient and would have unbalanced any closer relationship with so sensitive and finely poised a being as the Morning Star. The leopard, too, had its own matchless qualities but again there were basic disproportions of size and hubris of appetite and aggression to make it unsuitable, not least of all in the matter of its spots. Who could imagine, as Klara explained after my mother's reading, making us laugh with relief at the clarity and authority of her interpretation, the Morning Star — unstained and clear cut as the diamond in my mother's ring presented to my father by de Beers on their engagement — going about with a fudged and spotty bride? No, it could only be the lynx.

I remember how this conclusion quickened my pulse and warmed me through because, young as I was, I had seen the lynx already and knew him well. We had a couple breeding happily as pets on our farm but even more, in a remote complex of the hills which cut across the centre of it, one of which was high enough to earn it the title of mountain, several families still lived unthreatened in their natural state. I had been taken many times by senior members of a family of nature worshippers just to observe them. There was one favourite place where trellises and lattices of shade plaited in thick screens of bright green broom and blue brushes, dark wild olives and touch-me-not shrubs were presided over by some giant Euphorbia, like candelabra in a Byzantine church. The intense shadow thrown by an immense overhang of rock going grey with time, rippled like a wind on the water of a deep pond. There, repeatedly, I had seen how bright with flame and quick with light and colour the lynx was, so that his movement in that dark surround was like the flicker and flame of a vestal lamp. It explained why no pioneer ever spoke of him by any other name than red-cat.

But no sooner had the fateful logic and harmony of the union of Morning Star and lynx been established than all was darkened by the intrusion of the shadow of shadows. The female hyena appeared out of the night that was native to the carrion of which it was the dark, dishonoured royalty and without pretence or shame walked into the scene, naked with jealousy of the lynx. The turmoil and heightening of drama implicit in this shadowy entry were immediate.

I knew the hyena as well as the Morning Star and the lynx. The mountain of which I have spoken was not for nothing called the Mountain of the Wolves. The wolf was the pioneering name for the large, striped, powerfully shouldered hyena which could deprive a cow of its udder with one snap of its jaws. Our mountain was full of them. I had come to know the hyena so well already that in the half-light of an early morning on a long journey by carriage and horse with my mother, I had looked one in the eyes from some two yards away as it stood among the bushes beside the road where we had stopped to give our horses a breather. Its eyes, made for the dark, were already blurred and it held its head still so that it could examine with its nose the air between us. That look

was one of my most unnerving experiences. It was especially frightening, because of a profound melancholy in the hyena's eye, beyond reason and reso-
lution, deepened with a knowledge that it could never walk openly as do all
other animals in a world of light. It was frightening, too, because it revealed a
terrible insecurity, a suspicion and sense of irrevocable exile unrelieved by any
hint of trust in life. It could trust nothing except its unsleeping cunning and
deviousness and there was thus no discernible centre of integrity around which
it could weave, like other animals, a permanent pattern of vivid being and doing.
Indeed, it was so utterly aboriginal that it was like chaos and old night made
flesh and blood, and forced me to turn away and hide my face in my mother's
lap, full of a fear which had no name. Many years later I was to encounter a
summing up of the experience in a Bushman expression, 'the time of the hyena',
used the day I heard it to describe a state of madness which unbearable tragedy
had imposed upon a young Bushman woman; and again still later for describing
moments when not only the light of the mind was invaded by darkness, but life
itself was overcast with the approach of the goodnight of death. To add to my
heightening apprehension, I recognized the dread power of jealousy.

However much the grown-up world might pretend to be immune to such
primordial urges, we children knew better. However angelic the best of us may
have looked, we were not in danger of thinking of ourselves as 'only babies
small, dropped from the sky'. This embarrassing euphemism featured in a song
popular among 'respectable' young women of the day who had been shamed
into using it by Calvinist indoctrination. Exposed to all the processes of birth,
procreation and death that went on around us in the natural world from the
moment we ourselves were born, we had a more realistic view of life. We, therefore, instantly recognized, feared and were perpetually perplexed by adult hypocrisy and prejudices in primordial things. We knew and both gloried and suffered
daily from the fact that we were as open and subject to storm from all the
primeval urges as the sea is to the great winds that travel the world and time.
How could I, for instance, as one of fifteen children, not begin with jealousy of
the child that displaced me? Had it not been that the love available in our own
vast family was impartially accessible and at the service of all, envy, jealousy
and competitiveness could have distorted us. But happily I could not recollect a
single act of parental favouritism. Scrutinizing the family record as I have over
many years, I am uplifted by it. It was not until my mother was dying that I
discovered that she had had a favourite after all without ever having succumbed
to favouritism.

One began to learn early, therefore, that this basic form of insecurity,
jealousy, could only be experienced without damage to oneself and others and
ultimately one can only be redeemed from it and the fears it engenders, by a kind
of emotion of self-courage. This has to be induced by reconciliation with the
valid needs of others living in an atmosphere of love. This selfless love was the
centre of our family. It remains an irrefutable social and individual premise, that
no culture has ever been able to provide a better shipyard for building storm-

proof vessels for the journey of man from the cradle to the grave than the individual nourished in a loving family. This, though, is still a mere abbreviation, but what I have said is perhaps enough to indicate the impact that the appearance of the hyena made on me and explain the gallop of fear that took over as it proclaimed its intention of breaking up the marriage of the Morning Star and taking the place of the lynx.

The way the hyena set about it was sheer black magic and so convincing that I had no need then for a conscious grasp of the universal symbolism of what was happening and of which I attempted a cursory exegesis in *The Heart of the Hunter*. By the power of her dark art, she transformed the food of the lynx into a poison that progressively deprived the lynx of her will and spirit to live. Each stage of the deterioration was illuminated in the story with a bright bead of detail, as in those necklaces the primitive world of Africa prepares in mourning for their dead, until the final and seemingly unavoidable eclipse of the lynx and her banishment into outer darkness were imminent, and my heart was almost black with dread. Then, suddenly, the hope which was almost at an end in me stirred again.

The world of fairy-tale and folklore proclaims with irrefutable accuracy that no matter how many evil feminine forces and wicked masculine ones in the shapes of ugly sisters, witches, giants, uncles, step-fathers and step-mothers combine against creation on earth, somewhere always there is something built into life to counter them: a small, often despised something, a mere Tom Thumb, a crumpled old man, a humble, simple peasant couple like Baucis and Philemon, or even just a being of potential nobility disguised as a repulsive toad. In the story of the lynx the good fairy appeared in the shape of the lynx's vigilant sister who acted immediately and decisively. Just as the apparently doomed lynx was cast out of her hut and the hyena moved in, the gallant sister went to warn the Morning Star and told him plainly that his light on earth, his love of the lynx, and the reality of his own feminine soul, was about to be extinguished. Just as the love that is feminine cannot endure without male amour, and male power has no meaning without a feminine soul to serve, so the Morning Star instantly recognized the universal implication of the hyena's threat to heaven and earth, and took instant action. Fitting an arrow to his bow, and spear in hand, the story describes in language worthy of Blake's 'tiger bright', how the Morning Star descends swiftly to the earth, his eyes full of the fire of a just anger. The violence of his approach sends the hyena rushing from the hut in great panic. Swerving to avoid the spear of the Morning Star, its hind leg catches on the coals of the fire which were burning as usual on the scooped-out place in front of the hut. The hyena was burned so badly that it was condemned to the lopsided walk that it still has to this day. From that moment the lynx recovered, was fully restored in her honour and affections and she and all manner of things were well.

I could not have been more relieved and happy by such an ending and embraced both my mother and Klara in tears of sheer joy. I was all the happier on

being assured that the reason why the Morning Star continues to sit with an
eye so bright between night and day is that he has learned the lesson that not
only are the forces of darkness and evil which the hyena personifies on earth
built into the foundations of the universe and indestructible, but also that it is
only by an exercise of everlasting vigilance on the frontiers of the mind that he
can defeat them and prevent a triumph of night over day.

The effect on me of this story was so great that I woke early in the dark next
morning, and slipped out of the karosses, the rugs of soft animal skins in which
I always slept in good weather outside on the wide verandah which surrounded
our home. For a moment I hesitated. The howl of the perpetual recurring
Ishmael element in life which is implicit in the voice of the hyena reached me
and seemed to change into a minor scale the major key of the music of the stars
which resounded over the vast full-leafed garden beyond. There stood the trees
in their long robes of leaves, priests of their natural kingdom, heads bowed as if
calling for prayer from the minaret of the world. For a moment I shivered with
an involuntary spasm of the fear that the hyena's role in the story had induced
in me the night before, but then I recalled the impulse which had delivered me
from sleep. I went slowly to the very edge of the raised verandah and looked
over and out to the east of the immense garden and there, just lifting itself clear
over the dark crown of fig trees by the wall around the orchard, was the Morning
Star. Perhaps as a result of the story, it appeared to me brighter than ever, its
eye fiercer. An arrow was fitted to its bow, a spear was in its hand and the tips
of arrow and spear were aimed at the area of darkness on earth where the hyena
had just given a howl of self-pity, complaint, carrion intent and shame for itself.
The rush of emotion was so great that it stays with me still. It provided the
nursery in which a great tree of conviction and abiding hope grew, and I was
confirmed in the knowledge that there is a vigilant and indestructible element
of light in life that transcends night and day on earth as in heaven.

As for the hyena, the villain of the piece, a strange regret in me because it was
not killed was slowly resolved. Over the years the hyena has taken its proper
position in my mind. I realized why it had to live and have a hind leg permanently marked by fire. Fire was to become the great image of consciousness for
me and that seal of fire on the hyena was an assurance that the evil it represents
has been clearly marked. It is a sign of our conscious knowledge and experience
of the living reality and power of evil. For all its dominion in the night of our
unawareness and lack of vigilance, evil is so marked that man is free at last to
choose between light and dark, good and evil; a freedom not of escape or evasion
but a heightening of man's obligations to creation.

All this and much more was in the seed sown in me by a Bushman story
heard at a very early age. It is the most striking and unanswerable evidence of
man's need for enrolment in a true story if he is to endure and live his way towards his life's answer. The very next day, by a process of restless questioning
from me and solicitous answers from Klara and my mother, I learned how
Wilhelm Bleek and Lucy Lloyd had collected many stories such as this.

They drew them out of a group of little Bushmen convicts, condemned to the hardest labour: work on a new breakwater in Cape Town harbour. The crime had only been one of killing, when hungry, a sheep from one of the large flocks owned by men, white and black, who had stolen all their land from them. One of the most prolific sources of stories was a little Bushman called Xhabbo – a name meaning Dream, which Klara hastened to explain was a not uncommon Bushman name, because what could be more manly and responsible than to be connected to a dream. In due course I was given a copy of a colour portrait of Xhabbo of the Dream. It is still with me, together with a snapshot of a Bushman taken in the heart of the Kalahari some thirty-five years after Xhabbo first came into my reckoning. I keep the Kalahari photograph because it is of the hunter who told me one day when, greedy for more stories, I had exhausted him with questions, 'You see it is very difficult because there is a dream dreaming us.' And what could be closer to Shakespeare's prophetic soul, dreaming of things to come?

From that moment of illumination from the light of a star story, my appetite for Bushman stories, myth and legend grew and I clamoured for more. For years Klara and my mother complied. And as my interest in Bushman stories grew, the attractions of the fairy-tales of the Western world which were also thrust on me lessened, only the Greek myths and stories from the Old Testament still holding my imagination. It was not that I despised the Brothers Grimm, Hans Christian Andersen, or Andrew Lang but their characters were comparatively pale and remote proxies of those of men, animals and plants that were the heroic and anti-heroic material and settings of the Bushman stories. These were peopled with an immense cast of characters from the physical world into which I had been born and were the essential stuff of my imagination, dreams and being. There were even times when I felt sorry for European children fed on such anaemic food, so deprived of the trace-elements and forms of natural life that were lightning conductors of miracle and magic in my childhood. The more complex stories and literature of the West only moved into my imagination when the last Bushman story had been told.

Even then I seemed to know that the written literature which dominated my education and imagination was a mere dwarf poised on the shoulders of a giant of unwritten and oral literature that preceded it. It could never have had the meaning it possesses for me were it not for the stories of the living world which the Bushman had so reverently prepared for me. These stories, populated by the vivid natural life I understood and loved, remain with me. What I love most about them is that they are never obvious, and are intuitively Shakespearian in their wisdom. The Bushmen are never taken in by mere appearances and surface attractions. For instance, they are immune to the blasphemies of size, numbers and giant power and they do not measure the significance of man or beast by the ability to overcome and destroy those weaker than themselves. The heroes of the Bushmen, indeed, were almost invariably drawn from the physically insignificant.

The Stone-age civilization, of which I heard echoes in the Bushman stories of my childhood, spread over the greater part of southern Africa. It existed wherever the Bushman had enough permanent water and sufficient rain to make the earth fruitful. In Africa, nutritious roots, bulbs, tubers, wild fruit, nuts and berries grew in abundance. In no other continent was there so much game to be had. Consequently, the Bushman's struggle for survival was never so desperate as to engage the whole of his days. He had the leisure even to gather and add to his food an archaic honey that was like light on darkness and brought sweetness to the many rough and bitter tastes endured by his spartan palate. Typically he raised the search for honey into a kind of sacramental adventure. He joined to him as allies, not only the bird known as the honey-guide, one of the most miraculous elements of the air, a prototype of Ariel almost, but also the ratel or honey-badger, a Calibanesque phenomenon so close to the earth and its plants as to be almost clay made flesh. There was a magic and religious revelation in this alliance and to see it in successful action as I have been privileged to do, is to be overawed by a sense of how near the first men were to the miraculous. From the beginning, the human being was devoutly involved with nature.

Perhaps uniquely, therefore, the Stone-age Bushman had leisure and this explains why and how he could evolve the richest and most complex form of Stone-age civilization in Africa. That is why in *The Heart of the Hunter* I turned to the record of Bushman civilization and gave it preference over others I knew as well. I use the word 'civilization' rather than culture deliberately because of the Bushman's extraordinary achievement in the detail of his daily routine, and in the realm of the spirit through his myths, legends, stories, music, dancing and paintings. They are all without trace of the hubris to which Greek, Roman and Hebraic man were so prone that they feared it as the greatest source of evil. The inspiration of Bushman painting embraced not only 'magical' aspirations but all aspects of man and his surroundings, from the immediacies of his day to the most complex and subtle intimations of reality and immortality. Specialists in this field are usually not artists themselves. They tend to approach their subject with the preconceived attitudes imposed on them by the basic assumptions of their own discipline, conceived in a cultural context that could not be more remote and alien to that of the Bushman. I know of none among those who have written on Bushman art, for instance, who has thought it necessary to acquire in depth a knowledge of symbolism, comparative mythology and psychology. They need to recognize that the dream is the gateway to the meaning of our prehistoric past on which our sense of continuity and the totality of history depends. Indeed history is nothing if it is not so illuminated. Life is made intuitive and instinctive and inscribed in the forgotten language of the dream and its symbols. Dreams finally are the main instruments with which the meaning and achievement of Stone-age culture can be decoded, and the quintessential humanity of the Bushman unlocked. Indeed the Bushman was and, to an extent, remains what we, increasingly cut off from our natural selves and the little that is left of the natural world, can only dream of today. It is a constant source of amazement and of hope to me, that I have not been to a continent or island from East to West, where I have not found that when men fall asleep something like the Bushman awakes and beckons them.

Happily my introduction to the larger Stone-age man came at a time when he had not altogether vanished. I had only to ask and stretch out my hand to hear his authentic voice and touch his warm, smooth, apricot skin, and be startled by the electricity of immediate, utter humanity with which it sparked and against which we, in an arrogance of mind and hubris of our technological mastery of nature, are insulated. An illustration of this impoverished approach to Stone-age man, for instance, can be found in the work of a most worthy scholar who has dedicated his life to a study of Bushman painting and yet describes perhaps the greatest and certainly most tragic story ever told by the Bushman, as one of the funniest he has ever read. I feel certain this is because his studies were conducted in ignorance of the symbolism, mythology and, above all, the cypher of dreams in which their meaning is encoded.

It was not surprising that as my fund of stories grew, there were moments when the line so arbitrarily drawn by the exactions of contemporary consciousness between waking and dreaming seemed to vanish. I would often feel as if I were on an enchanted island in the sea of time at the still centre of the terrible storms, the aftermath of war, unrest, loss of faith and the prelude to an eventful catastrophic sequel which dominated the world of my parents. On this island I was surrounded with strange music and through these stories, it was as if the clouds for me too had opened as they had done even on Shakespeare's Caliban and allowed unimagined riches and splendours to pour over me, so that I wondered whether I was really awake and longed to sleep and dream again.

These stories were increasingly dominated by the Praying Mantis, the Hottentots' god as my ancestors called him when they landed at the Cape of Good Hope three hundred years ago. They attributed him to the pastoral Hottentots, an ancient nomadic people of Africa who were closest to the Bushman. Had they paused to ask the Bushman and tried to throw the tenuous bridge of a desire for comprehension across the abyss of spirit and being which divided them from him, they would have known that the Mantis was a Bushman and not a Hottentot god.

The Hottentots had their own highly evolved image of a god, subtle, complex, most evocative and, for me, intensely moving and real. They called him Heitse-Eibib and saw him in the red of the dawn which they held to be the blood of the wounds he had incurred in his everlasting battle with night for day. I was surrounded in childhood by even more Hottentot than Bushman survivors because the place where I was born was once the capital of what we as children thought of as the Kingdom of the Griquas, one of the last coherent Hottentot clans driven into the interior by the white tide of immigration from the Cape to the north. In the process they were subjected by well-meaning missionaries to a strange injection of biblical myths and stories which did not eliminate Heitse-Eibib but merely drove him intact to the core and inner keep of their spirit. They not only showered stories about him on me but at moments of crisis and emphasis still swore in his name. He became so real to me that I found poetic justice and continuity in the fact that he should follow in the spoor of the Morning Star, an heroic and wounded protagonist of light in the van of the passing-out parade of the military academy of the sky. I learned to feel his presence in the wind which stirred the leaves of the wild olives and great broom bushes where I crouched with burning cheeks and smarting, bare feet for relief from the heat of the great flaming days of summer. The Griquas had taught me his spirit was also always in the wind. But he would be most near me when I contemplated one of the heaps of smooth pebbles piled high in his honour in places from what is Zululand in the southeast today to where the mythological sun went down in the far west over deep ancient river-beds that run no more and where his people are no longer known. These piles were raised by Hottentots bound, out of their constant awareness of what was due to their sense of creation, to deposit pebbles in recognition of Heitse-Eibib's all-pervasive presence and help, wherever they had forded a river or stream. In my childhood those pebbles were as much wayside shrines to me as those encountered by knights of the Round Table and Holy Grail on their quest.

Knowing the stories they had evoked in the Hottentot imagination, the piles of pebbles were more sacred to me than the Calvinist churches I was marched into like a young recruit by the implacable sergeant-majors of law-bound elders thrice on Sundays. They produced a sense of the mystery of creation far more intense than anything in the Bible, many as were the stories in that Book that I loved. Many Bible stories in any case did not contradict or make implausible either Mantis or Heitse-Eibib, but placed them as neighbours in the inner propinquity of the authentic dimension of religious experience. In this regard, it could be said that by the time I reached the ripe old age of five, I was either as confused or enlightened and enriched by this exciting input of stories from these aboriginal sources as any Hottentot. More consciously and most important, I found them a great bridge from the primordial world of the child into the here and now of a rapidly growing boy. All I know for certain is that from birth I was exposed to influences of spirit which turned me into something new and strange which was native to Africa but not totally of it, compounded with something that made me also of Europe without being in it. And there I have always left it, without definition of myself, because the matter is doomed to be either indefinable or capable only of definition when it will have been fully lived out into the answer that we are all contracted to seek at birth.

But to return to the coming of Mantis. I dwelt on his comparison with the god of the Hottentots because the myths of Heitse-Eibib which reached me simultaneously joined in a preparation of the earth on which this great seed saga of the Bushman was to fall and take prodigious growth. I deliberately call this a seed saga because I accepted intuitively, implicitly, and without any hint of doubt what I now know consciously for fact, as the circle of a long life rounds, that each of the stories which composed it carried the seed of new being and increased awareness. Why this is so I do not know. 'Why' in any case is a severely limited question as the child discovers from the moment it begins to talk. It produces limited answers, limited as a rule to the mechanics and laws of the world, universe and life of man. But the human heart and mind come disheartingly quickly to their frontiers and need something greater to carry on beyond the last 'why'. This beyond is the all-encompassing universe of what the Chinese called Tao and a Zen Buddhist friend, in despair over the rationalist premises native to Western man, tried to make me understand as a newly-graduated man by calling 'the great togetherness' and adding, 'in the great togetherness there are no "whys", only "thuses" and you just have to accept as the only authentic raw material of your spirit, your own "thus" which is always so.' In and out of these great togethernesses it came to appear to me that the story brings us a sense of this unique 'so' that is to be the seed of becoming in ourselves during the time which is our lot.

This is what gives the artist in the story-teller his meaning and justification to go on telling his story, and sustains him, despite a lack of material reward or recognition, in poverty and hunger. Even though his work falls on stony ground and deaf ears or is trodden under the indifferent feet of the proliferating generations too busy to live in their frantic search for the joys and hopes of gaining the honours of the plausible world about them, this radar of the story never fails him. He does not even try to know but through an inborn acceptance of the demands of the gift which entered him at birth, spins his story in the loom of his imagination. The life in him knows that once a story is truly told, the art which this mysterious gift places at his disposal shall, when the time is ready – and the readiness is all – find listeners to take it in; their lives will be enlarged and the life even of the deaf and dumb around them will never be the same again.

This is the reason why parables are such irresistible seed stories, and the reason also, I believe, why Christ preferred to use them rather than hand out moralistic rules and recipes for human conduct. This is why, despite the scholar he was, Christ never committed himself to writing but totally to the living word, knowing that the word that was in the beginning would transform life in a way which no written word, however inspired, could. It gives one meaning to his remark that he had come to transcend the great laws which had preceded him. This, too, was the way the first masters of Zen stretched the narrow and pointed awareness of their long troubled age in China and Japan, and so restored imagination to its pilgrim self. This is why almost the first question asked by the child after it has been fed is, 'Mother, please tell me a story' and the mother, without question, complies.

In all this we are in the presence of a great mystery which does not induce mystification but a life-giving sense of wonder out of which all that man has of religion, art and science is born. It is a cosmic area and therefore universal to man and there is no dignified place here for presumptions like the Descartian, 'I think, therefore I am'. In the presence of this mystery at the heart of these great 'togethernesses', the human being knows how small is the area within himself where thinking is at the disposal of conscious will and preconceived purposes. He does not think so much himself but is compelled to be an instrument of life through which something beyond articulation initiates the thinking. The German language, though it may dive deeper and sometimes come up muddier and less clear than the lucid French, has acquired out of this plumbing Teutonic tendency the virtue of surfacing with incomparable expressions for these great intangibles that in time move mountains of imperviousness. It speaks of this mystery as an *Ein-fall* — literally a 'fall-in' which we call 'inspiration'. One does not want to diminish the value of the word 'inspiration' since it is a reality but it suggests something rare and privileged, whereas I believe it is as ever-present and natural to all men as breathing in and out, since it too seeks night and day to fall, as it were, into the mind and spirit; and from there it is breathed out through words, images and symbols to be transformed into behaviour. Mozart and Beethoven, if I remember rightly, use it in regard to their own work and Beethoven wrote of how he had to dream twice of one of his most moving pieces of music before he became obedient enough to the dream to compose it. Some such elaboration, which is minimal in relation to the vast orchestration of the theme available in the history of the human spirit, is necessary, I believe, to establish the primary importance of the role of the spirit and to silence the sophisticated, watch-dog mind which raises a frantic, baying storm of alarm when any form of awareness which is not rationally, logically and substantially demonstrable, approaches the door of contemporary intellect. Yet it all could still benefit, I feel, from two contemporary illustrations in depth; one basic, primitive and positive, and the other sophisticated and negative, and both significant in the process of the fermentation of Bushman yeast in my own spirit.

The first arises from a discussion I had with Jung about Bushman stories and my belief that whole civilizations had been destroyed because their stories had been taken away from them by the intrusion of a physically powerful and alien culture. At the end of an account still fresh because I had just come from the Kalahari Desert, he nodded his fine white head as the wind released a far-off refrain among the leaves of the trees he had planted as a young man at Bollingen, because they were living and viable thoughts of God to him. He went on, in that deep bass voice of his, to tell me at great length, how his work as a healer did not take wing — the metaphor is mine — until he realized that the key to the human personality was its story. Every human being at core, he held, had a unique story and no man could discover his greatest meaning unless he lived and, as it were, grew his own story. Should he lose his story or fail to live it, he lost his meaning, became disorientated, the collective fodder of tyrants and despots, or ended up, as so many did, alienated and out of their own minds, as had the patients in the Burghölzli Asylum to whom he owed this insight and who, despite the label of madness — tied like millstones round their necks by a criminal exercise of the power of conscious conformity passing for normality — had enriched his own life and work.

Indeed he told me ·of such a patient, a young woman who opened his medically sound spirit to this 'fall-in' and 'insight'. He had been warned against her by the other doctors who said she had been silent for years and could be dangerous. But as he watched her — often with the great father sun shining from beyond the high walls of the asylum through the leaves of the trees and occasionally weaving a halo as of gold around her head — deprived of voice, his colleagues believed for ever, he could not accept that this need be so. Something in him held that she could be restored to the light of her own day. But what and how? One day, watching her, there came the relevant 'fall-in'. She was making certain movements, when an irresistible urge came to him to go up to her, make the same movements, close his eyes and say whatever came into his head. Obedient he went towards her.

And here I must interrupt to add that real religious experience is not possible without a response to a glimmering of new awareness, however improbable and absurd, since it is always too mysterious and wonderful for understanding. In such a spirit of sheer obedience to the 'fall-in', Jung did just that and as he spoke a suspicious conscious self just had time, so immediate had been his response, to suggest that he might now be provoking the dangerous reactions of which his colleagues had warned him. But to his joy he heard a low feminine voice ask, 'But how did you know?'

From that moment, contact was established and communication grew so that they could speak of her dreams.

It was sixty years later when, piloted by this deep-sea navigator we call chance, I came across her case history meticulously kept in Jung's always young hand. Already, then, dreams were used in a way that surpassed any doctrinaire Freudian or other approach to the dreaming process, and confirmed in detail his description to me of how within six months, he could rule, despite powerful opposition from colleagues, that she should return to the sun and the world. But on her last morning before he signed the order of her release — and until then I felt I had never experienced the full meaning of 'order of release' — he called her to his office.

'Are you not anxious about going out into the world today?' he asked her solicitously.

'Of course I am,' she answered, aggressive with fearfulness.

'Did you have any dreams last night?' he asked.

'Yes, I did,' she answered, paused and added most emphatically with a good peasant adjective thrown in which I can only transcribe as 'bloody well', 'And for once I am bloody well not going to tell you what they were.'

The expression of joy on Jung's face at this point lives with me still and his voice was a chord of music as he concluded, 'You see, at last her dreams were her own, her story was her own again.'

He told me that he was never to see her again but he heard that she had gone with the years out of their sight without need of help or treatment again from 'the likes' of him.

So here was the positive confirmation of the importance which, without my knowing it in my childhood, the story of the Bushman had for me and for my own order of release.

As for the negative illustration, it belongs inevitably to my own deprived and diminished day. When I came to telling stories myself and the years went round like the swivels of lighthouses in the dark of the main behind me, I became apprehensive about the decline of the story in its most relevant and contemporary form, and its reduction to more and more archaic expressions in the cold, brutal sensation and action dominated fiction denied of soliloquy and inward vision. Stories were increasingly being strung along on thin, arbitrary threads of a bleak curiosity without a twist of fantasy, feeling and wonder in their making, or worst of all, reduced to adroit and nimble paperchases of intellect. They were written computer-wise without regard for humanity and its flesh and blood to give them life, as if all were mind – and the metamorphic spirit had no part in it. It struck me as a symptom of a deep and alarming sickness in the heart of our time, a loss of soul as the primitive companions of my boyhood would have called it, and as such an erosion of the power of increase and renewal that we and our societies so desperately needed. What or where, I wondered with increasing dismay, had all the stories gone? Why this decay of the great and meaningful orchestration of the story that had occurred everywhere in the nineteenth and beginning of the twentieth centuries? What made eminent critics say complacently and with an assumption of ultimate authority, 'The novel is dead', as if it were some kind of archaic technology of the imagination, to be superseded by something more up to date? I knew writers with imaginations so bankrupt that they no longer gave birth to the characters of their stories but went to research them in the world about them. There was no metamorphosis of fiction which is art but rather sociological essays on people without a breath of invention or fantasy to give life to them.

In the theatre, too, where some of the greatest stories of all have been enacted, not only the people who wrote for it but also distinguished talents in the service of the story in play like the Sybil Thorndike of my early years in London, declared, 'The theatre is dead'. Critics on the subject can be discounted, in a sense, unless they are writers of stories themselves, but the alarm could not be overlooked when these symptoms appeared among considerable novelists of the day like, for example, E. M. Forster. I quote him because I knew him and had admired his sensitive, compassionate, humane and original approach to the life of his time and always thought it tragic that what I believe was a fragmentation of spirit diminished contact between the artist in him and his natural self, and made him less creative than he could have been. I quote him, therefore, not to criticize or judge him in terms of what he could not be but strictly because I must evaluate what he said about the story on the magisterial level of the artist in him and the art to which he dedicated his life. In an essay of great merit called – with a modesty that was as admirable as it was unusual in a self-confident day – *Aspects of the Novel*, he asks the question, 'Must the novel tell a story?' and answers it to the effect that, 'Oh dear, yes, the novel must tell a story.' This answer to a vital question tells us a great deal more about E. M. Forster than the novel. He was through and through an 'Oh dear, yes' man, condemned never to be full-throated but capable at the most of 'the two cheers' of his celebrated remark: a ration of cheers, one suspects, that might have been uttered as an unenthusiastic 'Hurrah' not preceded by any 'hip-hip-hips'.

All this was brought acutely to my mind when I returned from the Second World War and saw Forster for the first time after a number of years. I went to fetch him from Benjamin Britten's home at Aldeburgh where he was already discussing the libretto for the composer's opera about Melville's Billy Budd as well as taking part in a special Festival evening. We went for a long walk on the wall beside the estuary which was the model of the water in Britten's *Curlew River*. The wall was raised above the Alde and the marshes were still wild and abundant with natural life and not plundered as they are today, almost like the invisible scene of the scorched earth of the modern spirit made visible. It was still early summer with the air a misty luminous yellow and the larks in such good voice that we could barely hear each other speak. He told me then he proposed reading an unfinished story of his to the Festival audience that night. I remember a strange quickening of intuition at the news and feeling hopefully, 'then the story must still live for him and this urge to tell it in public a sign to him and all of us that it wants to be finished and lived.'

I heard the story for the first time then with increasing emotion and ended by being profoundly impressed with its significance and urgency. It was, I remember, then called 'Arctic Summer'. I said to him that I found the fragment — because it was only the prelude of a story I had heard — one of the most important things he had ever written and begged him to set everything aside and finish it.

He shook his head sadly, almost tragically, and said with an 'Oh dear' nuance in his voice: 'I shall never finish it!'

I pleaded with him then and argued through the days that followed that all who had heard it found it important and wanted it finished. More, I urged him, despite signs of growing agitation in him, it was vital to him as a man and artist to finish the story. So why, oh why not?

'I cannot,' he declared finally with an emphasis highly dramatic in a man whose disposition excluded dramatics: 'I cannot because I do not like the way it will have to finish'.

The remark for me proved both how natural stories were to him and how acute was his sense of their significance, but at the same time revealed that his awareness was inadequate for the task the story imposed on it. It had to abort the story almost as soon as its conception was assured and an advancing pregnancy diagnosed. An irresistible and an immovable force had met and a condition of self-nihilism established. Yet I said no more. Perhaps for good or ill I realized this something was concerned with what Virgil called 'error inextricabilis', an error so profound that even some virtue can be dependent on it.

It was perhaps the explanation for why he never was more than he was. He had failed the story in him since he could not bend it to his own will and partialities. It was for me accordingly a most telling illustration of the power or forces at the disposal of the story in us and how the human spirit declines when they are denied. It remains one of the most illuminating experiences on my own doorstep of time of the sort of cancer of artifice, rationalism and one-sided spirit that is denying man the fulness of his own nature and devouring the cells of renewal and re-creation that are kept alive and dynamic in him by his story, his readiness to obey the story and to add his mite to it.

And here the last word on the subject, like the first, is with the Bushman. They are words spoken by Xhabbo, the Dream, who I have already mentioned. He was a convict – a man whom the establishment of European civilization had utterly in its power, and had not only violated his age-old right of occupation in his native land, but had also dishonoured his natural spirit, judged and punished him with the most extreme form of punishment short of death by hanging. He had been reprieved only as a result of the endeavour of this remarkable old German scholar I have mentioned. This old scholar noticed one day that Dream was sitting by himself deeply absorbed, silent and with a tragic expression on his face. Concerned, he asked what troubled him. Instantly there came from him who had never heard of, let alone known the Heidelberg and Cambridge which fathered the scholars and Forsters of this world, these words which remain for me the greatest statement ever uttered on the story. This is what Xhabbo, and the dreamer dreaming through him, said to the scholar he called master:

> Thou knowest that I sit waiting for the moon to turn back for me, so that I may return to my place; that I may listen to all the people's stories . . . that I may sitting listen to the stories which yonder came, which are stories that come from a distance, for a story is like the wind, it comes from a far-off quarter and we feel it. Then I shall get hold of a story . . . For I am here, I do not obtain stories; I feel that people of another place are here, they do not possess my stories. They do not talk my language . . . As regards myself I am waiting that the moon may turn back for me, that I may set my feet forward in the path, having stepped around backwards . . . I must first sit a little, cooling my arms that the fatigue may go out of them, because I sit and listen, watching for a story which I want to hear; while I sit waiting for it that it may float into my ear. I must wait listening behind me for when a man has travelled along a road and sits down he waits for a story to travel to him, following him along the same road . . . I will sit at my place, that I may listening turn backwards with my ears to my heels on which I went, while I feel that a story is the wind.

Even to this day I do not know how to describe the emotions these words and the long statement that followed caused in me. It can be measured best perhaps by the fact that both the light and the shadow they cast over me has not decreased but has become more intense as I have grown older. I remember as clearly as ever the moment – how I was sitting high on my favourite perch among the broad leaves of a gigantic mulberry tree planted in the centre of our immense garden some seventy years before by my grandfather. It was so high, wide and dense that no one looking upwards from underneath could see me, while the view over the orchard, all aglow with peaches, apricots, plums, cherries, pears, apples, quinces, pomegranates, purple and emerald grapes, contained between long walls of spreading fig trees planted in foursomes side by side to protect the fruit from the searing air which the burning hills of summer and the hot broad vale in their keeping breathed over them, all gave me a feeling as if I and the story were part of the beginning in the garden which our devout and constant Biblical induction, let alone our instincts, would never allow us to forget.

And then instantly the tragedy implicit in the scene and the meaning in Xhabbo's statement would join forces and become too much for my self-control with a sorrow too profound for tears. The scene, of course, had to come into the mood of the moment, because its fountains, and the stream of the otters, as the Bushman called it, which cut the garden in two but which also gave it the waters to nourish those alien trees and plants of Europe and China, had once made it great Bushman country. There was hardly a crest, ridge or dent in it which Klara had not endowed with some story or association with the history of her people. Yet, like the otters, the Bushman had vanished from the scene and left it as vacant and melancholy as a graveyard in which the mounds had been flattened and where only the walls remained, slowly crumbling, unattended and deconsecrated in the minds of their unnatural heirs and successors. A something without shape or name went through the calm and silence, so intense that there came to my ears a sound as of the congregation of blood singing deep within of unfailing metamorphosis to which even these broad Chinese leaves among which I sat bore witness by translation through worm into silk. The Bushman may have gone forever but whatever it was that had made him and fashioned his spirit remained undefeated in that earth and sky.

Of course, I do not pretend that on occasions such as this – and there were many – that I was capable of expressing my reaction in words such as these but they and much else beside were there as feelings only bearable because of their potential of catharsis and transfiguration which never left me. Evidence of how active all this was within me is to be found in a story that I wrote at the age of eight after my own father died. The story, to use the term which I defined at the beginning, fell into my imagination late in September 1914, despite its preoccupation then with the shattering impact of my father's death, the outbreak at the same moment of the First World War and a civil war which divided our large family against itself. The story, moreover, dropped in to me with such force that I had to obey it despite a theme which even I feared would appear so trivial to my elders and betters that I wrote the story in secret, and to this day have never shown or spoken of it to anyone. I thereby unknowingly set the pattern which I have followed ever since: not to let the world, not even its most trusted and beloved persons, sit in on what I am trying to create until I have done.

In this and many other ways the writing of this little story is perhaps the most important thing I have ever done. It was the first pilot scheme not only for my own vocation of writing but for my general behaviour and most things of meaning to me. It marked the beginning of an awareness that one's own small contribution to creation demanded the answering of apparently insignificant, improbable and, in the eyes of the world into which I was born, totally useless calls from within my imagination. I might even say in hindsight that obedience to the private and most intimate summons of imagination is to live symbolically and religiously: not so much by rational calculation and prescription, much as they are needed in the service of this obedience, but as if one were following the flight of a bird. I often shudder to think what would have become of me had I not allowed the will of this intangible to take over that September morning and confer a certain 'freedom of the borough' of the here and now on me as nothing else could have done. Although there have been times when I argued that the spirit of creation is infinite and would have given me other opportunities to seize on, I believe the process of education which already had me firmly in its grip, would have undermined the trust in the universal memory and instinctive knowledge of creation we bring into the world at birth and impaired my capacity to follow their improbable intimations as I obeyed them then and have tried to since.

This was the story which needs only some explanation as to why the 'flower', at the heart of the story, meant so much to me. September is the kindest of our months. It is the beginning of spring and towards the end of the month, if the season is good, it sees the appearance of the wild freesia in the hills and rocky ridges of the native interior. Since this part is exceptionally arid, the manifestations of spring produced there are bleak and deprived compared to the eruption and violence of flower, leaf and grass in England. The appearance of this rare and beautiful flower, therefore, had a miraculous effect on all of us — young, old, white, yellow and black. It was far more beautiful than the fat, lush, multi-coloured freesias on sale in Europe. It was clean-cut in shape and clear in colour and light as a star at midnight in a moonless sky of the southern hemisphere. Only at the bottom of its cup did it hold some distillation of the blue of heaven and a suggestion of the shades befitting a herald of a dawn also in the darkness of our black earth. Its scent, which for me is still incomparable, was both more intense and more subtle than the product the horticulturalists create in the belief that they can improve on nature. Indeed at night, when the dew began to fall, this scent would rise and travel the land and bring a sacramental quintessence to our senses. The scent combined with its star-like quality to make us call the flower not freesia but by its ancient Bushman name of 'evening flower'. Perhaps for a full understanding of this impact one has to consider how harsh and demanding the soil of Africa is; how powerful and in many ways ruthless a land it is, a giant among the continents of the globe. Yet it applies this power also to the protection of something so vulnerable and blessed as the evening flower. It explains, perhaps, as nothing else can, why we who are of Africa are bound to it and find it so great a source of wonder. It is not least of all because, even though it raises mountains to the moon, spreads outsize lakes among them, sends long rivers to the sea and rejoices in the creation of animals great and small, from the lion and elephant to the gazelle and springbok, it does not forget the fundamental significance for creation overall of the small, and the power of the minute of which the freesia with its star-light and scent of heaven at night-fall is plenipotentiary and which is at the heart of this Stone-age matter.

As a result, throughout September my generation would scout the vast land about them for freesias and when the first scouts returned with the news that the freesias were beginning to appear, everyone who could walk or even toddle, made for the hills in the afternoon and came back in the twilight carrying bunches of freesias like phosphorescent flares in their hands. Within days of their flowering the village was perfumed all over from dusk to dawn with the smell of freesias.

In this catastrophic September of the paradoxical year of our Lord 1914, freesias were unusually late in coming. This explains perhaps why my story begins with the fear of a young boy called Pierre, that no freesias would ever come again. This fear became so intense that it woke him early one morning and sent him off in haste to the hills. After a desperate search he found one sprig of freesia in bud. He resisted the temptation to pick it and hastened home where he refused to say why he had been gone so long. Early the next morning, he went to visit the freesia again and already it had begun to open and spray incense on the cool air. On a second morning the one flower had been joined by two more and left only one bud to unfold. On the third morning Pierre hastened back, excited by the prospect of seeing the bloom fulfilled only to find an animal had stepped on and flattened it just before his arrival. The shock was so great that he began to cry but then in the midst of crying he heard a voice saying beside him, 'Look up!'

Startled because he had thought himself alone and abandoned, he glanced in the direction of the voice. An old Bushman with a head of mottled grey hair, stood close behind him and repeated the injunction to look up. He did so and in the precise blue of a clear September morning directly above the crushed flower a small cloud was forming.

'Your flower is there helping to make a cloud for the rains to come. It will utterly flower one day again when its cloud joins the clouds to come and the rain has been made to fall.'

I have no doubt today that the story, expressed in the symbolism which night and day urges man into an enlargement of his being through an increase of his awareness, was telling me that the disaster all around us at the time was not the end and that the flower showed how creation was always a jump or more ahead of death.

But, of course, I did not analyse the story and failed to see any connection with the fact that once it was written I had made my peace with my father's sudden death, the World War and the civil war in our midst. But I never forgot it and even found comfort in it twenty-eight years later when I was told one night in a Japanese cell in Java that I was to be executed the next morning.

However, long before that I had inklings of how my little story could have more than a subjective reality and how it had grown out of the authentic first seed of Africa in my own native and aboriginal earth. One, for instance, was a statement made to Bleek about clouds by a Bushman in the course of a discussion on death. 'The hair of our head will resemble clouds when we die . . .' he told Bleek. 'We who know, we are those who think thus, while we feel that we seeing recognize the clouds, how the clouds in this manner form themselves . . .'

The connection between crushed evening flower and its translation into cloud then seemed more like part of a message of unfailing resurrection sent straight out of the earth of Africa to all life and greatly raised my conscious appreciation of the significance of the story. Hard on this came Xhabbo's great observation on the story and its connection with the wind that is our greatest image of the spirit of creation, indeed the only one which can explain our dread over the calm which enveloped the ship of Coleridge's Ancient Mariner and the surge of hope within our hearts and minds when at the end of Valéry's finest poem, 'The Graveyard of Sailors', we hear as a Reveille on a far-off bugle: 'Le vent se lève, il faut tênter vivre (The wind rises, one must try to live).'

All this combined to produce an unwavering emotion of revelation of the Pentecostal nature of the story and a full understanding why, as Xhabbo's statement to Bleek made plain, he was far more homesick for stories than people or places. Ultimately Xhabbo needed stories more than people and implied that they were a food without which the life of his spirit would die, destroying even the unique love of life of his kind and their will to live no matter what the odds. So when I began writing my first improbable long book on a little Mediterranean island, a place which, like Xhabbo's, was not my own and where, though the time for telling stories had come at home, I no longer 'obtained them'. Remembering this, I was back at once with Klara and my mother. In the undimmed recollection of what they told me I found unbroken the continuity between the writing my estranged grown-up self was attempting and the stories of my beginning, and the courage to work on my own unlikely and untried story.

The characters in these Bushman stories were, with rare exceptions, always insects, birds and animals and the most heroic chosen from among the small, insignificant forms of life, alien and abhorrent to European and Bantu senses and imagination. It was impressive how the first imagination of Africa rejected the great, imposing, splendid, powerful and glittering animals from its treasury. The elephant, rhinoceros, hippopotamus, lion, leopard, baboon, the hyena indeed, figured in his stories, sometimes prominently, but, even when respected, never in the Bushman's affections and innermost imagination. It was here that his sense of purpose and energies of creation were husbanded and grew great in his sense of the infinite in the small, like that of the Blake who had seen 'infinity in a grain of sand'.

The extraordinary forms of being that populated the world of Bushman stories were part of my own life, known to me personally, almost socially, a living texture of my own imagination; the beetles, lizards, house-mice, field, short-nosed, striped and long-nosed mice; birds, like the numinous hammerkop (hammerhead) charged for the Bushman with extra-sensory perception; his 'sister the vulture'; the blue crane; 'go-away birds'; honey-guide and countless others; the bee ants, ratel (honey-badger), hare, chameleon, porcupine, jackal, rock rabbit, mongoose; the cat family among which only the lynx was an image of his love of light; the steenbok, springbok and on through the immense antelope families where his heart ranged wide and free between large and small. Though most of all he concentrated on the beloved little gazelle, the springbok, he drew into his heart and inner aspirations the gemsbok, hartebeest and above all the imperial eland, which was his and Mantis's authentic guide to ultimate metamorphosis. Subtlest and of great transfigurative power, were elements of the sky: stars, moon, clouds, wind, particularly the great Gothic spires of whirl-winds, rain, pools of water, reeds and of utmost significance – an image inspired by the rainbow, which he called Kwammanga and allotted to his god-hero, the Praying Mantis.

It is perhaps understandable that European invaders, confronted with such an unfamiliar, improbable and promiscuous array of characters, and their organization into patterns of myths, should have been confused and bewildered into dismissing them all as primitive nonsense. But way back in the store of European literature, after all, there is Aesop who so effectively used animals for parables of wisdom which are eloquent and persuasive to this day.

Creatures of nature can live on and dominate a world of human society as, for instance, in the stories of Beatrix Potter whose own safe passage from child-hood in the claustrophobic confines of a house in London to unimpaired woman-hood and marriage, was due to the pets she kept in cages in her bedroom in Kensington and the fantasies she wove round them in isolation. The role of the mouse in her *Tailor of Gloucester* first excited me as a child, because it is similar to the role of the striped mouse in one of my first Bushman stories where it, too, is an image of the hidden fecundity and infinitely detailed little forces of great powers that live in the wainscots of our cat-like consciousness. They emerge only after dark and under the protective cover of the great objective unconscious to further causes of creation which can only be done in secrecy just as the seed can only germinate in the darkness and privacy of the earth. I can think of other instances from *Alice in Wonderland* to *Black Beauty*, *National Velvet* and *Animal Farm*. The animals from oysters to horses and pigs are epic and seminal material of the questing imagination of man when the abstract and cerebral word fails it.

They abound, too, in folklore and fairy-tales and in Africa, there are great Bantu nations who still put the soul of their people in the keeping of some animal and call themselves Men of the Crocodile, Elephant, Baboon, Duiker and so on. All these things are incontrovertible testimony to how new forms of life are not merely fresh stages in the mechanistics of zoological and botanical evolution, but each one of them a unique and truly proven achievement. They are a leap forward of spirit made visible and alive, and hence an organic and dynamic element of our being which instinct and intuition put at the disposal of the child.

By maintaining continuity of origin and destination and deepening our roots in aboriginal earth they promote a growth of awareness high and wide into the blue of our own day.

One example of the leap forward of spirit demonstrated by and made accessible through the story was the tale of the beetle and two kinds of mice. An attractive young beetle woman was imprisoned by her father, the lizard, in a house in the earth. The lizard is an image of awareness bound too closely to the earth and its rocks to be good for the future. Hence the beetle woman, its future self, though also intimately of the earth, was winged, capable and desirous of taking to that other great opposite of creation, the sky. But the father, as so many fathers throughout the masculine-dominated past and present, denies the daughter, the soul in him, the right to raise life towards the heavens and so fulfil the end to which it had been born.

At this point the Praying Mantis, who has appeared on Bushman earth as the instrument of ultimate meaning, has a dream and sees how life itself would be denied and arrested if the tyranny of the lizard were allowed to continue. He, therefore, sends the long-nosed mouse into battle against the lizard. We already know the reason for a mouse, but why a long-nosed mouse? Because the nose which informs life of things not seen in the night or hidden by distance and other forms of concealment, is one of the earliest of our many images of intuition. But like all intuition, wise and sensitive as it may be, like the dove in the realities of heaven, it lacks the cunning of the serpent which is necessary to overcome the lizard. Inevitably the long-nosed mouse is killed by the lizard and, though followed by countless gallant long-nosed kinsmen, all are killed and the lizard remains an adamant and triumphant impediment to 'becoming' new being. Happily, Mantis is informed of the disaster in a dream and decides to send the striped mouse into battle instead. The striped mouse, of course, has a sensitive nose but it is not too long, there is no hubris of intuition, and its stripes are of even greater significance. They are the outward signs that it is a more differentiated form of being and consciousness. Just as Odysseus was chosen to complete our Homeric quest, not because he was the bravest and wisest of the men who fought on the great plain of Troy, but because he combined without exaggeration in one person the best elements of all, so the striped mouse is elected as a Stone-age kind of Odysseus, to battle for the future of all. He kills the lizard, calling out as he does so, 'I am killing by myself to save friends', and hastens to free the beetle woman, the feminine in life, all in a manner I described in *The Heart of the Hunter*. All the dead forces of intuition, the long-nosed mice, are resurrected and there follows a most moving description of how this army of tiny visionary creatures are led back to the palace of the Praying Mantis, the Stone-age's supreme image of the infinite in the small. Jubilant and triumphant they follow the striped mouse and the beetle woman marching at his side, feeling herself 'to be utterly his woman'. As they march, they wave high above their heads like flags the fly whisks which the Bushmen of the great plains of the south alone had made out of animal tails.

It was for me, hearing this again and again, as though the earth joined in this triumphant waving like a kind of hosanna, not uttered but enacted. It was, and remains all the more so, because the story ends with the Mantis bringing up the rear, suddenly seeing that the wind has risen and everywhere the long, tasselled, green-gold grass is waving too. And this wind, I was told, came out of the East, the East where the new days are born. Seeing all this, Mantis leaned back, content because he had 'foreseen it all in a dream'.

Alone in the imagery of the stories told to me, Mantis was dealt with in epigrammatic form without extended definition because I was young and too affected by this tale. As a result, nothing more was necessary to underscore his importance in the rich mixture of stories poured on me like those splendours, the dreams of Caliban of the Island at the still centre of the storm in *The Tempest*. But this much and this approach were necessary to explain why the Bushman stories held me as no European fairy-tales did, though I came to love them too. The wolf, the fox, the bear, the giants, the bean-stalk, the sleeping beauties, the chocolate-box princesses and princes, came into my imagination at a more conscious level because they came later and were hearsay material to me. For me, the characters of the Bushman stories were all a direct part of the processes of growing up. Isolated from the great tides of civilization ebbing and swelling like the seas over Asia and Europe, the Bushman fought the battle for light and creation in his own triumphant way, transforming darkness into light and as he renewed and increased himself, he held back the forces that sought to deny life, until European and Bantu man arrived to quench him. Considering how long that old, old Africa had been there, a known unknown, a mystery in the full sun, and that none of the great civilizations surrounding it had been able to penetrate its natural frontiers and explore it, one would have thought this achievement alone would have entitled the Bushman to respect and been a passport to human consideration by the invaders. Yet despite all this, there appeared to have been something just in what he was which provoked all that was worst in the invaders and aroused the extreme selfrighteousness which can only be justified by the unconscious guilt for the wounds man inflicts on himself. It resulted in this compulsion to kill in the illusion that he would only have to remove the external reminders of this primordial unrest to calm his conscience forever. It was all summed up for me in the cry of explanation that both white and black sent echoing, like the voice of Cain, down the canyons of the centuries, 'You see. He just would not tame!'

What, then, was this hated being? It is too late, I think, to answer this question decently and in the round. It is, in any case, something so profound and so remote from what we have become ourselves that no answer perhaps, would ever have been complete. We would have been able to do better, however, had our ancestors paused before the killing to ask themselves the question and then looked, for instance, into what it was in the Bushman spirit that made him cover the rock of his native land with paintings of the external world and the world within him, covering all the aspects of art which the visual artists of the great cultures had explored: everything from the world about him, insect, animal and human, historical and immediate to his innermost world and his aspirations towards a meaning and reality beyond his here and now. It is so inspired and moving that it raises his painting to the order of that of an unusually articulate civilization.

We have incontrovertible evidence today that he was already painting superbly some thirty thousand years ago so that by the time Europeans and Bantu invaded his country, they had everywhere Louvres and National Galleries of paintings, still glowing with enough colour and light to brighten the darkest shadows of overhang and cave. Nor did the newcomers listen to their stories and music which made the Bushmen dance to the moon and under the stars and act out the meaning to come as it stirred within him and in the process gain access to those transfigurative energies which had entered him at conception. Luckily I was somewhat better placed. My family had over three centuries' experience of him, even though mostly only in battle; had been puzzled by him which was a beginning, however slight. It started a process of wonder which two little Bushmen, Klara, the Bleeks and Lucy Lloyd augmented to put me in closer touch with his spirit. Moreover, after the Second World War, I saw something of the original version still being lived in the central Kalahari and had a sufficient glimpse of his unique being to suggest some of the answers.

The essence of this being, I believe, was his sense of belonging: belonging to nature, the universe, life and his own humanity. He had committed himself utterly to nature as a fish to the sea. He had no sense whatsoever of property, owned no animals and cultivated no land. Life and nature owned all and he accepted without question that, provided he was obedient to the urge of the world within him, the world without, which was not separate in his spirit, would provide. How right he was is proved by the fact that nature was kinder to him by far than civilization ever was. This feeling of belonging set him apart from us on the far side of the deepest divide in the human spirit. There was a brief moment in our own great Greek, Roman, Hebraic story when his sort of being and our own were briefly reconciled and Esau, the first born, the hunter, kissed and forgave his brother Jacob, the strangely chosen of God, his betrayal. But after that Esau, like Ishmael before him, vanishes from our story and a strange longing hidden in some basement of the European spirit still waits with increasing tension for his return. Meanwhile, the divide in our consciousness between the Esau and the Jacob in man deepened and the Stone-age hunter and his values could not have been more remote and antagonistic to ours when we clashed increasingly in southern Africa. We were rich and powerful where he was poor and vulnerable; he was rich where we were poor and his spirit led to strange water for which we secretly longed. But, above all, he came into our estranged and divided vision, confident in his belonging and clothed as brightly as Joseph's coat of dream colours in his own unique experience of life. Where we became more and more abstracted and abstract, he drew closer to feeling and the immediacy of instinct and intuition. Indeed for him, his feeling values were the most important and the liveliest. Even the language he spoke was a feeling language, expressing reality not in ideas, calculation and abstraction so much as through the feelings provoked in him. He would speak of how the sun, feeling itself to be sitting prettily in the sky and feeling itself to be warm, believed it could make people on the cold earth feel warm as well. His language, therefore, was poetic rather than realistic and though, of course, he was not indifferent to a robust range of the sort of verbs we favour, all usages of his grammar, still warm from the presses of his aboriginal imagination, were contained in an assessment of reality and meaning through feeling.

This pre-eminence of feeling for natural forms of life was attached to him from birth. The family became his fundamental social and universal unit and his feeling of belonging was so wide and deep that all on earth and the universe were family to him. It was the unchanging rod in his bureau of standards by which experience of reality and a sense of future were measured. He seemed to have felt no need to organize himself into tribes or nations. He moved naturally as hunter societies do, in small family groups, and his contact with others of his own kind appears to have been unusually free of friction and dominated by the consideration that they were a family among other human families and one and all, they were part of a universal family.

He was never imperilled as we are by numbers, and the blurring of the human spirit which their collective standards and approximations exact today. He had as a result no national organizations or institutions, no ruling establishment and therefore no kings, queens or presidents. The highest and noblest titles he could bestow were those of 'grandfather' and 'grandmother'. And since the stars, with which the nights of the southern hemisphere are so densely packed that one can hear them straining at the seam of the milky way in the stillness, since they were family too, he naturally addressed the greatest of them as grandfather and grandmother, since there was no discrimination of value and dignity between the sexes. Two of the brightest, for instance, Canopus and Sirius, were female stars and since both were associated with one of his delicacies, the white ant-larvae referred to by my ancestors as Bushman rice, he would encourage and warm them from the cold with some of his own positive fire. For instance, he would call on a child, 'Give me yonder piece of wood, that I may put the end of it in the fire, that I may point it burning towards grandmother, for grandmother is carrying Bushman rice.'

Hungry, they would call on one of them, 'Thou shalt give me thy heart, with which thou dost sit in plenty: thou shalt take my heart with which I am desperately hungry, that I may also be full like thee.'

As important as the element of belonging was the feeling of being known. Perhaps this more than anything else sets him apart from us and the rest of Africa. In this connection we must not forget that the great black societies of Africa from which we derive our notions of the primitive, were and are not primitive at all. They were already extremely advanced in what we like to term the stages on the way to civilization; they, too, were people of property, with sophisticated concepts of life, law, order and makeshift ideological abstractions

of their own. Moreover, they had already succumbed to the heresy of numbers
and inflicted on themselves the stifling collective priorities in which socialism
and communism are now trying to imprison the life of our time, as if they were
the newest leap forward instead of a lethal somersault backwards into an amply
discredited pattern of spirit.

Relatively, of course, they had not gone down the road of cosmic anonymity
and unbelonging as far as we have done, thanks to the great natural world that
still contains and restrains them, but far enough nonetheless to hate Stone-age
man with a vehemence as great if not greater than our own. They, too, have
tended to lose, as we ourselves with rare, individual exceptions have totally lost,
this sense of being known. How many of us, for instance, have any emotional
understanding of what St Paul meant by his conclusion of what is for me the
greatest statement, not excluding Dante's, ever made on love: 'Now we see
through a glass, darkly; but then face to face: now I know in part; but then shall
I know even as also I am known'?

We have become perhaps the most bigoted collection of know-all cultures and
sects the world has ever seen but this sense of being known, which accompanied,
uplifted and preserved the Bushman from extremes and held him accountable
throughout his thousand and one centuries alone in the vastness of Africa, has
vanished from the heart of modern man. All that Klara told me, all I read, and
all I experienced of the Bushman in the years I knew him in his last keep in the
heartland of the Kalahari, almost overwhelmed me with nostalgia for this shining
sense of belonging, of being known and possessing a cosmic identity of one's
own, recognized by all from insect to sun, moon and stars which kept him company, so that he felt he had the power to influence them as they influenced and
helped him. All was two-way traffic and honourable reciprocity. I have already
anticipated some of this obliquely in the story of the Morning Star and his response to the appearance of Canopus and Sirius, the grandmother stars, in his
night sky but there was more of this in the practical detail of his everyday life.

For instance, as a hunter he would call on the stars to guide the hand that
released the arrow from his bow, with a certainty that was as much a command
as a prayer: 'Thou shalt take my arm with which I do not kill. For I miss my
aim, Thou shalt give me Thine arm.' He already knew himself well enough to be
in battle against error and fallibility and falsehood in himself and to turn to the
cosmic pattern of stars and constellations, in ordered courses where falsehood
and error did not exist, to overcome his own inadequacies.

In fact, one of my most moving memories is concerned with just this aspect
of his life in the Kalahari. One evening I went from my camp fire in the central
desert to see if all were well with a little Bushman group, desperate for food and
water, that I had encountered that day. As I came near their own fire, my Bushman guide and closest companion stopped me. Against the clear starlight I saw
the outline of a woman and as my eyes became more accustomed to the dark,
noticed that she was holding her baby, a boy, high above her head and calling
softly to the sky above.

I asked my guide what she was doing. Reproving me for not speaking more softly he whispered, 'She is asking the stars up there to take from her son the heart of a child and give him the heart of a star instead.'

'But why the heart of a star?' I asked.

'Because the stars are great hunters,' he answered with the condescension which my ignorance of what was essential and self-evident to him always provoked. 'And she wants them to give him the heart of a hunter too. If you listen carefully you will hear the sounds of their hunting cries up there.'

I listened and indeed a far sea-sound came from the stars to my ears.

'You hear!' he whispered, 'How they are calling out "Tssa!" and "Tssk!"'

These sounds needed no explanation. For generations all of us in Africa had used and were still using these very words to set our dogs after game. I had thought until then that they were of our own invention. But that evening I knew we had them from the Bushman and he had them from the stars. The word that was in the beginning came from the stars and the word was true.

That, of course, was more evidence of his intimacy and assumption of two-way communication with his universe long before this in-built pattern in life was revealed through the dream of a ladder pitched between another desert and heaven to a Jacob who had done a hunter and brother wrong. It is testimony, however, that should be amplified by the fact that the sun, too, made a sound for him, the same great ringing sound it made for Goethe and which he asserts as fact in the 'Prologue in Heaven' to *Faust Part I*.

As long as the Bushman heard this sound of the sun and stars and could include it in the reckoning of his spirit, all was well in his world but when the sound ceased, tragedy was upon him. It needed only one death, so clear was his identity, so at one with the family over all, that the sun ceased ringing and a star fell.

To use his own words, 'Since the feeling strings were cut, the sun has ceased to ring for me in the sky.' His heart cried out specifically on the death of a friend because that is what the cutting of strings meant; or more generally: 'When our hearts fall down, that is the time when the star also falls down. While the star feels that our heart falls over, as when something that has been standing upright falls over on its side — for the stars know the time at which we die. The star tells the other people who do not know that we have died.'

And the wind, the spirit that travels the world and time, would know it too, and in the cause of the precision and the symbolism of truth which presided over his spirit, would join in to perform the final rite on behalf of life that the man had served so well: 'The wind does this when we die,' he declared. 'Our own wind blows, for we who are human beings, we possess wind, we make clouds when we die. Therefore the wind makes dust because it intends to blow, taking away our footprints, with which we had walked about, while we still had nothing the matter with us, and our footprints which the wind intends to blow away would otherwise still be plainly visible. The thing would seem as if we still lived. Therefore the wind intends to blow, taking away our footprints.'

So even at the exit of the world, his spirit stood whole and fast, demanding accuracy in the last account with life and, compared to the longing for immortality which characterizes Western man, without complaint or regret. Indeed the hunger for immortality of the ego, too, had to preserve the proportions of creation and it plays the ultimate role as an instrument of truth and not as an impediment and source of confusion. Like rebirth and resurrection, death, oblivion and the wind were people of the early race, dark sisters who had their place among the first family of life at nightfall by his little fire with its spire of flame reaching up towards their cousins, the sun, moon and all the other stars.

For years I would watch the Bushman as I shall always remember him by countless such fires at nightfall, so confident and at home in his immense wasteland, full of an unappeasable melancholy. He was the Esau being we daily betrayed in our partial and slanted modern awareness and instead of blaming ourselves for the betrayal, we projected it on to him to such an extent that we had to kill him as Cain killed Abel. Yet, though he himself is vanishing fast from the vision of our physical senses as Esau vanished from the great story which contained as it fashioned the foundations of our culture, he lives on in each one of us through an indefinable guilt that grows great and angry in some basement of our own being. The artist and the seer, even though the priests who should have known it best have forgotten it for the moment, know there is an Esau, a first man, a rejected pattern of being within us which is personified by something similar to a Bushman hunter, without whom they cannot create and sustain a vision of time fulfilled on which a life of meaning depends.

As they create and dream their dreams by making his sort of being contemporary, by linking that which was first with what is new and latest and all that is still to come, they do work of cosmic importance and in the process are invaded with a compassion for this betrayed Esau element that leads unerringly to a love that is overall and which knew him long before we were made. Like that which created creation, named or not named, known or unknown, he is always there.

That this vital link with the first man in us is no subjective assumption of mine but objective truth is proved, I believe, by the striking parallels that exist between the basic images of his spirit and those of Shakespeare, Goethe, Blake and Valéry on which I have already drawn. I know of many more. But I believe these are enough to show how, in considerations such as these, we can proceed to dispel the lethal imperviousness in the cultures which compelled men to fear and extinguish him. Our diminishing civilizations can only renew themselves by a reconciliation between two everlasting opposites, symbolized by Cain and Abel, Jacob and Esau and, in our own day, by the Bushman and his murderer. We have no excuse left for not seeing how fatally divided against themselves the processes of civilization have been, and how horrific the consequences in the human spirit. Now there is only a re-dedication of man to knowing himself: the command of both Christ and Apollo which can lead him to rediscover the wholeness lost in the beginning in a contemporary and greater form. Something of this sort is the armour the spirit needs for a future imperilled by corruption from the power we have acquired over the forces of nature. Since this future has come to include man's journey to the stars, the proportions that our humanity needs to protect it from brutalization by hubris of power and extremes of greed demand that we should look back to the moment the first man summoned his son, his future self, and gave him a stick of light with his fire, his awareness, and pointed it to a great feminine star, a mother figure through which an overall father begets. In that slight exercise of what the anthropologists label Stone-age superstition, the journey to space was born and made inevitable, and we have an inkling of why the first man thought of the glittering men of heaven as hunters.

The hunter in the Bushman family, of course, was the person who provided the food needed for physical survival. But it is of fundamental importance to remember that for him, spirit and matter were manifestations of one another and the well-being of the body and the heart ultimately one. It was an axiom of his being that he could not eat without participating also in the character of the essential spirit he attributed to the source of his food. A Bushman father, therefore, would as soon as possible feed his son on the heart of a leopard, the bravest of the brave in the animal kingdom, so that his son would become brave and, as he put it, 'possess the heart of a leopard too'.

There presided always over his eating a sacramental element. His spirit was naturally so transubstantiative that he did not deny the animal reciprocity in the matter. In one of his most moving stories, like all great tales a frontier story and as illuminating and enigmatic as an early *Hamlet*, he tells of a lion who seeks to become a man. For this purpose a lion, significantly on his way to life-giving water, encounters a young hunter whom he overpowers and fixes firmly in the fork of a thorn tree with the intention of eating him when he has drunk his fill of the desert water of life. The young hunter, unknown to the lion, is merely pretending to be dead. Hurt by the rough fork of the tree, the pain forces tears to start from his eyes. Amazed, the lion licks away the tears with a strange tenderness and in that instant the relationship of lion and man is transformed and takes wing. It is as if the suffering of the young man is absorbed and understood by the lion and is translated into a compassion which establishes a bond between them that demands their union alive or dead. Sadly, as the story makes clear, it is a reckoning so royal, of such ultimate individuation and so transcendent a value that neither the community of the young hunter, the young man himself nor indeed the king of the greatest animal kingdom on earth, can yet achieve it.

In this, as in all else, the hunter for the Stone-age man was the image, the personification of the greatest of all the urges of his being, the hunger for food of the spirit, for meaning that would transfigure him. He felt himself without doubt or self-questioning a participant in the hunt that was on everywhere, not only on earth but in the expanding universe above and about him. The hunter was charged with the supreme image of all within himself that sought a truth that would transcend everything and quiet the unrest and the hunger for a reality beyond his here and now, his tiny allotment of time and space. He already knew instinctively what Baudelaire came to recognize at the end of one of his finest poems, 'Les Phares' [The Lighthouses], one of the most moving surveys of the meaning of the art of painting that I know. 'What is art, o lord, what is this ardent sob that breaks out and re-echoes from age to age?' he asks with a cry of anguish at the end of the poem and concludes, that it is also, 'A summons from hunters lost in the great woods'. This symbolic hunter was the Bushman's summons, the pentecostal element at the quick of his being that connected him to a process of becoming something other and more than he was in his given moment, always seeking to increase himself through his painting, story-telling, dreaming the great dream over all, making music and dancing his dances in sacred circles under the stars and the moon. And although I mention his music and dancing last, they were perhaps his most immediate way of linking himself to creation and the forces that raised the sun out of darkness; the stars and moon out of a bright day that blotted them out, so restoring them to the night that renews and reveals them in their lawful courses.

I was privileged to encounter the Bushman at a time when his culture was sufficiently whole to have preserved his music and dancing relatively intact and I marvelled at how, despite the diversity I uncovered in his highly differentiated stories, in the music and dancing from north to south, east to west, he was at one and his culture united and whole. Long after his story-tellers and painters had vanished from my part of Africa, fragments of his dancing and music remained. His last survivors had only to take a few dancing steps, utter a refrain or two for them to declare, with tears beyond our understanding springing to their eyes, as Klara and two little grey-haired old men had declared after a rehearsal of their history performed for me one unforgettable evening in the interior, 'But ah! How we have become young again'.

The steps and the music stayed with me so clearly that I recognized them forty years later as part of the patterns of the dances and the singing of Kalahari men. The dances were of all kinds but there were three that had a special meaning for me. There was first of all the dance of the little hunger that was performed to express the Bushman's need of food in his struggle for physical survival, and to enlist the help of the stars that knew no falsehood or impression but were always accurate and true. This was the dance that had its fulfilment in another performed to express gratitude to the animal which had allowed itself to be killed so that he could live. And there was the dance of the great hunger, not for the meat or fruit of the earth but for the food which the hunter within and his fellow hunters, the stars, were after. I suspect that this was the grand dance of which my ancestors spoke, the dance which fascinates the anthropologist of today almost to the exclusion of all other forms of his dancing: it is called the trance dance. This was the dance in which one of the dancers who had a gift of healing, of dreaming great dreams, of seeing visions and was, accordingly, a seer and prophet to his clan, summoned power, as it were, from the universe to reinforce his gift from life of healing the sick and anguished among his kind.

I have seen such a person also acquire similar powers and perform his healing in lesser dances but in this dance of dances, an awesome element and power was acquired that was not present in the others. It, too, was performed in a circle of mushroom magic, the image of mathematical completion, the sacred mandala of Tibet and the total rounding of the torn and divided soul which the modern psychologist tries to achieve in depth. It was danced like all the others, by the men, the women sitting close to the wavering margin of fire light, leaning against the black of night and providing the rhythm with song and clapping of hands while the dancers added to the beat by the pounding of their feet in the scarlet Kalahari sand and the swish of the rattles tied round their ankles. But it went on much longer than any others. In fact, the last great dance I saw in the Kalahari in 1954 started about four on an afternoon of clouds raised like temples in a sky illuminated with the revelation of lightning, and ended only at about midnight when the first heavy drops of rain began to fall. From time to time, one of the older women would jump up and break into the sacred circle to urge the men to greater exertion, until at the climax, as I watched it alone and apart in the dark, the whole of nature seemed to come alive and join in the dance and its call on the universe to appease a terrible hunger. The thunder became incessant, the lions suddenly began to roar, the ostriches to boom, the night plover to pipe its deep-sea call, the hyenas to howl and the jackals to bark as if they were a chorus of fate sent to swell the music and the prayer for appeasement and wholeness. The beat of feet, hands and voice indeed became so loud and regular that it was like that of a great time machine, and heard out of context on my taped recordings today, the beat sounds not so much human as like enormous pistons driving a ship at full speed ahead. At this moment the healer chose to lay his hands on the sick, pressing them tight against the ailing bodies before pulling them along and up to the top of the aching heads, uttering, as the hands left them, the defiant cry of the animal spirit with which the sickness was associated. At that moment the music would change; the frenzy left it and a mood of the most tender and delicate compassion took over, as if one and all knew instinctively what Paracelsus, the Einstein of modern medicine, as he has been called, knew in the sixteenth century when he declared that without love and compassion there could be no healing.

At that moment I realized why the dance had to last so long — fatigue was to the healer what drugs are to the psychiatrist; a means of lowering the level of consciousness and its wilful inhibitions so that the unconscious forces and the instinctive powers at the disposal of all life could rise unimpeded and be released in the healer. What these forces are I cannot define and would not be so foolish as to try to describe by anything save their consequences. Judging by those, they were as great as they were dangerous and only that prolonged and highly disciplined ritual of the dance could first contain and transform them into elements of healing. The danger, of course, was greatest for the healer. He was the lightning conductor to the great storm of primeval energies which had been released and when the healing was accomplished, he fell unconscious to the

earth. Another dance and cycle of song began to bring him back to the here and
now from this underworld of the forces which he had plumbed and released in
order to heal. When he opened his eyes at last and the water from a dozen or
more ostrich eggshells was poured down his parched throat, the look on his face
in that firelight was, I believe, the oldest I have ever seen on a human being and
the expression that of a pilgrim who could never tell others where and how far
he had travelled that night.

Yet despite all this, he did not bleed at the nose. I mention this because on
many rock paintings of dancers, the healers are depicted as faint and bleeding
profusely at the nose as if to demonstrate the Greek healers' dictum, 'only the
wounded physician heals'. I can only vouch that at the end of the dance I understood why holiness and being holy were one and the same, just as I and all
around me that night on earth and in heaven had felt to be one. And somehow
whenever I think of his dancing and how it renewed and made him whole, I
recall a dance I witnessed when his culture was intact. It was a dance to the full
moon, a moon as beautiful as any moon of Japan. When I asked them why they
performed that dance, they said with pity at my ignorance: 'The moon is about
to fall away and shall utterly die unless we show her by our dancing how we
love her not a little; how we feel we want her to live, utterly knowing that feeling thus, she will not die but return, lightening the night for our feet on which
we go out and return.' In all these and many other ways, out of his belonging
and being known, he felt responsible to the universe and capable even of in-
fluencing its course. Feeling thus, he was preserved from that erosion of meaning
and sense of participation in the wider plan of creation, which is eating out the
heart and will to be and to become of our bright technological day.

For all these and many other reasons, when I returned from nearly a decade
of war, I thought it well worth while to make one last effort to preserve the Bushman and his culture in the heart of what I called the lost world of the Kalahari,
and try to arrest there this age-old story of persecution and annihilation. I persuaded the British Government for the first time in our history to appoint an
officer charged with the sole duty of learning the Kalahari Bushman's language,
and to live with him and get to know, understand and defend him. I did not
mean to imply thereby that he should be preserved as some kind of living
museum piece. I had too great a respect for him and his potential for creative
re-evaluation. All I wanted was recognition of his humanity, his values that
were, at their best, precious qualities that we had neglected in ourselves and at
our peril, and his right to native land wherein his security was guaranteed so
as to give him time enough to find a way of his own into the world of the future.
'Give this officer fifty years with them,' I told a sympathetic administration, 'and
at the end of that time ask him for some recommendation on how to go on from
there.'

But I did not mean to leave it at that. I had experienced a Kalahari Desert that
had overflowed its arbitrarily imposed political boundaries from South West
Africa which today goes by the unhistorical and utterly contrived name of

Namibia, and up and over the river boundaries of Angola right to the outskirts of Moçâmedes itself. All this vast area was still recognizable Stone-age country and the Bushman hunter's life still a relatively coherent culture. Moreover, this land was a desert only in the sense that it had no permanent surface water and was covered with grass, shrubs, trees, bush, even forest, a dense lifegiving vegetation that made it the home of a rich and abundant animal population. Yet at that moment it had no great and lasting economic value in the modern sense.

So I had a dream of persuading all the governments who claimed sovereignty over this immense tract, to join forces and declare it an international heritage, transforming it into a unique reserve where both the first man and his attendant animal world would be protected and conserved. I began working at once with my friends to that end but we had begun too late. The world of Empire, which had this unique and precious earth in its keeping, collapsed and the forces of an archaic nationalism moved in to take its place. In the process, the Bushman was once more overlooked and his claims forgotten. He was not physically eliminated, but merely overwhelmed by a brash new world wherein he not only had no voice in his own future but had no command of any language which would have made sense to the powers that seized his secluded land in a cast-iron grip. Moreover, he had no immunities whatsoever to protect him against an infected world, sick with unschooled power and uncritical worship of its technological and material endowments. As a result when I went back recently, as I felt I had to in order to see what, if anything, could still be done to help him, I hardly recognized the man I had known in the nineteen fifties among the tragic fragments of families left behind like flotsam and jetsam on some desert island beach by the tidal wave of the mindless forces we had released and allowed to sweep over it.

As a result, he was being destroyed rapidly and more subtly now from within himself. To use his own metaphor, I found that his story had been utterly taken away from him. He could no longer live it and had only a fast receding memory of it left in the labyrinthine regions of his convulsed imagination, like an echo of the brave voice of the legendary hunter pausing to call farewell at the edge of his forest of the night before vanishing on his quest for the great white bird of truth. His culture was dying before our eyes and he and what was left of it, was about to vanish physically and spiritually into the bastard bloodstream of his unworthy conquerors. No doubt he will live on as other vanished and unrecorded men live on, and add a nuance or two to the being of the future, a look in the eye, a curl of hair, a tone of affirmative and indestructible laughter, a quickening of fantasy and expression on some face, that will stir men to wonder and to experience an inexplicable nostalgia of the heart and provoke a dream of new-old life in their sleep. This could be reward and treasure of an incorruptible kind. However, the horror of it for the moment was, to use a phrase I had learned out of the heart of suffering of Japan, 'an unbearable of life one had to bear'. There was nothing else to be done; neither he nor I and others who wished him well had any court or power in the world to whom we could appeal in our so-called enlightened day. The organizations that should have been the first to rush to his aid, like that whited-sepulchre of the hopes which had sustained us in yet another World War in which the best of my generation died, the United Nations, would not heed and had no ear for the voice of so tiny and powerless a minority as it has had no ear for the hapless Indians of Central America, Brazil, and other violated natural worlds.

Ironically, the much condemned apartheid country of South Africa was alone inclined to listen and concede the Bushman a certain recognition of identity and rights of his own. Far from perfect as that recognition is, it is more than anything practised by the apprentices to the nationalism fathered by the political liberalism which is the international fashion and dominant hypocrisy of our day. All we could do who had gone to the Kalahari to testify to the Bushman's human and primordial right to a pursuit of life, liberty and happiness in his own way, was to persuade dying fragments of his culture to re-enact for us such memory as they had of what I ventured at the beginning to call a Stone-age civilization. Added to the film record, *Lost World of the Kalahari*, I made in 1954–5, my book *The Heart of the Hunter*, and this film made with Paul Bellinger and Jane Taylor, what we have written here is in a sense, therefore, a last will and testament. Late, partial and hurried as it was in the doing, it will make those who ponder its fragmentary bequests nonetheless rich because they are all he had left to bequeath of the wealth of natural spirit out of which in his own day he gave so abundantly with all the grace, willingness and fulness of which he in his time on earth was capable.

For myself I can only record that on my last return from the desert my own world had never seemed bleaker. For not only was the sense of belonging and being known absent, but the individual self which was an instinct of his being and centre of his totality of imagination and doing was everywhere under powerful attack.

First man, as I knew him and his history, was a remarkably gentle being, fierce only in defence of himself and the life of those in his keeping. He had no legends or stories of great wars among his own kind and regarded the killing of another human being except in self-defence as the ultimate depravity of his spirit. I was told a most moving story of how a skirmish between two clans in which just one man was killed on a long forgotten day of dust and heat and sulphur sun, caused them to renounce armed conflict forever. He was living proof to me of how the pattern of the individual in service of a self that is the manifestation of the divine in man was built into life at the beginning and will not leave him and the earth alone until it is fulfilled. It is no mere intellectual or ideological concept, however much that, too, may be needed, but a primary condition written into the contract of life with the creator.

As I thought of the first man's instinctive sense for the meaning of life, I seemed to be more aware than ever of the loneliness creeping into the heart of modern man because he no longer sought the answers of life with the totality of his being. He was in danger of going back precisely to those discredited collective concepts and surrendering this precious gift of being an individual who is specific for the sake of the whole, an individual who believes that a union of conformity is weakness but that a union of diversities, of individuals who are different and specific, is truly strength. A grey, abstract, impersonal organization of a materialistic civilization seemed to be pressing in on us everywhere and eliminating these life-giving individual differences and sources of enrichment in us. Everywhere men were seeking to govern according to purely materialistic principles that make us interesting only in so far as we have uses. It was true even in Zululand, let alone Paris and London.

I was speaking once to an old Zulu prophet who, when I asked him about their First Spirit, Unkulunkulu, said to me: 'But why are you interested in Unkulunkulu? People no longer talk about him. His praise names are forgotten. They only talk about things that are useful to them.'

This ancient reverence for the individual, so clear and unprovisional in the Bushman, has been lost, this individual dedicated to a self that is greater than the individual, who serves something inside himself that is a microcosm of the great wheeling universe. This individual who, by being his self, is in a state of partnership with an overwhelming act of creation and is thereby adding something to life that was not there before, is being taken away from us. We no longer feel the longing, the wonder and the belonging out of which new life is raised. In the depths of ourselves we feel abandoned and alone and therein is the sickness of our time.

Human beings can enjoy anything except a state of meaninglessness of which it seems a great tide is creeping down upon us. Apparently nothing but conformity will do. Take, for instance, the concept we hear so much about – the statistical notion of the average man. When you come to think about it, there is no such thing as an average man. It is like the average rainfall, which never falls. But because numbers have replaced unique and human considerations in the faceless abstractions of our time, we feel lost in a world where nobody cares any more for what we are in ourselves. Inevitably we cease to care in return. One of the most awful consequences is that as we lose touch with the natural man within, which demands a unique self of us, we lose respect for him. And as the natural man within loses honour, so too does nature without. We no longer feel reverence for nature, and defoliation of spirit and landscape are everywhere to be seen.

It is only now that we have lost what I re-found in the Kalahari in the nineteen fifties when, for months on end, I moved through country no 'sophisticated' man had ever set eyes on, that I realize in full what it meant and did for my own senses, brutalized by years of war. It was as if I had been in a great temple or cathedral and had a profound religious experience. I returned to the world, knowing that unless we recover our capacity for religious awareness, we will not be able to become fully human and find the self that the first man instinctively sought to serve and possess. Fewer and fewer of us can find it any more in churches, temples and the religious establishments of our time, much as we long for the churches to renew themselves and once more become, in a contemporary idiom, an instrument of pentecostal spirit. Many of us would have to testify with agonizing regret that despite the examples of dedicated men devoted to their theological vocation, they have failed to give modern man a living experience of religion such as I and others have found in the desert and bush. That is why what is left of the natural world matters more to life now than it has ever done before. It is the last temple on earth which is capable of restoring man to an objective self wherein his ego is transfigured and given life and meaning without end.

Looking back with a nostalgia that I am powerless to describe and which often wakes me aching in the night and walks like my own shadow at my side, I must testify with all the power and lucidity of expression at my command that this lost world was one of the greatest of such temples, in which the first man and the animals, birds, insects, reptiles and all, had a glow upon and within them as if they had just come fresh and warm from the magnetic fringes of whoever made them. He and they were priests and acolytes of this first temple of life and the animals dominated his stories, his art, his dancing and imagination because they followed neither their own nor his will but solely that of their creator.

Follow, I would add today, the first man in ourselves, as well as the rainbow pattern of beasts, birds and fish that he weaves into the texture of the dreams of a dreaming self, and we shall recover a kind of being that will lead us to a self where we shall see, as in a glass, an image reflected of the God who has all along known and expected us.

This is as far as my own words about my experience of the being of the Bushman can carry me and yet there is more. The word that was at the beginning and shall be at the end is a living word. The living word and the living truth are always more than statistics and facts. Neither can be imprisoned in any particular expression of themselves however valid and creative, but must move on as soon as that phase of themselves is fulfilled. The concepts, cultures, whole civilizations, indeed, are not terminals, but wayside camps, pitched at sunset and broken at dawn so that they can travel on again. As end and beginning round to meet in my own life there seems only one lasting form without inbuilt obsolescence of any kind in which their nature can be conveyed from generation to generation and that is through the story. And it is in a great Bushman story that I sought and found refuge from the sense of doom of the Bushman idiom of primitive man that assailed me on my return to one of our cities where, to use Xhabbo's words, 'I no longer obtained stories'.

It is a story which is, in a sense, like a symphony wherein many notes and chords are struck on a diversity of instruments to compose a whole. I must begin the story, therefore, with a description of the characters and elements that are the instruments, the notes and chords and associations. Thus preauditioned in imagination, when the full orchestra is assembled, the key and scale determined, the listeners' minds will be wide open to the subtle alchemical intent of the story.

The principal character in such a seminal story, of course, is Mantis; the others that appear in it are Kwammanga who is described on this occasion as Mantis's son-in-law; Kwammanga's son; Kwammanga's shoe-piece; and Mantis's shoe-piece. It also includes a pool of water where reeds stand; honey; an ostrich feather; an eland; and the moon. As these characters and elements appear they strike chords of association in the minds and emotions of all those listening because of the roles they have played from the time of the first story on and through the age-old story-telling process that leads to ultimate communion.

I begin with Mantis as he is the supreme plenipotentiary of creation on Bushman earth; his is the clearest image of the Bushman's acute sense of the infinite in the small, and as such is endowed with powers of creation himself. He is, indeed, so much the child of light that the children of the world appear far wiser in their generation than he. They, like his wife the rock rabbit, his son and grandsons are constantly reproving him for his apparent foolishness without realizing that it is god-inspired and that that which is still to come always looks impossible in the eyes of what is. He it was, after all, who stole fire to give to the Bushman; he is the Prometheus of that world, and significantly, one of the nick-names conferred on him after my ancestors arrived at the Cape was 'old tinder-box'. With him, the miracle of consciousness — of which fire is our supreme symbol — came into the Bushman's world and set him apart from the animals who, an early story tells us, ran away in great fear from mankind with whom they had been at one, when his first fire was lit. Here already is an example of the great divide, the separation and polarization of life-giving opposites, which consciousness inflicts on man with such a nostalgia for the whole that preceded it. With consciousness, inevitably, came the word because it was Mantis, it is said, who first gave things their names, declaring, for instance, that 'Your name shall be tortoise and you shall be utterly tortoise to the end of your days'.

All these associations and many more which I have analysed in *The Heart of the Hunter*, were alive and active in the imagination of listeners when Mantis walked on to the earthly scene in this story. However strange or absurd his elevation to such a role may appear to men today who have only to see an insect to rush to the nearest chemist for the latest insecticide, it was not strange to the Greeks who recognized his qualifications for such a role and gave him the name mantis, seer, which meant he was a prophet of sorts to them as well. Besides, even my ancestors, for all their imperviousness and other inhibitions, were compelled to think of him as an insect at prayer and so not without numinosity. Not surprisingly, he carried for the Bushman a charge of the numinous of the kind Moses experienced, when he saw fire in the burning bush. I do not know what the Bushman name for Mantis meant but I do find it of the highest significance that among the thousands of Bushman paintings I have examined, I have not found one of Mantis, implying that he, too, did not allow images, painted or graven, to be made of him. Hence it is as a bringer of consciousness and as an instrument of enlarging human awareness that he figures most of all in this story.

Kwammanga, his son-in-law, his future self in the law of creation, is not flesh and blood, not even insect or anything tangible but an element visible at times in the rainbow. Since we know that the rainbow in our Hebraic story was an arc of the covenant set by God in the sky as a sign that he would never flood the world again, never allow unconsciousness on a universal scale to overwhelm consciousness again, it is not surprising that as son of Mantis, he, too, represents consciousness of a kind. It is consciousness of the beginning in the here and now and far more circumscribed than the larger awareness for whose increase Mantis is uniquely responsible.

He and his sons, all images of Mantis's future selves, are in the business of living out today new stages of consciousness imposed on their reluctant and conservative selves by Mantis; they are the politicians and statesmen, as it were, in the parliament of the totality of Mantis's complex and diversified being; converting Mantis's vision of the impossible into the art of the possible. As more evidence of the Bushman's gift for universality, all this would have been dear to the heart of Goethe, who also thought of the rainbow in a similar way, especially as a natural image of consciousness. As for the two shoe-pieces in the story, they are there as images of man's conscious way through life, his consciously adapted behaviour. Kwammanga's shoe-piece is the image of his role, his influence on the way of man in the restricted here and now; that of Mantis is the image of the greater awareness which compels Stone-age man to think beyond the here and now and serve the being to come. As a result, Mantis becomes in most of the stories the great, incorrigible disturber of peace and social order; the trickster who twists, convulses and confounds fireside complacency and is forever at war with the gravity of human inertia. Although his strange family is forced to obey him, it fears and mistrusts him, complying with his wishes with an air of 'Oh God, what next?' which in many stories was such irresistible comedy for my ancestors. As the fear of the Lord was the wisdom of the Old Testament Lord, so it is with Mantis and at the end of the long and complex Mantis saga, I have emerged again and again with a searing re-perception of how the love of creator for the created is darkened not only by a separation from the created but also by a lack of reciprocity of love from the created. These stories are full of illustrations of Mantis's love of *all* things but none of an equal reciprocity. It is as if there is implicit in the way he carries on the task of creation regardless, an assumption that that is precisely what creators are for. Without that thought, I would not have had an inkling of what the story of Job might mean nor that appointment with a cross in Palestine.

The pool of water is a symbol of the lifegiving and transfigurative energies in the collective unconscious. Just as in the Bible, wells, rivers and watering places are the material of miracles and settings for fateful and sacred encounters, so they are in the saga of Mantis in particular, and of Stone-age man in general. For instance, it is in such water that Mantis resurrects his son killed in his great

war against the baboons, by dipping his dead child's eye – his vision of the future
– deep in the pool.

Perhaps most moving of all because it is from a story told with singular
delicacy and tenderness, it is in such a pool that a Bushman of the early race,
hungry and dispirited, sees the wind that represents the living spirit, spiralling
over the stricken wasteland. It lifts an ostrich feather to which one tiny speck
of dried blood is clinging and deposits it deep in the pool, where it is transformed
into a perfect ostrich chick. The pool in the story to be told is surrounded by
reeds, marking it as an area of growth dear not only to the water but to the
wind that sings in passing as they sway and swish in the rhythm of its movement, a song of birth, death, resurrection and eternal life-giving change.

The honey, which recurs in many a story, was dearer even to Mantis than to
the Bushman for whom it was miraculous and a source of sacramental tran-
substantiation. The Bushman, the most perceptive and experienced naturalist
and botanist Africa ever produced before our coming, had observed the bee
faithfully and long, even as Solomon the Great had commanded the men of his
day to observe the ant and become wiser in the process. For the Bushman
the bee was an image of wisdom and foresight in action; the patience, industry,
perseverance, selflessness, attention to miniscule detail, and devotion of all to
transcendent value, which was the life of the bee, made a profound impact on
the Bushman imagination. Bees and his permanent water were, according to
my ancestors, almost the only two fixed material elements he was prepared to
fight for as for his own life. In going about the business of promoting the welfare
of his own highest value, which significantly was feminine, the bee was also an
instrument of universal creation, fertilizing the flowers and fruit of his world
and transforming their essences into honey. For this pagan African honey, with
its wild flavour and texture so translucent with archaic light and made of the
essences of the flowers of creation itself, brought sweetness to the Stone-age
man's palate in a way equivalent to the light of his eye in the night of his spirit.
In the logic of an imagination wide open to the wonder of creation, inevitably
honey became the ultimate symbol of the wisdom that leads to the sweetness of
disposition which is a love that transforms and the only source of power that
could not corrupt. That this was already so in the beginning is made clear in a
story which describes how one of the first deeds of Mantis was to give the animals
their different colours and in so doing fixed each colour with honey. He was
clearly devoting all the sweetness, the love in his disposition, to the task.

The feather that follows, of course, represents the bird which, in a land so rich
in bird life as Africa, is never far from the story-teller's imagination. Plato, who
described the mind of man as a cage of birds, would not have marvelled at the
fact that for the Bushman, too, the bird represented inspiration, the thoughts
that come into the mind of man, winging of their own accord out of the blue of
the imagination and demanding to be acknowledged and followed.

One of Klara's first stories to me was of the Bushman hunter who, as a result
of just seeing the reflection of a great white bird in the water of a deep, blue pool

at which he was drinking in the heat of the day, lost all his passion for hunting game. He devoted the rest of a long life to an exhausting and apparently vain quest for the bird whom he knew only by its reflection. Close to death, he had travelled far and wide enough to reach the foot of an unscalable mountain on top of which the bird was reported to roost. Convinced, as he watched the sheer cliff soaring into the blue of evening above him, that he would now die without ever seeing the bird itself, he lay down in despair, until suddenly a small voice said, 'Look up!' In the red of a dying day, he saw a lone white feather come floating down to him. He stretched out his hand and grasped it, and in grasping it, I was told, he died content.

When I asked for the name of the bird, Klara told me, 'It has many names but we think of it as the bird of truth'. It has remained a key story of my life and a source of illumination of many obscure things.

The feather in this story may not be a feather of the bird of truth itself but nonetheless the association with it is important because it is also a servant of the living truth that the great white bird symbolizes. It is specifically an ostrich feather, a feather of the bird from which Mantis stole the fire that is consciousness and which he gave to man. As a consequence of the natural precision which characterizes Stone-age symbolism, fire, the inspiration which is the image of the source of the greatest transformation of life on earth, could only be represented by the biggest bird of all – a bird, moreover, which was deprived of the gift of flight after the theft of fire as a sign that consciousness had come down from heaven to earth forever.

After the feather, the inspiration: the eland, the greatest of African antelopes, charged with a grandeur of creation in a measure that exceeds all others of its kind no matter how impressive their beauty and grace, is the central element and instrument in the symphonic story. For the Bushman he represented creation in its highest animal form, food for survival in its greatest abundance, and in its most nourishing, reassuring and alchemical measure; so much so, that the eland was associated with the miraculous and given a eucharistic role in Stone-age culture not accorded any other animal. He was, I was told, dearest of all to Mantis and in some stories, Mantis is depicted seated between the horns of the eland. In one story told to me in the Kalahari, Mantis is seated between magnetic toes that release sharp electric clicks which echo as the eland walks, magisterial in the silence of the desert, lifting one patent-leather hoof after the other. It is what I have often heard and observed him doing and in this bleak European scene, I ache in my heart for the wonder of it all. It is as if we are being told symbolically by Stone-age man that Mantis positioned between the eland's eyes, directs its seeing so that his vision and the eland's are one, and that positioned also between the eland's toes, Mantis is showing us that the eland's way is Mantis's way. The symbol could not be more complete and meaningful and all this is given additional force by the fact that no animal figures more frequently, diversely and beautifully in the rock paintings of Africa than the eland. There is not a phase of his physical existence and his importance to the

welfare of Stone-age man that is not a subject of rock paintings from the mountains of Natal, the plains and hills of southern Africa through to the Kalahari
and on to Namibia. But more significantly still, his numinous character, his
eucharistic role, his translation into a bridge between the divine and man is
greatest in the Bushman's dances and in the best of his paintings.

I think of one particular painting in this regard, perhaps the most remarkable
of all. It is painted on the fragmented and scoured canvas of rock of what was
once a great cave in the mountains between Natal and Lesotho. There, in the
quiet, a great herd of eland graze at peace, unstalked and unhunted and move
across the rock to the music of a fall of water nearby. But suddenly there rises
from among them the awesome shape of two beautifully painted Bushman
Titans. Tall as the Bushman always walked in his own imagination he has never
walked as tall as in these shapes. The instinctive authority and power of the
Titans in the painting left no doubt that they were deliberately raised by the
artist out of a passionate longing for a state of being far beyond that on earth
below. High above the placid herd, a mystical animal is depicted as the goal and
food for yet another ascent of the spirit of man. It is in a true sense both a
mythological and a mystical painting and the way the numinous and pentecostal harmonize with the natural and normal progression of the herd made
me tingle all over. Like the story to come which also has an eland at its core, the
painting rises fountain-wise in a place of Stone-age spirit where man experienced the revelation of the divine.

Finally, there is the moon which he loved as man loves woman. In one of his
first stories, I was told, the moon looked down on the people of the early race
and saw how afraid they were of dying. Moved in its heart by compassion, the
moon summoned the fastest animal nearby, the hare, and commanded, 'Run.
Tell the people on earth to look at me and know that as I in dying am renewed
again, so they in dying will be renewed again'.

The hare in its haste — and in Bushman mythology as in many others, haste
was invariably a source of evil — got the message wrong and told the people,
'The moon wants you to look at it and know that unlike it, who in dying is
renewed again, you in dying will not be renewed'. The moon was angry and it
bit the hare in the lip so hard that it was split, as it remains to this day, as a
sign that it bore false witness in a matter of universal truth.

All these instruments combined in the following story of Mantis and the eland
to strike great chords in the memory of Stone-age man and swelled as in the
climax of a great symphony, soaring to reinforce the urgent music of the spheres
beyond the stars.

So this is the story. Once upon a time, Kwammanga took off part of his shoe
and threw it away. Mantis picked up the despised piece and took it to the water
at a place where the reeds stood. It is as if Mantis is aware already that the spirit
renews itself out of what is despised and rejected by our worldly selves. It is an
eternal axiom of 'becoming' as expressed in the biblical observation that the
stone the builders rejected became the cornerstone of the building. Hence Mantis

soaks the piece of wornout leather, or the spent way that needs renewal, in the water or the transfigurative element of the unconscious. He goes back later and finds that the rejected element has already been transformed into a tiny eland and, since it is still small, he leaves it there until it is strong enough to emerge from the water by itself. Then Mantis rejoices, dances and sings to it, and fetches it honey. He summons, in fact, all the love and wisdom at his disposal and rubs the honey into it to make it beautiful, strong, wise and great. Mantis becomes so moved by his creation that he weeps as he fondles it. For the magical number of three nights, he leaves the little eland to grow great within the pool by itself and then returns to call it to come out of the womb of the unconscious onto firm conscious earth. The story says the eland 'rose forth', and came to Mantis in such a manner that the ground resounded with the power and glory of his coming, and Mantis composed and sang for joy a song about it before once more rubbing it down with honey. Only then did he return to rest at his home.

The story proceeds from there to disclose in detail how Mantis's rainbow aspect and grandsons, his future selves, become aware of his creation and in Mantis's absence combine to kill the eland and cut it up for food. Mantis comes on them in the process and weeps for the eland but his sorrow, by implication, is not just caused by the killing, as there is no other way in which the eland can be made food not only for the body but for the spirit. He weeps also for his suffering which is being exacted under a clause of the law of creation itself that separates and sets apart the creator and his creation. Mantis is in the role here of a Stone-age Moses who can lead others to a promised land of new being which he is not allowed to enter or participate in himself; his bitterness for the moment is extreme and is depicted in a furious argument with the gall of the dead eland.

The gall was one part of an animal that even Stone-age man could not swallow. And it seemed for a while as if Mantis would not succeed in swallowing and digesting the gall of the consequences of the separation his creation had forced on him. The gall warns Mantis that if it is pierced and dispersed, it will burst and overwhelm him with the darkness of hate and despair. In the end, however, Mantis pierces the gall which, as threatened, covers him all over so that indeed he can no longer see. The bitterness has become so great that he has no vision left at all and he has to grope along the ground in hate and despair, feeling his way like an eyeless animal. He finds at last an ostrich feather – a flicker of consciousness that was fire in the great bird's keeping. It is enough to brush the last vestige of negation and unconscious resentment out of his eyes and to make conscious the meaning of what Mantis had done intuitively and so make his suffering bearable: since all suffering is bearable once a meaning is discerned within it.

Free in heart and mind again, he throws the feather high up into the sky, committing the flame of light that emancipated him into a permanent light of heaven, calling out to it, as it soars up: 'You must now lie up in the sky. You must henceforth be the moon. You shall shine at night. You shall by your shining light up the darkness for all man. You are the moon, you do fall away, you return to life, when you have fallen away, you give light to all the people.'

In a total recall of the role of this story in my own imagination from childhood over the long random years of a life that is rounding fast, I remembered something I read in my boyhood lying on a dune beside a gleaming Indian Ocean, a mirror of unfathomed sea darkened as by a cats-paw of wind with reflections of longing to travel then from a halfway to a full house of history and spirit. It was a passage from the Upanishads to which Indian friends in Port Natal had directed me. It describes a scene at the court of the great King to which the sage Yajna-valkhya had been summoned.

'By what light,' the king asked him, 'do human beings go out, do they work and return?'

'By the light of the sun,' the sage answers.

'But if the light of the sun is extinguished?'

'By the light of the moon,' the sage replies.

And so question and answer proceed; if the moon is extinguished, then by the starlight, — if even the stars are cancelled, by the light of the fire but if the fire too is quenched, what then, the king finally wants to know.

'By the light of the self,' is the conclusive reply.

I had no doubt that in this story Mantis was teaching the spirit of Stone-age man a discovery of the self in which the great sage who never knew them put all his trust as well. For without this moon of renewal to transfigure our partial, bright daytime selves spent under all that is symbolized by the great sun of reason, men shall lose themselves in light as stars are lost in morning even before the nightfall of their time. This moon which lifted Mantis out of hate and the black rejection, is an image charged with evocation of the capacities with which life has equipped the human spirit to see through the darkness that falls when his conscious self fails. It is the symbol of all the feminine values, the caring, feeling values, the receptive spirit charged with wonder and hope and the glow, as the shining of the moon, that is intution and its shy intimations of new being and becoming that make the opaque past, the dark present and obscure future, translucent with inner light, as was the comb of wild African honey that Mantis used to make the eland great and Stone-age spirit new.

We live, I wrote at the end of a long desert exploration some thirty years ago, in a sunset hour of time and need the light of this moon of Mantis, this feminine Ariadne soul, which conducts the travel-stained prodigal son of man on a labyrinthine journey to the innermost chamber of his spirit where he meets the 'thou that heals'. Had it not been for the Bushman I myself would not have the confirmation, the certainty and continuity of hope in the wholeness of an origin and a destination that is one and holy. And I wish I could take each one of these anonymous fragments of those remaining Stone-age men and women by the arm and say to them before they vanish: 'Thank you, and please go in the dignity that is your right. You and your fathers were not beasts and cattle but hunters after meaning: painters of animal eucharist and metamorphosis of man on canvasses of rock; tellers of stories that were seeds of new awareness; dancers of dances that restored men to the fellowship of the stars and moon and made them heal one another; and makers of music in which the future sings. They have altogether travelled a way of the truth that would make men free.'

In this, I know, they did not live in vain, however much the desecrated present denies their children. We need their spirit still. We who loom so large on the scene are not better than they, only more powerful with a power that corrupts us still. It is we who shall have lived in vain unless we follow on from where their footprints are covered over by the wind of the moving spirit that travels the ultimate borders of space and time from which they were redeemed by their story. Woven as it is into a pattern of timeless moments, their story may yet help the redeeming moon in us all on the way to a renewal of life that will make now forever.

Bibliography

Alexander, J. E., *An Expedition of Discovery into the Interior of Africa*, 2 vols. London, 1838; Cape Town, 1968.
— *A Narrative of Exploration*. London, 1837.
Anderson, A. A., *Twenty-five Years in a Waggon in the Gold Regions of Africa*, 2 vols. London, 1887.
Andersson, K. J., *Lake Ngami; or Explorations and Discoveries during four Years' Wanderings in the Wilds of South Western Africa*. London, 1856; Cape Town, 1967.
Arbousset, T., *Narrative of an Exploratory Tour of the North East of the Cape of Good Hope*. Cape Town, 1846.
Baines, T., *Explorations in South-west Africa*. London, 1864.
Barrow, J., *An Account of Travels into the Interior of Southern Africa in the Years 1797 and 1798*. London, Vol. 1, 1801; Vol. 2, 1804.
Biesele, M., 'Old K"xau'. In *Shamanic Voices* by J. Halifax. Harmondsworth, 1979.
— 'Aspects of !Kung Folklore'. In *Kalahari Hunter-Gatherers*, edited by R. B. Lee and I. de Vore. Cambridge, Mass., 1976.
— 'A Note on the Beliefs of Modern Bushmen concerning the Tsodilo Hills'. In *Newsletter of SW Africa Scientific Soc.*, 15, 3/4, pp 1–3, 1974.
Bleek, D. F. (ed.), *The Mantis and his Friends*. Cape Town, 1923.
— *The Naron: A Bushman Tribe of the Central Kalahari*. Cambridge, 1928.
— 'Customs and Beliefs of the /Xam Bushmen', Part V: Rain; Part VI: Rain-making. In *Bantu Studies*, 7, pp 279–312 and 375–392. 1933.
— 'Customs and Beliefs of the /Xam Bushmen', Part VII: Sorcerors. In *Bantu Studies*, 9, pp 1–47. 1935.
— 'Customs and Beliefs of the /Xam Bushmen', Part VIII: More about Sorcerors and Charms. In *Bantu Studies*, 10, pp 131–162. 1936.
Bleek, W. H. I. and **Lloyd, L. C.**, *Specimens of Bushman Folklore*. London, 1911.

Burchell, W. J., *Travels in the Interior of South Africa*. London, Vol. 1, 1822; Vol. 2, 1824.
Callaway, H., *Nursery Tales, Traditions and Histories of the Natal Nguni*. Natal, 1868.
Campbell, A., **Hitchcock, R.** and **Bryan, M.**, 'Rock Art at Tsodilo, Botswana'. In *S.A. Jnl. of Science*, 76, pp 476–478. 1980.
Campbell, J., *Travels in South Africa*. London, Vol. 1, 1815; Vol. 2, 1822.
Chapman, J., *Travels in the Interior of South Africa*, 2 vols. London, 1868.
Cooke, C. K., *Rock Art of Southern Africa*. Cape Town, 1969.
Cumming, R. G., *Five Years of a Hunter's Life in the far Interior of South Africa*. London, 1850.
Dornan, S. S., 'Notes on the Bushmen of Basutoland'. In *S. Afr. Jnl. Phil.*, 18, pp 437–450. 1909.
— *Pygmies and Bushmen of the Kalahari*. London, 1925.
Ellenberger, V., *La Fin Tragique des Bushmen*. Paris, 1953.
Galton, F., *Narrative of an Explorer in Tropical South Africa*. London, 1853.
Hart, R. R., *Before van Riebeeck; Callers at South Africa from 1488 to 1652*. Cape Town, 1967.
Holub, E., *Seven Years in South Africa, 1872–1879*, 2 vols. London, 1881.
How, M. W., *The Mountain Bushmen of Basutoland*. Pretoria, 1965.
Inskeep, R. R., *The Peopling of Southern Africa*. Cape Town, 1979.
Johnson, R. T., *Major Rock Paintings of Southern Africa*. Cape Town, 1979.
Katz, R., *Boiling Energy*: Community healing among the Kalahari !Kung. Cambridge (Mass.) and London, 1982.
Kolben, P., *The Present State of the Cape of Good Hope*, 2 vols. London, 1731.
Lee, D. N. and **Woodhouse, H. C.**, *Art on the Rocks of Southern Africa*. Johannesburg, 1970.
Lee, R. B., *The !Kung San: Men, Women and Work in a Foraging Society*. Cambridge, 1979.

Lee, R. B. and de Vore, I. (eds.), *Man the Hunter.* Chicago, 1968.
— *Kalahari Hunter-Gatherers.* Cambridge (Mass.), 1976.
Le Vaillant, F., *Travels into the Interior Parts of Africa by the way of the Cape of Good Hope in the Years 1780–1785.* London, 1790.
Lewis-Williams, J. D., *Believing and Seeing: Symbolic meanings in southern San rock art.* London, 1981.
— *The Rock Art of Southern Africa.* Cambridge, 1983.
— 'The Economic and Social Context of Southern San Rock Art'. In *Current Anthropology,* 23, 4, pp 429–449. 1982.
— 'Ethnography and Iconography: aspects of southern San thought and art'. In *Man* (NS), 15, pp 467–482. 1980.
Lichtenstein, H., *Travels in southern Africa in the years 1803, 1804, 1805 and 1806.* Cape Town, Vol. 1, 1928; Vol. 2, 1930.
Livingstone, D., *Missionary Travels and Researches in South Africa.* London, 1857.
Marks, S., 'Khoisan resistance to the Dutch in the seventeenth and eighteenth centuries'. In *Jnl. of African Hist.,* 13, pp 55–80. 1972.
Marshall, L., *The !Kung of Nyae Nyae.* Cambridge (Mass.), 1976.
— 'Marriage among the !Kung Bushmen'. In *Africa,* 29, 4, pp 335–365. 1959.
— '!Kung Bushman Bands'. In *Africa,* 30, 4, pp 325–355. 1960.
— 'Sharing, Talking and Giving: Relief of Social Tensions among !Kung Bushmen'. In *Africa,* 31, 3, pp 231–249. 1961.
— '!Kung Bushman Religious Beliefs'. In *Africa,* 32, 3, pp 221–252. 1962.
Moffat, R., *Missionary Labours and Scenes in South Africa.* London, 1842.
Orpen, J. M., 'A Glimpse into the Mythology of the Maluti Bushmen'. In *Cape Monthly Magazine,* 9, pp 1–13. 1874.
Pager, H., *Ndedema.* Graz, 1971.
— *Stone Age Myth and Magic.* Graz, 1975.
Paterson, W., *A Narrative of Four Journeys into the Country of the Hottentots and Kaffraria.* London, 1789.
Philip, J., *Researches in South Africa,* 2 vols. London, 1828.
Schapera, I., *The Khoisan Peoples of South Africa: Bushmen and Hottentots.* London, 1930; New York, 1953.
Shostak, M., *Nisa: the Life and Words of a !Kung Woman.* London and New York, 1981.

Silberbauer, G. B., *Hunter and Habitat in the Central Kalahari Desert.* Cambridge, 1981.
Sparrman, A., *A Voyage to the Cape of Good Hope.* London, 1789.
Stow, G. W., *The Native Races of South Africa.* London, 1905; Cape Town, 1964.
Stow, G. W. and Bleek, D. F., *Rock Paintings in South Africa.* London, 1930.
Theal, G. McC., *Chronicles of the Cape Commanders.* Cape Town, 1882.
— *History of South Africa.* London, 1903; Cape Town, 1964.
Thomas, E. Marshall, *The Harmless People.* London and New York, 1959.
Thunberg, C. P., *Travels in Europe, Africa and Asia, made between the years 1770 and 1779,* 4 vols. London, 1795–6.
Tobias, P. V. (ed.), *The Bushmen.* Cape Town, 1978.
Tobias, P. V., 'The Evolution of the Bushmen'. In *Am. Jnl. of Phys. Anthrop.,* 14, p 384. 1956.
— 'New Evidence and New Views on the Evolution of Man in Africa'. In *S.A. Jnl. of Science,* 57, pp 25–38. 1961.
— 'The Physique of a Desert Folk'. In *Natural History,* 70, 2, pp 16–25. 1961.
— 'On the Increasing Stature of the Bushmen'. In *Anthropos,* 57, pp 801–810. 1962.
— 'Stature and secular trend among the southern African negoes and San (Bushmen)'. in *S.A. Jnl. of Medical Sciences,* 40, 4, pp 145–164. 1975.
van der Post, L., *The Lost World of the Kalahari.* London, 1958.
— *The Heart of the Hunter.* London, 1961.
Vinnicombe, P., *The People of the Eland.* Pietermaritzburg, 1976.
— 'Motivation in African rock art'. In *Antiquity,* 46, pp 124–133. 1972.
— 'Myth, motive and selection in southern African rock art'. In *Africa,* 42, pp 192–204. 1976.
Wendt, W. E., 'Art-mobilier from Apollo 11 Cave in SW Africa'. In *S.A. Archaeol. Bull.,* 31, pp 5–11. 1976.
Willcox, A. R., *Rock Paintings of the Drakensberg.* London, 1956.
— *The Rock Art of South Africa.* Jo'burg, 1963.
Woodhouse, H. C., *Archaeology in Southern Africa.* Cape Town, 1971.
— *The Bushman Art of Southern Africa.* Cape Town, 1979.
Wright, J. B., *Bushman Raiders of the Drakensberg.* Pietermaritzburg, 1971.

Index

Figures in **bold** refer to captions.

Acknowledgments

The publishers would like to thank the following for supplying photographs for reproduction in the book: H. C. Woodhouse: 29, 30, 31; David Lewis-Williams: 44; Norman Mankowitz: 64, 65, 66, 70. All other photographs are by Jane Taylor (agent Sonia Halliday).

N | II

968.
1
VAN

Please renew/return items by last date
shown. Please call the number below:

Renewals and enquiries: 0300 123 4049

Textphone for hearing or
speech impaired users: 0300 123 4041

www.hertsdirect.org/librarycatalogue
L32